Recycling Reconsidered

Urban and Industrial Environments

Series editor: Robert Gottlieb, Henry R. Luce Professor of Urban and Environmental Policy, Occidental College

For a complete list of books published in this series, please see the back of the book.

Recycling Reconsidered

The Present Failure and Future Promise of
Environmental Action in the United States

Samantha MacBride

The MIT Press
Cambridge, Massachusetts
London, England

For information about special quantity discounts, please email special_sales@mitpress .mit.edu

This book was set in Sabon by Toppan Best-set Premedia Limited. Printed and bound in the United States of America.

Library of Congress Cataloging-in-Publication Data

MacBride, Samantha.
Recycling reconsidered : the present failure and future promise of environmental action in the United States / Samantha MacBride.
    p.   cm. — (Urban and industrial environments)
Includes bibliographical references and index.
ISBN 978-0-262-01600-1 (hardcover : alk. paper)
1. Recycling (Waste, etc.)—Government policy—United States. 2. Refuse and refuse disposal—United States. I. Title.
TD794.5.M285   2011
363.72'820973—dc22
                                                                        2010053623

10 9 8 7 6 5 4 3 2 1

Contents

To Mark, who is everything to me.

Acknowledgments

This book has been the work of my adult life and the consequence of many people's influences, ideas, and encouragement. First and foremost, I thank my mentors at New York University: Robin Nagle, Neil Brenner, and above all Harvey Molotch. Each in their own way revolutionized my thinking, and each was incredibly generous in their intellectual and moral support. I cannot thank them enough.

I am very grateful to Clay Morgan, my editor, and Robert Gottlieb, the series editor, as well as the MIT staff for their support in completing this book, as well as to the four anonymous reviewers who provided extremely helpful comments.

I also thank those scholars who were formative in my thinking: Vivek Chibber, Stephen Lukes, Eric Klinenberg, the late Dorothy Nelkin, Paul Mattingly, Jochen Albrecht, Sonia Ospina, and Rae Zimmerman all left me indelibly changed for the better. Over the years, other scholars, starting with A. Wallace Deckel and continuing on to Sydel Silverman, have shaped my view of the world, as did my first teachers: David Tafe, Whitney Blair, Frederick Christie, and Richard Pike.

At New York University, where I studied and wrote my dissertation, I was fortunate to know Michael McQuarrie, Aaron Passel, Aaron Panofsky, Aaron Major, David Schleifer, Monika Krause, Curtis Sarles, Noah Norberg-McLain, and Dorith Geva, who all helped me think through things and challenged me with their own ideas as we all developed together. I thank Nitsan Chorev for her friendship and generous intellectual inspiration; it has been my privilege to know her. I also thank Phaedra Daipha for her crucial comments on my book title.

My professional colleagues have been bold in sharing their world views to support the trajectory of bureaucracy in socially progressive directions. Robert LaValva, Venetia Lannon, Pat Grayson, and most of all Robert Lange made this book possible. Christine Datz-Romero,

Kate Zidar, Chris Neidl, and Carl Liggio are among those whom I thank in the "waste world" of New York City. I also thank staffs at the New York City Public Library Archives, in particular Thomas Lannon, and the Cross Mills Public Library, in particular Ulla Virks and Ray Brennan, for their support.

I wouldn't be here without my family: my mother, Laidily, my father, Robert, and my grandmother, Margaret, who were all authors and scholars; my extended family among the Mahoneys and Greens, especially Janice, Patti, and Dan; and my friends, including Andreas Lachnit, Michael Muse, Judy Kreid, Kirsten Noyes, Erin O'Brien, Laurie Obbink, Anthony Bossis, Chris Robinson, Patty Fitzpatrick, and Paul Kuhn, who encouraged me every step of the way. But most of all I thank my husband, Mark, who has inspired and helped me with selfless support, insight, and wit. I love him very much, owe him everything, and dedicate this book to him.

Acronyms and Abbreviations

ACC	American Chemistry Council
BEACC	Business Environmental Action Coalition Committee
C&D	Construction and demolition
CIWMB	California Integrated Waste Management Board
CPI	Consumer Policy Institute
CRI	Container Recycling Institute
EAC	Environmental Action Coalition
EDF	Environmental Defense Fund
EPS	Expanded polystyrene
E-waste	Electronic waste
GCMI	Glass Container Management Institute
GRRN	Grassroots Recycling Network
HDPE	High-density polyethylene
LDPE	Low-density polyethylene
LULUs	Locally unwanted land uses
MRF	Materials recovery facility
NRC	National Recycling Coalition
NRDC	Natural Resources Defense Council
NSWMA	National Solid Wastes Management Association
NYC WPC	New York City Waste Prevention Coalition
NYPIRG	New York Public Interest Research Group
OPA	Office of Price Administration
OPM	Office of Production Management
OWN	Organization of Waterfront Neighborhoods
PET or PETE	Polyethylene terephalate ethylene
PP	Polypropylene

PS	Polystyrene
PVC	polyvinyl chloride
RCC	Resource Conservation Challenge
RCRA	Resource Conservation Recovery Act
U.S. EPA	U.S. Environmental Protection Agency
USGS	U.S. Geological Survey
WRI	World Resources Institute

Introduction

We are at an important moment in natural and social history. State action and widespread public concern, organized at scales ranging from local to global, are rapidly mounting to confront material burdens of industrial production and mass consumption that have accumulated over past centuries. The unintended consequences of the overuse of nature's resources and services are increasingly and violently forcing their way into people's lives. Action and concern over environmental problems take many forms, ranging from international conventions (United Nations 2009) to the mainstreaming of "green" calculus in the business model (Hawken, Lovins, and Lovins 1999; Gunther 2006) to struggles for environmental justice that are increasingly networked across borders (Pellow 2007). Within this complex of thought, communication, and action, **solid waste**—commonly known as *refuse*, *garbage*, or *rubbish*—is one trace of the interrelated problems that manifest themselves today in climate change, ecosystemic loss, and risks to health. This book is about solid waste—how it poses problems and how solutions to those problems have fared in the United States since solid waste began to be thought of and dealt with in the framework of contemporary environmentalism in the late 1960s.

Solid waste in the United States has several characteristics that make it a useful entry point into consideration of larger environmental problems. The first is the disproportionate U.S. contribution to its quantity. It is beyond dispute that most metrics of environmental burden situate the United States as lead consumer of resources (Harrison, Pearce, and AAAS 2000; GFN 2008). Among many other indices is the per capita rate of generation of municipal solid waste, a category that covers wastes arising from activities of collective consumption—including residential life; government operations; and retail, office, food service, and other nonindustrial commerce. At an estimated 4.6 pounds per person per day, the U.S. rate exceeds that of any other nation (Harrison, Pearce, and AAAS 2000).

Disposal of municipal solid waste has direct local consequences for pollution. Although today's landfills and incinerators are greatly improved from earlier decades in terms of containment technologies, they still entail the concentration of toxic substances diffuse in garbage, which in the long term will be released into air, water, and land (Nemerow, Agardy, Sullivan, et al. 2009). There are also extralocal impacts. Waste-disposal activities represent slightly more than 2 percent of total U.S. greenhouse gas emissions (U.S. EPA 2009a). Transportation of municipal solid waste from points of collection through consolidation at transfer stations and eventually on to disposal is a major source of truck-related diesel exhaust. But the direct environmental problems associated with municipal solid waste disposal are relatively small in relation to others associated with acute hazard or widespread ecosystemic disruption that are taking place at multiple scales all over the globe. What makes municipal solid waste most relevant to the complex of problems that we today call "environmental crisis" is its status as end product of the materials economy as a whole. This economy, organized in stages of extraction, manufacture, distribution, and consumption, sets the trajectory that natural substances follow during their sojourn in the social realm. The last stage in this economy is wasting—the reintroduction of substances back to nature. Garbage is the material artifact of a great range of steps prior to wasting. Its existence signals larger, more diffuse problems. In it, we see the last vestige of havoc wreaked by materials as they flow globally.

In a country of unevenly distributed but comparatively great wealth, U.S. citizens frequently express concern over garbage as a manifestation of environmental crisis in toto. Trash, a pollutant that arises daily and visibly in the household, is always at hand as an object upon which to work up environmental concern and action in the realm of everyday life. "Recycling," defined in this context as separating certain materials for collection and routing them back into beneficial use, is a well-structured outlet for direct action. Reducing personal consumption, conscious purchasing, repairing and reusing discards, and contemplating how and why so many find themselves participating in a "throwaway society" are less-developed actions institutionally but increasingly discussed with great fervor in the virtual and real public spheres, along with recycling in the sense defined here.

Over the past forty years, citizens have organized politically to challenge how solid waste is managed. Those who began to organize as the antitoxics movement in the 1970s, followed by the environmental justice movement starting in the 1980s, have said "No!" to the risk from sited solid-waste facilities (Szasz 1994; Bullard 2000). They have spoken and acted with a clear objective—to remove hazards from their bodies, homes, and communities. Saying "close it down, move it out, don't burn it here," they articulate and object to one commonly constructed problem of solid waste: its toxicity (Walsh, Warland, and Smith 1997). The antitoxics and environmental justice movements are quite different from organized citizens protests premised on the slogan "Not in My Backyard" ("NIMBY"), whose aims are to protect property values and neighborhood character. In resisting the infrastructure of waste, the antitoxics and environmental justice groups seek not just to prevent facility siting, but to set the groundwork for new, better, and more just environmental policies and practices and to refuse to accept certain risks as "inevitable" consequences of development. Crucially, the goal of the antitoxics and environmental justice movements is not to *even out* environmental risk, depletion of resources, or health effects across the population at large. Instead, it is to insist that the handling of discards be ultimately organized without posing risk, and to point out that risk is inherently unjust. The scale of these movements is local and transnational; their range of action has to do with where repositories of solid waste are built and operated as well as with social justice. As a whole, they have radically changed how industrial facilities are sited (Bullard and Johnson 2000).

With regard to U.S. problems of solid waste, however, the antitoxics and environmental justice movements have not engaged primarily in the technological and programmatic development of waste solutions. This sphere of action is led by different groups of citizens who may or may not live in polluted communities themselves. This array of groups, which I refer to in this book as the "recycling movement" (with portions now in transition to become the "Zero Waste movement" in the twenty-first century) has since 1970 articulated a different set of objectives than those held by the antitoxic and environmental justice movements. Although recognizing the harm and inequity of sited hazards, the recycling movement counts among its aims the reduction or elimination of the need for siting and building of solid-waste repositories in the first place by cultivating alternatives to disposal. It means not only to shut down local sited risk, but to offer local employment and to reach beyond the local to the global and to protect the forests, ecosystems, waterways, and even sites of labor far afield, often—and this is a crucial point—by working *with* businesses and industry associations in collaborative partnerships.

The recycling movement's accomplishments are now solidified into municipal practice and thriving private industry, and reflected in widespread general public support of recycling in general. For this reason, recycling is often hailed and celebrated as a vibrant and growing expression of environmentalism (Bell 2004; *Congressional Quarterly Researcher* 2007). It is important to point out, however, that its goals of saving the earth, saving trees, conserving resources, and cleaning the economy are far from being realized. The vast majority of solid wastes generated from extractive, industrial, business, and residential activities are still burned or buried (see appendix I). The recycling that takes place routes discarded materials back into remanufacture but has not yet made a dent in the increasing rates of global materials extraction (Kraussman, Gingrich, Eisenmenger, et al. 2009). Furthermore, as I discuss in detail in this book, although recycling does create jobs, the way that most recycling takes place today makes these jobs dull, hard, and harsh ones. Using recycled inputs for remanufacture does save energy in comparison to using virgin ones, but the current configuration of recycling in cities means that there is still considerable pollution from diesel trucks that collect and transport recycled materials in the first place.

This book looks at what has happened given all the work and progress to date and finds that the recycling movement, since its emergence in 1970, has often fallen prey to a form of derailment that the term *co-optation* only imperfectly describes. In some cases, grassroots groups have been co-opted overtly to advance the interests of firms that would seek to keep solid-waste policies from threatening their autonomy (Rathje and Murphy 1992; Gould, Schnaiberg, and Weinberg 1996; Rogers 2005). In other cases, however, the recycling movement has hobbled its own potential by selectively focusing on certain realms of social experience and de-emphasizing others that would be more effective areas of concentration. In particular, it has overfocused on the individual consumer, the local scale of economy and governance, and a global realm that is only vaguely defined. Less in its agenda have been the role of the individual as political participant, the national scale of economy and governance, and participation of importing and exporting nations with varying degrees of wealth and power in the exchange of materials internationally (Wallerstein 1974). Mirroring these emphases has been a preference for consensus over conflict (Maniates 2002; Hahnel 2007) and an implicit theory of social change rooted in notions of education and moral/psychological growth rather than in state regulation or structural reform (D. King 1995; Gould, Schnaiberg, and Weinberg

1996). Finally, the recycling movement has tended to conceive of businesses as capable of maintaining profits while stepping down their ecosystemic harms—provided enough leadership and creativity are applied (Hershkowitz 2002; Murray 2002). To the recycling movement, "clean, green production" can and will come to constitute the materials economy as a whole, even if that has not yet happened, as firms that are environmentally responsible are cultivated and encouraged (McDonough and Braungart 2002). At its peril, this movement has been reluctant to acknowledge the extent to which all firms are ultimately constrained by competition to compromise on responsibility when profits are at stake.

Table I.1 summarizes areas of greater and lesser emphasis that characterize the movement's approach to problems of solid waste. Make no mistake, all elements in table I.1 have been present in the discourse and practice of the recycling movement as it has struggled since 1970 to identify solid-waste problems and to seek solutions. Indeed, the rich and often contradictory history of development of solutions to solid-waste problems in the United States offers a great deal of hope, but it is also cause for concern. The movement's simultaneous advocacy of contradictory positions, I argue, has again and again led to outcomes in which there is a great deal of activity, the appearance of progress and improvement, but an underlying stasis or, worse, a net growth in the material dimensions of the solid-waste problems that such solutions set out to address in the first place.

Table I.1
Summary of Emphases of the Contemporary Recycling Movement

MORE	LESS
Individual as consumer and project manager	Individual as citizen (voter, party member, protester)
Consensus	Conflict
Individual change → social change	State regulation and alteration of physical and institutional structure → social change
Local (community) scale	National scale
Global (the earth)	Trade in materials between developed and developing nations (North and South)
Win-Win (profit–environment protection)	Win-Lose (profit–environment protection)
Win-Win-Win (economy, environment, equity)	Pursuing equity and environmental goals nonsimultaneously

I call this condition "busy-ness." Busy-ness is a fulfilling sense of work and achievement that often brings positive side effects but fails to reach the central effect. If progress is a flowing stream, busy-ness is an eddy, moving vigorously but not forward. How and why busy-ness has characterized so many solid-waste solutions is historically contingent but, I argue, at heart reflects the structure of contemporary society. It is an outcome of the exertion of power by businesses, organized as industrial sectors, that controls transformations of natural materials in today's economy. These businesses are bound by the basic requirements of market competition to proceed so that profits eclipse environmental protection as an economic goal if and when the two come into conflict, which they often do when solutions to solid-waste problems are considered. They desire above all to be left free to pursue their interests, and they have found busy-ness an effective means to deflect social movements that might challenge this freedom. Busy-ness is a handy method of maintaining the status quo yet is simultaneously active, optimistic, and often makes people feel better. For this reason, to critique its diversionary aspects tends to come across as nay-saying, discouraging, or failing to advance a constructive alternative. In this book, I explain why I think such critique is necessary and why it does not have to lead to dismal nihilism.

Busy-ness and Business

My perspective takes business (capital) as the central focus of analysis with respect to the creation of and solution to environmental problems. Rich literatures exist that question whether capitalism can ever be an ecologically or socially viable system of meeting human needs, given that capitalist production subtracts materials from nature and reintroduces them back to nature in ways that are predictable only in their tendency to deplete and pollute (Schnaiberg 1980; O'Connor 1998; Burkett 1999; Foster 2000). Equally developed are schools of thought that see the reinvention of business as the antidote to past centuries of unintended devastation (Hajer 1995; Hawken, Lovins, and Lovins 1999; Mol 2001). This latter view, often termed "ecological modernization," envisions a reinvented capitalism that is conscious of material impact, learns from natural systems, and maximizes human creativity expressed through technology, with the capacity to reverse and stabilize trajectories of devastation, sometimes but not always enlisting the state's helpful but steadily guiding hand (Janicke 2006). Aspects of both perspectives, and sometimes neither, inform the hard work on the ground that grassroots recycling activists and community-based enterprises carry out daily (Freilla 2005; Hess 2005; ILSR 2005). Folks who handle discarded materials and transform them back into objects of use as well as those who fight for government resources (funding, contracts, services) and against large, disposal-service corporations conceive of the business model in abstract as one capable of good or bad—best if kept small and employing local labor yet capable of growing and morphing into a powerful complex at odds with the public good.

At the risk of oversimplifying massive amounts of scholarship, the perspectives of those who see capitalism as inherently unsustainable, and of those who see it as amenable to correction, can be reduced, when it comes to on-the-ground policy and action of those who roll up their sleeves and plunge their hands into waste, to whether business cannot or can be trusted. Do we believe that business, without calling it "evil" or other childish names, is not immorally but rather amorally premised on profit and profit alone and thus can never be trusted to limit its activities to those that are ecologically beneficial? Or do we believe that business has acted terribly in the past but need not do so in the future if its leaders are wise and moral and its size kept on the human scale? If we believe the former (as I do but constantly seek to evaluate, consider, and admit the latter), then we must watch business like a hawk and channel its activities from outside a business calculus, mainly through state structures of regulation and taxation, using the science of ecology and Kant's moral imperative as our guide, and treating the inherent creativity of business as a useful monster to be kept on a short leash. If we believe the latter, then our role is to encourage business's voluntary reorganization, letting it free to work and only reluctantly engaging with its mechanisms by altering the costs it faces (preferably through state subsidy). In the latter conception, "business" is not monolithic. Some small or even large but sustainable businesses can be great forces for public good and, if fostered through subsidy, can flourish incrementally to the point of taking over whole spheres of material activity. If there is an evil in the world, this latter view holds, it is within ourselves and our own greedy or perhaps lazy nature, and in a similarly incremental fashion we can educate and effect moral transformation, translating this transformation back through the production chain to factories, mining sites, or forests, primarily via the mechanism of consumer choice, but also through different ways of thinking.

The information presented in this book sets out an empirical basis for my belief that business (including the market mechanism) cannot be trusted with solutions to ecological problems, and with this view comes an associated argument about the relatively minor role that consumption choice and personal transformation can ever play in society's struggle for a sustainable world. Instead, I argue that business's creativity and efficiency must be harnessed collectively, with the harness applied through a combination of intense civic monitoring and state regulation. The empirical basis of my argument begins in the study of the history of methods of disposing or recovering solid wastes in the United States, in which the role of business has been central from the outset.

With little exception, the relation of business to the existence of and problems associated with solid waste went unchallenged and unnoticed until the first stirrings of the contemporary environmental movement in the late 1950s (Szasz 1994). As this movement gradually gained followers and momentum, it began to mount opposition to the "business as usual" practiced by manufacturers of commodities as well as by the waste-disposal industry, prevailing upon the state to set standards, provide services, make investments, and gather data such that firms were constrained to change their modes of operation, often though not always with a financial cost to themselves. In the post–World War II era, the environmental movement and, specific to this story, those groups within it that were focused on problems of solid waste forced the development of business as a whole in directions it would not have taken on its own.

The largest impact of this push from outside has been the development of a strong, vibrant industry organized around the recycling of paper, metal, plastic, and glass separated out of municipal solid waste by residents and businesses and collected for processing by governments, firms, or government–firm partnerships. This industry, I maintain, has next to zero impact on resource conservation measured in global scales and delivers only weak results in terms of pollution reduction or energy savings. On the contrary, national and global environmental burdens from materials extraction, manufacturing, and distribution show no signs of abating (WRI 2001; Rogich, Cassara, Wernick, et al. 2008). Ever growing and unevenly distributed, these burdens have been largely unaffected by the recycling, composting, reuse, prevention, and consumer choices that constitute solid-waste solutions in the United States today (M. Smith 1997; Gardner and Payal 1999). Nonetheless, recycling as an industry is a great success economically. Today, it employs about 1.1 million people, generates an annual payroll of $37 billion, and grosses $236 billion in annual revenues (NRC 2001). And for every ton of waste handled, recycling entails 10–25 jobs for every one that disposal offers

(ILSR 1997). The success of the recycling economy is mirrored in the status of recycling as a success story for environmentalism. By far, recycling is the most thoroughly developed practice for doing something with solid waste other than burying or burning it. It is flourishing, and it is popular. As has often been repeated, more Americans recycle than vote.

The achievements of the recycling movement have thus been remarkable; without the efforts of activists on its front lines, cities likely would be still disposing of all of their wastes except metal, and in some cases paper (for reasons that I discuss in this book). In a few happy cases, the development of recycling industries in particular places and times has led not just to economic activity but to good, local jobs and an infrastructure in which to expand the range of alternative methods of diverting wastes from disposal (for example, the nonprofit Ecocycle in Boulder, Colorado, or Eureka Recycling in St. Paul, Minnesota). In most cases, however, the development of the recycling industry has proceeded as an ancillary activity carried out by large firms who still derive the bulk of their profits from disposal, thus placing recycling at a fiscal disadvantage (Crooks 1993; Rogers 2005). But regardless of the social or fiscal qualities of any recycling business, recycling as we know it addresses at most one third of all municipal solid waste produced and leaves untouched other far larger waste fractions, those emanating from extractive and manufacturing activities (see appendix I).[1] Burying and to a lesser extent burning continue to be the major forms of dealing with billions of tons of wasted material annually, some of it containing hazardous constituents. Moreover, although recycling in its current incarnation has flourished, most alternatives advocated by the recycling movement since the 1970s (including laws that restrict producers' freedom by taxing, banning, or requiring product take-back) have been actively and often successfully opposed by businesses and still struggle to gain foothold, and others—in particular those addressing industrial by-products—have remained outside consideration and contemplation entirely.

The history of solid waste in the United States that I lay out in this book shows case after case of business pushing back against the recycling movement's initiatives, resisting laws, regulations, and requirements that would be imposed by the state. This push-back is not hard to understand— it occurs when immediate profits don't accord with a particular ecologically beneficial way of addressing waste. It also occurs even when profits would be minimally impacted in the short term, but the autonomy of business to take future actions freely is impugned (where business fears a "slippery slope"). Push-back has taken place in a variety of familiar ways. Producers, organized into trade associations, agitate to block regulation through lobbying, campaign finance, and use of the courts. Leveraging economies of scale, large, for-profit disposal conglomerates absorb or outcompete small nonprofit recycling startups. Such conflict is out there for all to see and has not escaped the recycling movement's notice.

If this were all there were to it, reaching the goal of an ecologically beneficial future for solid waste would be basically a matter of keeping up the fight. If businesses want to work with the recycling movement and the state to reform, redesign, and refrain from ecosystemic harm, great. If not, prepare for battle. But the core and contentious argument I am making is that there is far more to it, and that some of the deepest contradictions and hence barriers to achieving the goal of sustainable waste (or materials) management reside within a set of ideas and practices that are core tenets of the recycling movement itself, generalized among U.S. citizens who love recycling and are concerned about garbage. The history of solid waste in the United States that I set forth suggests, without the need for conspiracy theories or notions of good and evil, that citizens' impulse—individually and collectively—to mount challenges that pose a threat to business has been preempted before it can get started. The result is that waste-oriented ecological citizens wear comfortable and increasingly sophisticated but invisible shackles that they themselves have forged in collaboration with business. Making these shackles visible—mainly through data, but also through a challenge to cherished American notions such as freedom, individuality, responsibility, and symbolism—is what I undertake in this book.

Diversion and Power

As I mentioned earlier, using metrics of tons flowing globally and ending in waste, rather than the vibrancy of the recycling industry or the popularity of recycling, it is fair to say that solutions to solid-waste problems today are not achieving outcomes in a materially meaningful way. From one perspective, this dilemma can be faced with a pragmatic "not yet." In this view, what are needed are more and different solutions that go beyond collecting bottles, cans, and papers in cities. This perspective is in the United States today organized under the rubric "Zero Waste," a set of concepts and practices that aspires to no less than defining waste out of existence (Murray 2002). Building on the recycling movement's achievements, Zero Waste holds that redesign of industrial technology, the diffusion of new values and behaviors among consumers, and a proliferation of community-based enterprises for recycling, composting, and reuse are key to the goal of completely (or nearly) eliminating solid waste (GRRN 2008a). In its embrace of local enterprise, its willingness to work with and harness the power of good green business, and its emphasis on personal consumption choice, this movement has some characteristics of the "business-trusting" perspective I associated earlier with ecological modernization. As with any real-world phenomena, however, the movement advocates potentially conflicting tactics as well, supporting, for example, mandatory extended producer responsibility policies that require unwilling industries to pay for or physically manage spent products, or both, and the banning of certain materials (such as plastic bags or expanded polystyrene foam) from sale. Many of its scholars write eloquently on the antiecological role of a waste-management industry that provides recycling services along with disposal. They fiercely rebut the faulty data and misleading logic of industries that, along with sympathetic municipal-solid-waste managers, advocate combustion or gasification of municipal solid waste for energy as an ecologically sustainable alternative to disposal, one that is akin to recycling, composting, prevention, and reuse. In this aspect, their distrust of business comes through in a clarion call.

Holding two contradictory positions is anything but hypocritical; it is the hallmark of full and free thought and is the basis of dialectical reasoning and communication. At the same time, when social movements discursively or practically admit contradictory policies and programs, they inadvertently open the door to powerful actors within business or the state to act strategically to foster solutions they like in place of those they don't. The exertion of this kind of strategic power has been studied over the years within the context of environmental problems. Research has examined the emergence of recycling programs that entail curbside collection of mixed residential recyclables by private firms contracting to municipalities (Cummings 1977; Gould, Schnaiberg, and Weinberg 1996; Weinberg, Pellow, and Schnaiberg 2000). Each study interpreted the flourishing of such programs as interfering with more materially and socially meaningful alternatives (deposit laws in the case of Cummings, community enterprises in the case of the others). Matthew Crenson (1971) and Thomas Beamish (2002) studied the social conditions in which a material environmental problem is *not* constructed as one in social terms. Crenson called this phenomenon "unpolitics": the case of a serious problem no one is politically interested in and no one talks about. If busy-ness is at the overactive end of an axis of ways to underaddress a problem, unpolitics is at the other. Outside the sphere of environmental issues, Nina Eliasoph has investigated the dynamics of American voluntarism that lead concerned, informed, and enthusiastic citizens to "tamp down" public-spirited critique in favor of what is "do-able close to home" (1998, 12). Her findings are compatible with what I see as the downside of the "can-doism" that is rampant in discourse about solid-waste problems. It is widely acknowledged that any action that "gets the word out," "helps even one person," or is "a start" is part of an overall positive trend (Crompton 2008). To suggest, as I am doing, that busy-ness does not in fact constitute diverse, collaborative progress on multiple fronts requires a theory of why it might be otherwise. Here the work of Steven Lukes (2004) on power is a useful start.

Lukes identifies three dimensions of power, with power defined as an instance in which A gets B to do what he would otherwise not do. The first dimension is overt and common to the everyday sense of exerting power. Through force, coercion, or fair fight (as in a battle of votes), A succeeds and gets his way; the victory is there for all to see. The second dimension of power has to do with less overt and formal means—by controlling the agenda. Peter Bachrach and Morton Baratz (1970) describe this process as the "mobilization of bias." Much of the work behind this type of exertion of power is done outside formal structures in which an outcome is supposed to be decided. Lobbying, influencing the media, and other discursive tactics take place so that certain matters never come up for a vote, laws are not passed, options are not considered. Linguist George Lakoff (2004) has written about this phenomenon as "issue framing." In this case, A controls the agenda such that B cannot attempt to do what he would otherwise do; B may gripe about it, but his gripes have no context in which to become a basis of a fight (fair or otherwise). Nevertheless, the victory can be detected with some research on B's preferences and ideas, even if A and B do not engage in a contest with a clear outcome.

The third dimension of power is, as Lukes states, the most insidious.[2] In this case, A consciously or unconsciously prevents B from even considering what he would otherwise do. Stated another way, A has enough control over the production of knowledge that he sets the rules of the game from the outset; his agenda represents all that is conceivable. Given this background, B acts against his own interests and in the interests of A, all the while thinking that he (B) is in fact acting in his own interests. The nature of this form of power is what Antonio Gramsci called "hegemony." It is able to be carried out without detection and in a wide sphere, sometimes even without A's own awareness, because the development of individual consciousness and freedom of will takes place within a set of preexisting constraints and opportunities that have been shaped in the past more by those in power than by those without it. As Raymond Williams puts it, "The whole lived social process is practically organized by specific and dominant meanings and values" (1977, 109).

Using the A–B power formulation, busy-ness as an outcome of the successful exertion of power can be thought of in the following way. Imagine a case in which B has finite resources and can pursue only one of two alternative options to achieve his goal, which is against A's interest. Option 1 is highly effective, and Option 2 is either less effective or ineffective. Through direct exertion of power, A may prevent B from pursuing Option 1. Or A may work behind the scenes such that B sees Option 2 as feasible but Option 1 as impossible. Griping, B will turn to Option 2 while still acknowledging the superior effectiveness of Option 1. Finally, A may exert power to the extent that the superiority of Option 1 is no longer known. B will come to consider both options as equally effective, compatible, or constitutive. Moreover, A may extend the idea that B is free to pursue both options if he is able to muster the resources; he may suggest that Option 2 is a first step to Option 1. Working on Option 2 keeps B busy and A free.

Essential in this example is that B cannot devote full resources to pursuing both Options 1 and 2. Also essential in the example of busy-ness being cultivated by power in its third dimension is that A knows that Option 2 is less effective than Option 1, but B does not. There are two reasons for the superiority of A's knowledge. First, A is in the business that both options seek to affect; B is an amateur. And A knows certain rules of the game ahead of time because these rules are his bread and butter. Second, A has won before. He controls knowledge and the production of knowledge. B is new to the game, learning as he goes.

In this book, I demonstrate that in the realm of solid waste, each of these three dimensions of power play out in the diversion of B toward Option 2 (busy-ness or unpolitics). These exercises are not theoretical; they take place in flesh, blood, tonnage, and toxicity. We will see packaging firms fiercely opposing legislated fees and taxes that would force the return of their spent products to them. We will see some of these same firms realize consumer-based recycling programs as an "Option 2" and promote them actively via grassroots environmental organizations. We will see consortiums of waste-producing industries argue against having to account for and safely manage their own huge tonnages of solid waste even as they laud residents and municipalities for doing so with their far smaller tonnages. Other industrial groups will take the stage as well, promising jobs and efficiency through recycling, but at considerable public expense. All are examples of the first and second dimensions of power such that the much celebrated "recycling" turns out to be defined narrowly as the collection of bottles, cans, and paper in mixed form from residents' homes and some businesses for sorting and selling on uncertain global commodity markets.

The exertion of the third dimension of power, as Lukes has extensively discussed, is harder to demonstrate. In some cases, Option 2 will be the opposite of busy-ness; it will be an absence of socially constructed attention where one would expect it given the material qualities of the problem (as in cases investigated in Crenson 1971 and Beamish 2002). Why do environmentally concerned individuals and groups care so passionately about glass waste but do not really consider textile waste as the same type of problem? Why are more questions not asked about the massive tons of industrial waste that go unrecycled and unmonitored each year, when focus on municipal recycling rates is intense to the point of obsession? Why is the promise of recycling so rooted to the idea of the community enterprise, when this scale leaves most municipal waste to be handled through disposal or industrial-scale recycling? Why is recycling more types of plastic called for by citizens as a solution to the problems of plastics in general even though it does nothing to reduce risks from plastics to health and ecosystems? The attention to some features of solid-waste solutions (glass recycling, municipal recycling rates, local economic development, plastic recycling) suggests missing or inaccessible knowledge about the problems of textile waste, industrial waste, the scale of waste solutions, and the ecology of synthetic polymers. Data on these topics are not being gathered and disseminated as they should be; there is a problem in the social production of knowledge. There is also a problem with the definition of social problems to begin with—a problem with the notion that personal responsibility, visibility, locality, and closeness to home are overused to understand what is wrong with solid waste and all environmental ills.

Within the profession of waste management, the word *diversion* refers to a measure, expressed either as a rate or weight in tons, of discards that do not make their way to disposal in landfills or incinerators but are diverted to beneficial use through recycling, reuse, or composting.[3] Diversion is a measure of material success in solid-waste solutions. More generally, the term has common meanings that include "routing via an alternative" and in other contexts "fun" in the sense of being taken away from the dreary realities of life. This fortuitous coincidence of definitions sums up what this book is seeking to analyze and reveal.

The Chapters

Each chapter of this book consists of an historical account of tensions and struggle around solid-waste problems, involving groups in industry, civil society, and government. The problems chosen are meant to shed light on cases in which the recycling or Zero Waste movement holds contradictory positions that open the field for powerful business interests bent on derailment of concern away from change and in harmless directions. Chapter 1 contrasts two waste materials, glass and textiles, asking why the former is so subject to concern as waste among the recycling movement, but the latter far less so. Chapter 2 examines a clash of policy mechanisms: those that partially tax producers (through container deposits and product fees) and those that completely tax consumers (curbside collection of recycling). Chapter 3 considers a disparity between sectors of waste generators—urban residents and manufacturers—and investigates why so much attention is invested in the former's solid waste, when the latter's tonnages are so much greater. Chapter 4 looks at scales of recycling, questioning the popular contemporary focus on the community/ local scale as a space of material exchange. Chapter 5 returns to the clash of mechanisms examined in chapter 2, this time focusing on plastic wastes. The conclusion makes concrete proposals, calling for a strengthened federal role in gathering industrial statistics and proposing a set of material-specific urban-waste policies. It also invites the recycling public to embrace a humble process—composting—that holds real transformative potential to cultivate people and heal the earth.

The historical periods are sequential, with chapter 1 starting in the late eighteenth century, following the fate of glass and textile discards through both world wars, through the economic transformation known as Fordism, and up to the cusp of the first iteration of the solid-waste "crisis" that would be felt in U.S. cities in the late 1960s. Chapter 2 starts on Earth Day 1970, with the emergence of the contemporary recycling movement, charting the rapid development of curbside recycling (of which glass was part, but textiles were not) and the onset of the second solid-waste crisis organized around the infamous Mobro 4000 garbage barge of 1980. Chapter 3 begins around 1980, reviewing the successes and failures in congressional attempts to address different problems of industrial solid waste during fiercely antiregulatory presidencies as knowledge about the billions of tons of such waste remained absent in the overall imagination of environmentalism of the time. Chapter 4 takes place in the 1990s and 2000s with the emergence of Zero Waste as a new framework for civil-society organizing around waste solutions, with heavy emphasis on turning waste into wealth as a local tool of economic development. Chapter 5 starts in the present and looks to the future, examining new forms of activism and policymaking around producer responsibility as well as the management of materials so as to slow climate change. The conclusion is also future oriented, with policy recommendations, and invites future discourse about the role of ecological citizenship and human relation to the soil.

The Actors

Three major groups of businesses have been active over this history. The first includes firms that extract raw materials or manufacture products of use. Although some were and are "mom and pop" enterprises, in the main they are huge global industries whose manufacturing decisions entail vast quantities of materials. And although their products are varied, they share a strong desire to be left free, especially by government but also by citizens exerting pressure on them, to conduct business as they see fit.

A second group is far smaller—the scrap industry, which hails its origins in the rag-tag alliance of peddlers and junkmen that gradually professionalized and organized during both world wars. Today the scrap industry is a strong but not extremely powerful sector of the U.S. industrial economy. Its stance toward government and citizen involvement has been mixed. While chafing under periodic pressure to move its unsightly operations away from public gaze, this sector has also sought and sometimes gained from direct collaboration with state and civil society, making the case that it has a role to play in making good use of society's discards.

A third group constitutes a rival to the scrap industry. An outgrowth of a different historical alliance of garbage collectors and dump owners, the waste-management industry of today controls nearly all disposal of urban wastes and competes with the scrap industry for state contracts to recycle municipal paper, cans, and bottles. With vast disposal-site land holdings, access to networks for long-haul waste transport, and government contracts for collection and disposal across the United States, this oligopoly has consolidated power by treating disposal and recycling as opposite sides of the same waste-management coin. Recycling is what it does if municipalities are willing to pay, but disposal is what it does best.

Municipalities and counties, which have the responsibility for collecting trash and recycling, either through public workforces or contracting out, are the first set of government actors to have to deal with waste. By and large, they treat waste as an immediate problem to be dealt with, something sitting on the curb that has to be taken away—and soon. States lead in enactment of laws that curtail producer freedom. All returnable-container deposit laws in the United States are enacted at the state level. States also, to widely varying degrees, engage in solid-waste-management planning and enforce federal solid-waste regulations (Scicchitano and Hedge 1993). Some have advanced institutions of governance that conceive of solid-waste solutions on scales larger than the local; others desire nothing more than to be left alone. The federal government, with a few exceptions, has been a relatively minor actor in the management of solid waste, but, I argue, it has promise to do more. The environmental movement has not fully tested or even called on this potential to coordinate solid-waste policy at an effective and meaningful scale. Cynicism about the federal role is more than deserved, given its almost forty years of retrenchment and ineptitude after a brief flourishing in the early 1970s (Dunlap and Mertig 1992). Nonetheless, I argue that this role merits reconsideration and that such reconsideration goes beyond addressing questions of solid waste to potential arenas for enhancing democracy (Beck 1995; Lake 2002).

Within civil society, the two predominant constellations of actors are, as described earlier, community-based forms of activism (including the antitoxics and environmental justice movements) and what I call the "recycling movement." The recycling movement includes organizations and institutions that promote recycling, composting, and reuse and that encourage prevention of waste via purchasing choice for environmental and social reasons, not just as business. Many of these organizations are or started as community-based ecology centers that included an educational and neighborhood-building mission along with material goals. Others are the large national environmental lobbying groups, notably the Natural Resources Defense Council (NRDC) and the Environmental Defense Fund (EDF), that were formed in the late 1960s and early 1970s. These groups use legislative participation and the courts to fight for policy changes on a wide range of environmental issues, among which solid waste is but one. Another set of groups is more explicitly focused on solid-waste policy, seeking to integrate local action with the gathering and dissemination of information and sometimes critical analysis. These groups include the Grassroots Recycling Network, the Institute for Local Self-Reliance, INFORM, and other organizations working for Zero Waste.

The Method

My research method involves following material metrics and social meaning associated with waste tonnage and toxicity. In considering any question of risk, injustice, resource squandering, social benefit, or any other claim related to solid waste, I first ask how much of the particular waste type in question is being generated, what it consists of, and how it compares to other waste quantities. I then examine socially constructed attention to the waste in question, expressed in public discourse and public policy. For both types of inquiry, I draw on information published in primary sources, including newspapers and trade journal articles; reports from a wide range of state agencies, nonprofit research organizations, and trade associations; the archives of grassroots recycling groups; and the text of proposed and enacted legislation at the federal, state, and local level.

Research on social meaning requires looking at what people say spontaneously in conversations over time. To this end, I have followed dialog and debates on GreenYes, the listserv of the Grassroots Recycling Network, for roughly ten years and a wide range of other listservs and blogs. In the course of my research, I also conducted ten semistructured interviews with government officials and nonprofit researchers that focused on their experiences gathering waste statistics. Their frank discussions of the political ramifications of asking industry for data were premised in my keeping their names anonymous. I cite four of these interviews directly; the remainder informed where I went to look for published evidence.

Research on material metrics requires longitudinal statistics on waste quality and quantity. For these statistics, I relied heavily on data reported annually by the U.S. Environmental Protection Agency (EPA), as compiled by its long-time contractor, Franklin Associates, and reported in a publication called *Municipal Solid Waste in the United States: Facts and Figures*. "Franklin data," as this information is colloquially known in solid-waste circles, is admittedly imperfect. It is based on an extrapolation of discard-material generation, disposal, and recovery that starts with a monitoring of domestic manufacture and import of products and is combined with estimates of product life span. This projection of what, in total, Americans are going through per year in terms of consumption of stuff is then compared to data compiled by various disposal and recovery industries to estimate how much is disposed and how much is recovered for recycling, reuse, composting, or other beneficial application. None of these calculations is transparent. Although Franklin does discuss its methodology in general, its actual calculation methods and raw data sources are proprietary. Critics have pointed out these insufficiencies (Knapp 2008). Nonetheless, I consider Franklin data as useful a baseline as any upon which to build arguments about tonnage. Comparing these estimates to those that are directly measured in various cities—namely, waste-characterization studies—does generally confirm the overall portrait of waste that Franklin paints.

I have drawn information on toxicity, in contrast, from a wide range of primary and secondary sources that discuss both well-established and speculative concerns about the effects that waste materials have on human health and ecosystems. These effects are felt in various ways. They stem from out-and-out creation of new compounds (dioxins) as a result of incineration; dispersal of heavy metals and a wide array of chemicals in air, water, and soil as near and long-term impacts of landfilling or incineration; as well as the ingestion of residues of consumption (especially in the case of plastics). They also include the established health impacts of activities inherent to solid-waste handling but not to the waste material itself—most notably emissions from diesel trucks. My role as a sociologist is not to evaluate systematically all competing claims to the toxicity or safety of materials, transformative processes, and containment technologies, but to identify areas of extreme concern among the public, as compared to no concern, and to remark on instances in which such concern appears not to match the magnitude of material metrics or the policies enacted. This approach leads me to concede, among other things, that contemporary waste-to-energy technologies (i.e., those that burn waste to produce power), which account for a large percentage of disposal in Europe and Japan, are in the near term relatively safe in terms of emissions (orders of magnitude safer than past and in some cases present technologies used in the United States), but at the same time to reject waste combustion as unacceptably risky on the basis of a much more complex precautionary principle.

This book grew out of my academic research but has been equally informed by my professional experience as a midlevel bureaucrat working in the recycling field within a large municipal agency. In that capacity, I have been granted access to facilities and have had frank conversations with engineers, managers, secondary materials brokers, and trade lobbyists who, I strongly suspect, would not have been willing to talk to me in the context of a formal research endeavor. What I have learned has guided my formal research on documented material practice but—out of ethical considerations and plain fairness—has not been reported as research data in this book. Industry individuals' reluctance to speak frankly about the materials they manage and their interests as a group, I should stress, does not stem from any concern about the political ramifications of a critical analysis of their material practice. My experience is that those in the waste and recycling industries as well as those representing manufacturing and retailing are utterly unconcerned on that score, but that they are quite concerned over proprietary information and competition with others in their industry as well as averse to enhanced regulation that scrutiny of their activities might engender.

Unlike many studies of waste from a social science perspective, I conducted no participant observation among communities burdened by waste facilities or among groups benefiting from positive alternatives (although I have spent time in both locations on and off over the years). This choice in part stemmed from my professional role, the need to avoid conflict of interest, and the desire not to abuse my status as a government official. My research, furthermore, did take me abroad literally and virtually, but comparative policy remains outside the scope this work. For this reason, there will be little discussion of rich, interesting, and quite different social movements and institutional forms at work to reduce waste in Canada, Europe, Japan, China, India, and Africa—all of which I have "visited" online or in person in my ongoing sociological study of waste.

What I contribute instead is a joining of technocratic, often difficult-to-access information on materials and their flows to the discussion of environmental justice, sustainable cities, and the politics of the environment in the United States.

My Politics

I have already stated that my analytic impulse is to mistrust business as a whole to consistently and coherently make products without ongoing harm to ecosystems and people. My political perspective urges an informed, skeptical ecological citizenship, cultivated through deliberative, discursive democracy, that will guide the state in steering and controlling capitalism's tendency to harm. Dangerously, however, the critiques I make of the recycling movement in this book bear superficial resemblance in some cases to those made from a diametrically opposed right–libertarian perspective (Scarlett 1994; Tierney 1996). The sole point that this perspective and I have in common is the rejection of symbolism as a reason to value recycling or any other waste-diversion activity. The right–libertarian perspective points out instances in which recycling does not make economic sense in order to argue for the full privatization of recycling where and when it is economically advantageous to the business sector. I point to the same lack of economic basis to argue for the displacement of financial responsibility from municipalities and taxpayers to commodity-producing businesses. Right libertarians argue that the "feel-good" aspects of recycling participation lead to irrational policy. Their project here is to discredit systemic concern among the public over manifold environmental problems. I acknowledge and investigate the same "feel-good" quality as a symptom of political immaturity on the part of the relatively privileged in our deeply unequal society. Proponents of waste-to-energy, furthermore, are beginning to respond to the erroneous linkage of personal to industrial waste that, as I explain in chapter 3, has unfortunately begun to be articulated in popular environmentalist discourse. Although correctly pointing out the faulty logic behind such linkages as well as the fact that data on industrial waste are very old, conservative pundits nevertheless argue that industrial waste is no longer a problem (M. Hall 2010). I examine the age of these same data as a problem in and of itself and a more recent social construction of the personal–industrial waste linkage as dismaying in its unhealthy individualization of systemic phenomena. If there is anything a reader should take away from this book, it is that I am deeply allied with those concerned about environmental and social problems involved in waste. But I can't stay silent on the contradictions I have observed for fear of uttering a discouraging word.

The Promise

As I sift through data and consider conflicts and consensus among different groups in society, I always have in mind the recycling public—people who participate in recycling at home or at work and profess to care about problems of solid waste. In my professional work, I meet people like this every day who have questions and concerns about their own contribution to solid-waste problems and who wonder—rightfully so—why more can't be done to turn the crap that we continue to throw out into something useful. Their numbers are measured in recycling rates, public-opinion surveys, and electoral response to changes in recycling laws and are reflected in the discourse of popular magazines and online media. As Allen Hershkowitz of the NRDC says, "People understand recycling—it's the most widely practiced environmental activity in the U.S." (*Congressional Quarterly Researcher* 2007, 1). Recycling is not a phenomenon of the American affluent only; strong recycling participation extends across income, race, and class (Taylor 1997). I find promise in these numbers. When I argue, as I do, that recycling is at present a cramped, inappropriately commodified and potentially self-defeating reflex in the face of environmental risk and loss, I also recognize the great promise in people's enthusiastic participation. With this book, I hope to address the U.S. recycling public that, as I have found in my academic and professional travels, thirsts for information about waste and its consequences. Rather than discouraging recycling as it is currently practiced, I invite readers to think about recycling in all that it might be.

1

Rags and Bottles

In 2002, I toured a glass-beneficiation facility, a plant whose sole purpose was to ready recycled glass to make new bottles, fiberglass, and high-end sand substitute. Beneficiation facilities are a second stop after glass containers go through a first round of sorting at a materials recovery facility (abbreviated as MRF and called a "murf" in the recycling business). Bottles and jars that residents set out with their cans, plastics, and other recyclables rarely arrive at materials recovery facilities intact, but even those that do are sure to get broken as they proceed. As mixed recyclables move along a conveyor belt, a combination of magnets, electrical currents, air jets, and hand picking remove metal, plastic, and paper, leaving only glass. As glass is sifted out of the moving mix, it emerges crushed, mixed with food residues and bits of label. In this form, known as "dirty mixed cullet," it is not good for much. At best, it can be used as low-grade fill or as what is known as "alternative daily cover," a substitute for the earthen layer that must cover each day's load of trash at the landfill. If it is going to become anything more, it has to be shipped to a beneficiation facility to get cleaned and color sorted.

In the facility I visited, what was being delivered looked like something you would find under your car's backseat if you hadn't cleaned it for ten years. To me, it was unrecognizable as glass. But as this mass of gooey, crunchy, whitish material moved through the facility, it was bathed in water, dried with high-speed jets of air, and crushed to a uniform size. Gradually, it began to look like glass again. Optics took over from there—beams of light calibrated to the refraction of clear, brown, and green hues shot through each shard, classifying and then sorting it, with a blast of targeted air, off the belt and into a bunker below. As the now sparkling, gemlike pieces moved along the conveyor, they were neatly blown into gleaming piles by color. After optical sorting, small pieces of plastic and metal as well as an interesting array of china and ceramic bits were left over, all destined for the landfill. The point of glass beneficiation was to yield green glass that could be shipped to Europe to make new wine and beer bottles, brown glass that would stay in North America to be used to make beer bottles, and the highest-value output—clear glass that could substitute for as much as 30 percent input in the production of a new bottle or jar. Pieces too small to be color sorted were crushed to a fine dust that was utterly indistinguishable from sand. Safe to pick up and handle, this material would also go to beneficial use as sand substitute.

As I watched this amazing technology at work, part of me was awed at the precision of the optics and cheered by the restoration of a mass of muck into cleanly sorted piles of useful material. Another part of me was dismayed, however, at the long journey and expenditure of energy and money that these pieces of glass had needed to take from the moment they were set down beautiful and intact in someone's home. Had the shards in question been extremely valuable, rare, or toxic, such costly, transport-intensive, and painstaking attention might have made sense. But as I discuss in this chapter, none of these qualities applies in the case of glass.

Several years later I worked on a large and fascinating project whose goal was to sample and classify what was in the garbage that residents of my city discarded everyday. Crews of workers stood around tables, carefully teasing apart the contents of black trash bags into categories of organic and inorganic material. Each category had its own bucket into which sorted items were tossed; these buckets surrounded the sort tables, filling up with separated rotting food, diapers, unrecycled metals, plastics, paper, variously colored glass, and other wastes. Among the buckets were two marked for textiles—one for clothing, another for linens and home furnishings. To my surprise, the clothing bucket filled to overflow each day with clean, intact, and often fashionable apparel. In the other bucket, forlorn but still fluffy stuffed animals, lace curtains, and towels with tags on them burgeoned. Dirty rags were a rarity in these buckets, which daily filled up with an enticing array of quality merchandise. I was again dismayed. Why hadn't people donated these textiles to thrift shops? Why was so much useable material being thrown away?

The quantity of textiles in the trash was a striking and unexpected finding, one borne out when the data were analyzed over thousands of samples. Close to 5 percent, or almost 200,000 tons, of textiles were going to landfills each year in my megacity jurisdiction. This tonnage was similar to the quantity of glass containers thrown out annually by local residents, only about half of which was being properly recycled at the time. (NYC DS 2007; see also appendix II). As it would turn out, national statistics suggested that textile and glass wasting were taking place in roughly equal quantities across the United States.

In this chapter, I look at the histories of glass and textile waste to understand how they came to occupy such different statuses in waste policy and public concern today.

Glass and Textile Wasting in the United States

In the contemporary United States, comparable tonnages of glass[1] (7.2 million tons) and textiles (8.5 million tons) are disposed of each year as municipal solid waste, destined for landfills or incinerators (U.S. EPA 2009b; see also appendix II). The quantity of glass diverted from disposal, however, is roughly double the quantity of textiles diverted. Some 2.8 million tons of glass as compared to roughly 1.5 million tons of textiles are reclaimed for reintroduction into the economy each year, yielding a diversion rate of 28 percent for glass as compared to only 15 percent for textiles (U.S. EPA 2009b; see also appendix II).

Diversion of each of these materials is organized under quite distinct arrangements. Both local and regional governments intervene heavily to promote the recycling of waste glass. Nearly all municipalities include glass bottles in mixed recycling collections, along with plastic, metal, and paper recyclables (*Waste News* 2010a). In addition, 10 U.S. states have container deposit laws (also known as "bottle bills") that encourage redemption of glass beverage bottles as well as plastic bottles and aluminum cans, at point of sale, for recycling. As a result, more than one-quarter of container glass is recycled or beneficially reused each year. Municipal funding for collection of used textiles, however, is a rarity, nor do states impose deposits or other waste-related fees on clothes, shoes, linens, or other textile materials. Instead, textile reuse (through resale) and recycling (to produce composite fabrics) is organized through networks of nonprofit social service organizations (thrift shops), with consolidation and supplementary collection of waste textiles accomplished via the private textile-scrap industry. Given the comparability of the amount of waste materials involved, why are the prevailing methods for recovering glass and textiles so different? In particular, if comparable amounts of waste glass and textiles are going to the dump, why do recycling programs target one substance but not the other?

From a standpoint of pure economics, there is little reason for local government to involve itself in reclamation of either material from municipal waste. Landfilling and incineration have been and continue to be the easiest and least-expensive methods to handle most municipal trash (Miller 2000). Contemporary policies of reuse and recycling instead reflect political will to do something better with waste than dumping it. This political will began to emerge in 1970, when a nascent ecology movement first cast waste prevention, reuse, recycling, and composting as environmentally beneficial methods of handling waste (De Bell 1970). Demand for local governments to organize and implement reclamation of materials from municipal solid waste was rooted first and foremost in goals of pollution reduction, resource conservation, and beautification of the surroundings (Murphy 1994). The ecology movement also pointed to economic benefits that would accrue (in jobs through recycling, revenue sharing from the sale of valuable recyclables), but these benefits were secondary to ecological goals.

The institutionalization of municipal recycling collections, which are now commonplace for metal, glass, paper, and certain plastics across the United States, has been a successful achievement of the U.S. environmental movement. As recycling has emerged as an environmental "success story," so has a common understanding of what is a solid-waste "problem" and what is a desirable "solution." In this common understanding, waste glass is a problem, and recycling is the solution, but waste textiles remain largely outside discussion and activism. This disparity in attention, it turns out, is the inverse of the ecological and economic qualities of both materials in waste. Glass is, relative to textiles and many other materials, of low concern environmentally and in fact a massive drain on recycling economics, whereas textiles have serious environmental impacts at all stages of the lifecycle and are traded on a thriving secondary market.

Neither Impacts nor Prices

Glass is an inert material that does not contribute to pollution in landfills or incinerators (Reindl 2003a, 2003b). It is produced domestically from plentiful raw materials, primarily silica (GPI 2006). New bottles can be produced with substitution of up to 30 percent clean, crushed, color-sorted recycled glass for virgin inputs. Such a mix saves some energy and reduces some emissions in comparison to using 100 percent virgin inputs, but these benefits are minor in comparison to comparable benefits for reuse of paper, metal, and plastics (Saphire and Bluestone 1994). Mixed-color broken glass may also be used as a substitute for sand and gravel in road building. Such uses are less costly but yield even more marginal environmental benefits (Reindl 2003b).

In terms of disposal impacts, glass is far more benign than other materials that municipalities routinely collect for recycling, including paper and certain plastics. In a landfill, the decomposition of organic materials, including paper and cardboard, release methane, making landfills the third-largest source of such greenhouse gas emissions in the United States (U.S. Census Bureau 2008). Although the most frequently recycled metals are relatively inert, some varieties—such as heavy metals—can leach from landfills into groundwater and contribute to the pollution of aquifers (Barlaz, Green, Chanton, et al. 2004). In waste-to-energy plants, the combustion of plastics in particular has been identified as a source of toxic emissions (Gilpin, Wagel, and Solch 2003). It should be noted that the pollution resulting from modern landfill and combustion is highly dependent on the technological controls used, and its inevitability is highly contested (Commoner 1995; Nemerow, Agardy, Sullivan, et al. 2009). What is salient to this discussion is the contrast of the relative risks of disposal of waste textiles with the absolute absence of such impacts for waste glass.

Glass also contrasts with other materials at earlier stages of the product life cycle. Extraction of virgin timber, minerals, and petroleum that are used to make paper, metal, and plastic products has wide-ranging impacts on resource availability and pollution, with complex effects on ecosystems. Manufacturing processes associated with each are energy intensive and have pollution impacts that far outweigh those for glass production. Glass, in contrast, is made from materials that are plentiful and available worldwide (GPI 2006). Their excavation is not without impacts, but these impacts pale in contrast to those produced by other types of materials extraction (Saphire and Bluestone 1994). Unlike other commodities, glass is not generally traded globally; it is fabricated and used in its country of origin (an exception involves trade in glass for certain beverage containers—the United States and the United Kingdom import continental beers and wines and with them foreign glass) (CA DEC 2006). Transportation pollution from the glass trade, at least on a global scale, is therefore not as pronounced as for other commodities. Nor is the glassmaking industry a major polluter. The glassmaking process is somewhat energy intensive, but it generates far fewer air or water impacts than do paper, plastic, and metal manufacturing processes (Saphire and Bluestone 1994).

dered in terms of "cradle-to-grave" impacts, in fact, textiles are environmentally significant than glass. The disposal impacts of natural and synthetic fiber textiles are comparable to those for paper and plastics, respectively. The textile and apparel industry is one of the most energy-intensive and heavily polluting manufacturing sectors: petroleum refining, pesticide application to cotton, and finishing and dyeing processes have substantial impacts on air, water, and ground pollution (Slater 2003).

Despite these facts, an argument might be made to include glass in municipal recycling programs if its value on secondary markets served to subsidize the extra costs associated with recycling more ecologically relevant materials. But recycled glass commands a far lower price per ton than other secondary commodities and then only after costly processing to clean, color sort, and crush glass to useable specifications.[2]

Low prices for clean, color-sorted cullet and long transport distances to the few bottling plants in the nation that take cullet as an input mean that the use of recycled glass in new container production is economically viable only when heavily subsidized by the state and sourced through deposit redemptions (which facilitate a clean, presorted source of glass).[3] Most municipalities struggle to find outlets for their mixed, broken glass, often resorting to using it as "alternative daily cover," a substitute for the layer of earth applied on the landfill at the conclusion of each day's dumping.

In contrast to glass, the market for used textiles is strong and vibrant. Once donated, old clothes enter a complex system of grading that sends materials, by quality, to a cascading range of end markets. The best-quality clothing and shoes are retained for sale domestically in thrift and consignment shops. Serviceable clothing of lower quality is baled for export to markets in eastern Europe, South Asia, South America, and Africa. Linens, towels, and ripped, torn, or stained clothing are sold in bulk to intermediary scrap processors, who grade it for use as industrial wiping rags or, as last resort, for uses more akin to recycling than to reuse—such as the production of low-quality composite fabrics used to line auto trunks or as padding. Like trade in metal, paperboard, and plastic recyclables, the used-textile economy is a global one, with flows of materials emanating from rich, developed nations for processing and use in the developing world (Schor 2002). Demand for used textiles is high and a source of profit for the scrap-textile industry, yielding profits as well as funding for charitable social service programs. Nonetheless, it succeeds in diverting less than 15 percent of all textile waste generated annually (U.S. EPA 2009b; see also appendix II)

To summarize: a low-value, relatively environmentally benign material receives massive concern, state spending, and municipal attention, whereas a high-value, environmentally significant material of equal presence does not. Municipal glass-recycling programs divert 25 percent of all waste glass, a rate considered by the environmental community as too low (CRI 2008), but the nation's network of thrifts shops and for-profit rag dealers diverts only 15 percent of waste textiles, with the recycling public and most environmental groups uninterested in this outcome. The present arrangements for reclamation of glass and textiles do not appear rational from a contemporary ecological *or* economic standpoint.

To understand why and how this irrational situation came to be, I turn to the history of materials reclamation in the United States before the emergence of the contemporary recycling movement in 1970.

The History of Rags and Bottles in America

In the eighteenth-century and early-nineteenth-century home, materials that came in as purchased commodities stayed for a long time, passing through stages of use and reuse in creative ways (Strasser 1999). The point at which a housewife would trade rags from the rag bag for a trinket or sell them for a penny was one at which they were heavily worn. Glass jars, used in home canning, and glass bottles, which generally contained alcoholic beverages, tonics, and medicines, were rare and expensive during this period because they were hand blown. This is not to say that waste of either material did not exist, but that it occurred after the material had a long and varied career within the early American household.

The value of waste glass and textiles on nascent secondary-materials markets of the eighteenth and early nineteenth centuries was high enough that the vast majority of such materials were recovered, once discarded, by a network of traveling entrepreneurs who either exchanged them on a piece basis or channeled them into larger networks of junk consolidators. Peddlers generally sold bottles for refill, often for illegitimate use in containing inferior products (Beverage World 1982). This rogue form of refill was, in fact, such a problem for legitimate bottlers in the nineteenth and early twentieth centuries that *Scientific American* profiled invention after invention meant to prevent the reuse of a bottle beyond its product's original intent (*Scientific American* 1896). During this same period, demand for old rags grew rapidly as inputs for paper production (Zimring 2005).

Technological advances in automated glass blowing and pulpwood-based paper production, which emerged at the turn of the nineteenth century, began to change the uses to which old bottles and rags were put. Refill of branded bottles with beverage product many times over became a requirement of the burgeoning milk, beer, and soda industries emerging in the first decades of the 1900s (Beverage World 1982). As a result, beverage makers applied their own deposits on bottles bearing their mark or label. Given the cost to transport heavy, bottled beverages, these systems remained on a local or at the most a regional scale well into the twentieth century. In the late nineteenth century, parallel innovations in mass-production technologies brought about a rapid shift in the feedstock used in making paper (Zimring 2005). Wood pulp replaced rags as the economically rational raw material for most paper production, although textiles continued to be used to make high-grade paper, especially when stocks of pulpwood became scarce (during both world wars). Overall, trade in rags took a back seat to trade in steel and other metal scrap, but alternative end markets for rags continued (Zimring 2005). As the scrap industry grew and became more formally organized in the early decades of the twentieth century, several international markets for rags emerged—for industrial wiping cloths, for unraveled wool yarn, for wool composite (known as "shoddy"), and for certain other uses, including batting and silk fiber (New York Times 1913).

The fact that glass waste was not recognized as a commodity worth targeting by the scrap industry is an important detail in the history of U.S. glass reclamation. By the early twentieth century, the scrap industry was professionalizing, seeking to shed the stigma of junk and prove its worth to the U.S. economy. A 1913 article detailing the second annual meeting of the National Association of Waste Materials Dealers described "five general classes" into which the members would be divided, including "rubber, metals, paper stock, cotton and woolen rags, and scrap iron" (New York Times 1913, 2). As in all such accounts, glass was not included. This is not to say, however, that glass waste didn't exist. In the 1920s, many consumers' failure to return empty milk bottles led to the enactment of state and local laws to protect dairy interests by requiring deposit redemption under penalty of civil fine (New York Times 1921). Despite these efforts, the breakage and littering of bottles were noted and decried. In the pre-Depression era of prosperity, commentators lamented the appearance of glass litter along roadsides that pleasure drivers left behind (Los Angeles Times 1921). In the 1930s, assays of discards in municipal dumps led to government and citizen concern over the "useless waste" of bottles that was found (*Los Angeles Times* 1931). Overall, glass waste was critiqued in public discourse as a moral failure and as evidence of a malfunction in the branded refill system upon which the beverage industry depended. Waste glass had little or no value as an input to new production, however, as other scrap materials did. In other words, glass was not recycled into new bottles because there was little economic reason to do so. For glass "scrap" to recover value, it had to be reused, and, for this reason, glass's equivalent to the scrap industry was the beverage and bottling industry itself—a fact that would become highly relevant as the nature of bottling changed in the 1960s.

The emergence of mass-production technologies for domestic consumption and export of finished goods as well the growth in international trade accompanied a rapid increase in household consumption from the mid–nineteenth century onward. Although periods of home mending, repair, and frugality with textiles as well as other materials had peaks during the Depression era and the world wars, the tendency for homemakers to repair and reuse cloth diminished overall (Strasser 1999). Whereas previously even the wealthy had "made over" the few fine articles of clothing they wore, passing them on finally to servants for years more of use, now greater and greater quantities of unwanted clothing and other consumer goods were accumulating in the basements and attics of the well to do (Strasser 1999). A newly emerging model of charity identified the opportunity to solicit such materials as donations a model based not on alms but on the spiritually and economically redemptive qualities of work. In the late nineteenth century, two parallel Protestant movements, Goodwill Industries and the Salvation Army, organized institutions that combined poor relief, job training, and self-funding through sale of rehabilitated, donated material goods—including furniture and clothing (Lewis 1977). There is some evidence that the scrap trade considered these groups as competitors to their profit-driven, export, and industrial-oriented trade (*New York Times* 1924). In other instances, both Goodwill and the Salvation Army made forays into different models of material recovery than the "thrift shop," in particular collecting and selling paper between 1920 and the late 1940s and working with the emerging ecological recycling movement in the 1970s (*Los Angeles Times* 1949; De Bell 1970). However, the rag trade operated in parallel to the collection and sale of used clothing via the thrift shop. As this trade does today, it absorbed unsalable textiles from charities and supplemented its collections with inputs from scavengers, overstock, and industrial cuttings.

As privately organized textile-scrap reclamation became larger in scale and more formally organized, so did municipal waste management. City governments organized street cleaning and sanitation departments, moving into the reclamation business themselves by licensing and letting contracts to organized scavenging companies or by developing factories of their own to sort and grade dry discards for sale to scrap dealers. The entrance of the local state and a professionalizing private sector represented the "scientific management" of waste disposal and recovery in the first decades of the twentieth century (Melosi 1981). The scavenger, a key figure in the early history of scrap reclamation, was forced out in favor of different, more bureaucratic structures organized around waste reclamation. Municipal dumps closed themselves off to freelance collectors, or "trimmers," as they were called. Municipalities entered into contractual arrangements with junkmen. As opposed to "rag men," "junk men" were businessmen with ties to established scrap-dealing firms. They worked on commission, buying and consolidating grades of scrap from rubbish sorted at public expense in centralized municipal facilities.[4]

World Wars: Foreshadowing Can-Doism

As Hugh Rockoff (2007) observes, wars provide a unique opportunity for economic historians to examine market processes in a context in which unusual levels of state intervention and social norms of self-sacrifice and solidarity apply. In both World War I and World War II, major shifts in the availability of virgin imports as well as in markets for recovered materials required new roles for the citizenry. Aspects of these roles would be reprised in the ecology movement that organized around recycling in 1970.

Prior to World War I, much of the nation's scrap supply depended on foreign inputs of both primary and secondary materials. When the war began, textile export embargoes imposed by France and other European nations left the United States with an undersupply of both pulpwood and rags. One 1916 article predicted, "The war is causing a shortage of the material essential for the manufacture of paper and the old-time rag bag will assume its former importance" (*Los Angeles Times* 1916, III16). Before the war, rags had been used only in making the best grades of paper. But the cessation of cheap pulp exports from Scandinavia cut off paper's primary feedstock, driving up demand for scrap cotton and linen. U.S. powder makers, furthermore, were vying for rags to produce gunpowder for military use, paying extremely high prices that crowded out the paper trade. Paper prices climbed precipitously (*Los Angeles Times* 1916). And citizens were called on to supply rags as a patriotic duty.

New York City, which let revenue contracts to firms for the right to rag pick, experienced record high bids in 1916, shortly after the United States entered the Great War (*New York Times* 1916). The paper industry, desperate for rag feedstock to substitute for wood pulp, turned directly to householders to boost supply. "The prevention of waste on the part of the general public will do much to relieve the situation," said R. P. Andrews, president of the Retail Merchant's Association, which represented the paper industry. Noting that "any old cotton or woolen rag has a value today, no matter how old and soiled it may be," Andrews exhorted the public to "save old rags instead of burning them," for which they would be duly compensated. The industry appealed not just to patriotism, but to the history of American pioneering spirit. As Andrews explained, "Years ago every family had its old rag bag and made a practice of selling rags. This applied to the country family and the city family alike. In those days peddlers traveled around the rural districts in their big vans and traded dishpans and other tin utensils for rags. The United States supplied all the rags it needed in those days, but not so at present. Today, the average family throws old rags into the trash and they are burned" (Andrews, qtd. in *Los Angeles Times* 1916, III16).

By the time the United States was poised to enter World War II, export rather than input was driving the scrap economy. When the National Association of Waste Materials Dealers held their annual meeting in 1939, stagnating prices were attributed to "lack of cargo space, high cargo rates and regulations governing exports to belligerent nations" (*New York Times* 1940). Once the United States entered the war, domestic demand for scrap skyrocketed. The Office of Price Administration (OPA), the federal agency charged with stabilizing prices and materials flows for the duration of the conflict, set the maximization of domestic scrap supply as central to its mandate (Bartels 1983). In 1941, the OPA's Bureau of Industrial Conservation launched a year-round drive to promote waste saving and collation for "materials of all types necessary to defense" (*New York Times* 1941b). As during World War I, the public was called on to refrain from the profligacy of modernity and to reembrace the thrift of a now mythic colonial or frontier epoch. In 1941, the conservation chief of the Office of Production Management (OPM) declared that "we are the world's greatest wasters" (*New York Times* 1941a). "Bundles for America," an OPM-sponsored contest to encourage housewives to sew clothes from rags, was "designed to show American women 'how they can recapture the pioneer spirit of independence which contributed so much to the building of the United States'" (*New York Times* 1942a, 22).

Children were important to this appeal to moral civic engagement. The OPA called on the Boy Scouts and Girl Scouts to "inculcate the educational facts regarding salvage so that the needs of our country will be met by proper habits of conservation in the home" (*New York Times* 1944a, 42). Yet despite the widespread enthusiasm for citizen-led scrap drives, the actual practice of collecting scrap from the public was plagued with inefficiencies. As early as 1941, critics cited problems with the "work, save and fight" effort marketed to households (*Washington Post* 1941, 7). OPM director General Knudsen alluded to the fact that "mistakes had been made in the recent 'pots and pans' aluminum campaign conducted by Civilian Defense Chief Mayor F. H. LaGuardia," a notorious incident during the summer of 1941 in New York City in which stocks of donated aluminum languished in scrap yards because the OPM insisted on dealing directly with smelters instead of with scrap dealers. Director Knudsen "emphasized [that] the regular commercial channels of junk collectors and scrap dealers" would be used to consolidate civilian drives, noting that "it was 'silly' to attempt to short-circuit the sorting and stripping function of the dealers" (*Washington Post* 1941, 7).

Nonetheless, the scrap industry found itself ignored and sidestepped as the government and the public joined forces to turn as much scrap as possible out of cupboards, attics, and basements. At the same time, the industry was facing problems in processing the rapidly growing quantity of collected industrial scrap because of manpower shortages (Enright 1942). By 1944, other economic problems emerged. A scandal in which some waste-paper dealers held back sales and sold paper scrap for "non-essential production" surfaced in 1944, with the OPA and the scrap industry collaborating on a criminal crackdown. Paper dealers were having difficulty coming up with the "tremendous tonnages required" by the OPA, maintaining that even if it were to set prices higher, this adjustment would "merely shift [back] to a lower level of prices and would not of itself bring out the tremendous tonnage which is demanded by industry" (*New York Times* 1944b, 25). This situation highlighted a fact not prevalent in the discourse aimed at citizens. Industrial production, not the war effort per se, was most in demand of waste. And industrial scrap, not household sources, furnished the majority of supply.

Nonetheless, the citizen effort was championed and highlighted to the extent of ushering in a protocurbside recycling program in New York City. After Fiorello LaGuardia's 1941 aluminum fiasco, the New York City Police Department appointed "salvage wardens" to support the air-warden corps with state-sponsored junk collection. "This salvage warden system forms an orderly and systematic supplement to the work of the Boy Scouts, Girl Scouts, Salvation Army and other charitable organizations," wrote one commentary approvingly (M. Adams 1942, SM13). Plans exceeded execution, however. That same year New York City housewives complained about the lack of a "regular system for periodical collection" of the tin cans, old paper, and scrap rags they were instructed to save (*New York Times* 1942b, 14).

In his study of World War II salvage drives among citizens, Rockoff (2007) tracks the tonnages of materials collected and the uses to which they were put (or not put) in the context of the nation's overall need for materials in industrial production. He concludes that citizen scrap drives had a very limited impact on the economy but were promoted by local and federal governments primarily because of their effect on morale. In this overtly propagandistic application of "can-doism," we see the first glimmers of what would become a far more subtle utilization of genuine community concern and willingness to "pitch in" with little material outcome. In the decades to follow, however, it would not be the state's war interest that would cultivate such symbolic civic efforts, but rather firms' interest in deflecting onerous taxation and deposit legislation.

Crisis, Cans, and Synthetics

The postwar era experienced a rapid escalation in waste generation after a period in which it had been on the decline, as pent up demand for luxury and convenience goods was unleashed on a thriving manufacturing sector. Within the scrap industry, oversupply of paper, metal, and rag waste materials meant that tonnages were "moving freely," but at "prices lower than were in existence 10 years previous" (Gebel 1954, 3). The effects of increased postwar production and consumption on waste generation would not be explicitly identified until a few years later. In 1954, scrap dealers were still wondering if oversupply were "still the effect of the large (wartime collection) campaigns indoctrinated over the years" (Gebel 1954, 3)—an unlikely explanation given Rockoff's argument about the inefficiency of such drives and the rapidity with which other postwar behaviors changed.

At the same time, municipal solid waste generation was on the rise as well. Per capita rates of municipal solid waste reached their highest in the 1940s, largely due to quantities of ash from coal and wood burning. As such forms of heating were replaced by oil and steam, tonnages declined per capita, reaching lows in the early 1950s (Walsh 2002). Between 1960 and 1970, levels of municipal solid waste started to increase again, rising from roughly 88 to 120 million tons annually over the decade, with changes in composition (see appendix III). In the trash were increasing quantities of paper, metal, and glass packaging, reflecting the fruition of a radical change in product delivery that had been in the making since the end of World War II. In 1946, at the annual meeting of the Packaging Institute, representatives from box and wrapping industries discussed the "unprecedented era" of "vast growth" that would revolutionize the food-retailing industry and establish the United States in a new role of economic preeminence. With the "peacetime application of modern scientific packaging in international trade," the United States would be in the position to import "goods, raw materials, finished articles, fruits, and vegetables" from the Far East and other distant sources as well as to export manufactured goods to these emerging markets (*New York Times* 1946, 51).

The rapid escalation of in municipal solid waste, combined with new regulations for how it could be disposed of in an increasingly urbanized and suburbanized nation, brought on the onset of a "waste crisis" (Melosi 1981). By the mid-1960s, this crisis was experienced first and foremost by municipal sanitation departments and highway administrations charged with roadside cleanup. Commentators described an "avalanche of waste and waste disposal problems" as an "impending emergency" and a "national disgrace" (Hill 1969, C38).

On the glass front, major changes were occurring that would mean an explosion of glass waste. In 1949, the number of bottling plants reached the highest level since pre-Depression years, totaling more than 6,900. According to the beverage industry, "this total reflected many small plants which had been favored with special sugar allotments to provide soft drinks for servicemen" (Beverage World 1982, 46). With the war's end, the decline in the number of small, marginal bottling plants was "rapid and drastic" (Beverage World 1982, 46). In 1950, 250 bottling operations closed, and such closings continued throughout the decade. The reason was increasing cost and complexity of production and distribution methods. As the industry's leading trade journal noted, "the efficient operation of a soft drink plant now required more and better machinery and equipment. Bottling machine producers were forced to increase machine speeds each year. More and more automatic devices were developed. Some closed plants were turned into warehouses in an effort to control production and distribution costs" (Beverage World 1982, 46).

The steel beer can, which had been introduced with limited success during World War II for use overseas, had made significant inroads into the market share for beverages by the 1960s. Its light weight made it economical to transport over long distances; its shape and material precluded refill. The convenience of the "one-way," "no deposit, no return" beer can was so great for both consumers and distributors that by the late 1950s the bottling industry was compelled to imitate to compete. By 1960s, technologies for bottle production and transport had advanced enough to make it profitable to do what in prior decades would have put beverage makers out of business: cease refilling bottles. With this shift, the scale and geographic structure of the beverage industry changed. The number of bottling plants decreased dramatically as their size grew. Distribution networks for soda became national in scale, as large brands such as Coca-Cola and Pepsi crowded out local pop varieties. Facilities that had housed local-scale beverage plants shifted to use as warehouses, receiving and then distributing loads of bottled drinks trucked via long-haul tractor trailers from centralized bottling hubs. As marketing of one-way beverages increased in total and per capita, roadside litter ensued. The aesthetic blight of litter sparked widespread concern starting in the mid-1960s. In this context, glass waste emerged as particularly alarming: with its ability to cut hands, feet, and paws, it constituted not only a nuisance, but a danger.

The textile-scrap industry was hit hard by a parallel industrial development of the 1960s—synthetic fibers. Synthetics were not absorbent and therefore not suitable for resale as industrial wiping rags, a major end market for scrap textiles, nor did they lend themselves to unraveling and reweaving, a practice that was already on the decline for wool and silk by the 1960s as the prestige of the "virgin" label was cultivated by the wool apparel industry. Additional sorting and processing began to be needed to separate natural fibers for sale on existing end markets, which cut into profits. As other branches of the scrap industry thrived, the textile branch found itself struggling to retain a foothold. Starting in 1970, its weakness would become particularly pronounced as it failed to engage with a newly emerging motivation for reclamation: ecology.

Recycling to Save the Earth

It is hard to overstate the suddenness with which the concept of "recycling" emerged within environmentalist discourse on waste problems. Before 1970, engineers had used the term to describe processes of oil or water recirculation (see Harbin 1926). In 1970, the recycling process burst into broad ecological consciousness as the best way to manage the waste crisis, springing forth as if a new concept. In preparation for the first Earth Day, Garrett De Bell wrote, "The principle of recycling is to regard wastes as raw materials to be utilized; this is the only ecologically sensible long-term solution to the solid waste problem. . . . The environmental crisis has come into the public consciousness so recently that the word 'recycle' doesn't even appear in most dictionaries" (1970, 215). The activities organized around Earth Day and other events that preceded and followed it were used to, as the community group Bay Ridge Ecological Action toward a Healthier Environment put it, "reach people on an individual basis and make them more aware of the problems facing not only our specific area but the whole country and the whole world and to educate them as to how they can help improve things" by sorting and consolidating "glass, tin cans, and newspapers" (BREATHE 1972). These three materials, and not rags, were the targets of the community recycling movement from the outset. As the decade proceeded, plastic bottles would be added to this list, but from the start rags were not within the movement's scope.

The scrap industry as a whole seized on the proliferating interest among community-based ecology groups, urging, often to no avail, that municipalities and residents not overlook the industry's centuries of experience in consolidation and marketing, as had so disastrously occurred with LaGuardia's aluminum fiasco. A 1972 editorial in *Secondary Raw Materials*, the scrap industry's trade journal, described the sudden emergence of "collection centers. Here, charitable organizations and other groups tote their discards either for the aesthetic notion behind pollution abatement or for monetary return. . . . They have become quasi 'stockpiles' from which it is expected mills will draw upon when these items are needed." Such stockpiles, noted the editorial, tended to grow as demand stagnated or declined, with scrap dealers "left out of the picture" as the U.S. EPA encouraged such centers to sell directly to industry. In the "retrospect" of 1972 looking back to 1970, stated the editorial, "'recycling' is a well intentioned goal. However, the means now being used to attain this end are both misguided and erroneous. We have an industry with all the expertise necessary to carry out the goals of recycling. There is no need for amateurs or bandwagonners to get in on the act" (*Secondary Raw Materials* 1972, 13).

As in past decades, the scrap industry did not concern itself with glass reclamation. In fact, since the demise of refill in the early 1960s, no one had. Into this role reentered the beverage and bottling industry itself, now for very different reasons. Whereas bottlers had previously been dependent on redemption and refill to make beverage distribution economically viable, now they found themselves the subject of attack by a public organized around the litter and municipal solid waste crises. Among the initiatives sought by environmental groups and directly by states burdened with waste tonnages and litter problems were bottle bills, which would return the husbandry of the bottle back to the bottler after a two-decade vacation. The activities of Keep America Beautiful, a packaging industry interest group, to forestall such efforts by constructing litter as an individual choice have been well documented (Rathje and Murphy 1992; Rogers 2005). But container industries also intervened directly to foster an alternative for the much larger volume of glass waste that was not litter, but rather municipal trash. The answer, they stressed, was postconsumer recycling—collecting broken glass after it had been used and feeding it as raw material back into production.

The Glass Container Management Institute (GCMI), the bottling industry's trade group, began as early as 1967 to study the contexts under which glass recycling—not refill—might work. Technology was not the issue. For millennia, glass blowers had known that a clean supply of broken glass and the appropriate additives could be used in place of sand to make new glass. The question was instead how to get the recycled glass to the bottling plant and how to do it with minimal added cost to the producer. To this end, the GCMI organized voluntary drop-off programs at the 92 facilities that were by then producing glass bottles in 25 U.S. states (*Hartford Courant* 1970). Residents were urged to collect and transport glass directly to these plants or to organize their municipalities to do so for them. But such efforts, even the GCMI acknowledged, would never be more than token because of the extraordinary amount of labor and transportation involved. The same transport economics that had limited bottlers to local or regional scales in the days of refill applied in reverse with glass recycling. The larger scales of distribution were a major reason why bottlers fought bottle bills so fiercely; the costs of taking back bottles that had contained their product stood to damage the allocation of labor, technology, and transportation that worked with one ways. Richard L. Cheney, director of the GCMI, summarized that the "long-range solution to the waste problem" would be the "separation of all components out of waste and returning them for reuse [sic] to their respective industries, such as paper back to the paper mill; aluminum back to the smelter; scrap iron to the foundry; and glass to the glass house" (Christian Science Monitor 1970, 10). And here the glass house meant emphatically not the refilling plant, but the producer of new bottles.

In the decades to follow, recycling advocates would take up the GCMI's recommendation and would pressure municipalities to collect glass, along with metal, paper, and later plastics, at curbside for recycling. It would fall to municipalities to pay for glass beneficiation or to seek out low-end alternative uses, such as road making, to keep glass out of landfills and off highways. If glass recycling was extraordinarily costly, the hope and expectation were that cities, with enough commitment and know-how, would "make it work."

These conditions in 1970 determined the emerging environmental movement's scope of interest concerning waste. The foundering secondary-textile industry failed to make the connection between its trade and the emerging eco-consciousness. In 1971, Richard Frankel, head of the textile division within the National Association for Scrap Materials Industries (the new name for the National Association of Waste Materials Dealers since 1970) pointed out, "When it comes down to textiles, we find the public generally unaware of the textile deposits in solid waste. Unfortunately, it has been a hidden fact, for most of these collections are accumulated in local areas all across the country, and the environmentalist, seeing only a small amount of used clothing and discarded rags, has told us 'there is no problem'" (1971, 104).

Conditions for the thrift shop had ironically never been better. Through the 1960s, thrift shops were stigmatized outlets for the poorest consumers. In 1970s, however, the notion of "vintage chic" emerged concurrently with the contemporary ecology movement. The appeal of retro clothing would stay strong in the decades to follow, and thrift shops would flourish among the rich even more than among the poor. In the 1980s and 1990s, as community-activist recyclers succeeded in transferring the duty of collecting, sorting, and attempting to market glass and then plastic bottles along with metal and paper for recycling, textiles were not considered. There was, after all, a thrift shop in every town.

In Defense of Glass Recycling

The fierce reaction to the suspension of glass from New York City's recycling program in 2002 is but one indicator of the importance placed by the public on including it in any curbside recycling program. In the fiscal crisis following the events of September 11, 2001, Mayor Michael Bloomberg cut glass collection from the curbside program, citing the drain on collection and processing budgets that glass recycling entailed for the reasons explained earlier. The response was rapid and outraged. Hundreds of citizens wrote the city in protest. Public Advocate Betsy Gotbaum warned of the backsliding in public education that would result if portions of the program were suspended "for any length of time." Among the benefits of glass recycling were, per Gotbaum, to "preserve our neighborhoods and deal with our huge solid waste issues." Although this decision had no impact on the New York State bottle bill, Gotbaum remarked that "before we had the bottle deposit law our parks and playgrounds were awash in broken glass. If we end recycling, the playgrounds will again be unsafe for kids because maintenance staff in the Parks Department has been cut to the bone. We need recycling" (2002). A reworking of the city's municipal contracts so as to maximize the value of metal and plastic and thus offset the costs of glass processing ultimately enabled the reintroduction of glass to the program in 2004. Today, New York City pays $65 a ton to have its commingled metal, glass, and plastic recycling taken by a private scrap-metal dealer. If glass were not included in that mix, the city would receive revenue at minimum of $12 a ton, although far lower tonnage would be diverted from disposal.[5]

Among contemporary environmentalists, it is highly controversial to acknowledge the lack of value of "scrap" glass (an industrial contradiction in terms) or to question the environmental benefits of glass recycling at all. GreenYes is a listserv maintained by the Grassroots Recycling Network, a progressive "North American network of recycling and community-based activists who advocate policies and practices to achieve zero waste, to end corporate welfare for waste, and to create sustainable jobs from discards" (Platt and Seldman 2000, i). A 2003 exchange illustrates the contentiousness of critiquing the environmental marginality of glass recycling. The executive director of Coast Waste Management Association, a progressive affiliation of municipalities, recyclers, waste handlers, and nonprofit groups in British Columbia, wrote:

GLASS is a problem. Glass is heavy. Glass markets are more and more just a second use as opposed to closed loop. Glass is inert in the landfill. Glass, in single stream programs, contaminates other materials. It's no wonder many recycling collection operations are considering removing it from the recycling stream. . . . Let's look at the big picture. If we have to make a choice between recycling organics or recycling glass, I say spend the money on backyard composting promotional programs, or curbside chipping & collection. I'm a dedicated recycler, so I want to recycle as much as possible. But just because we've recycled glass in the past doesn't mean we have to continue, especially when faced with tough financial choices. Is glass recycling lower priority than other materials? I put the question to you. (Telfer 2003)

Responses to this provocative post, which, one participant remarked, "touched a lot of nerves" (Spendelow 2003), fell into two groups. Some concurred with the poster, citing comparative data on greenhouse gas emissions, pollutants, and energy usage per ton of virgin versus recycled glass in relation to the recycling of other materials, to make the case for the relatively minor environmental benefits of glass recycling. These voices supported expanding bottle bills and other forms of producer responsibility for glass waste as opposed to curbside collection. Helen Spiegleman (2003), executive director of the Product Policy Institute, another progressive waste-reduction organization, argued forcefully that the GreenYes community concede the futility of glass recycling as it was currently configured. The opposing group, consisting of recycling managers and others who did not so identify, took umbrage at the critique of glass recycling in this dialog. Objections took several forms. Some argued that the environmental and economic benefits of glass recycling would become apparent if only the footprint were drawn widely and accurately enough. With each call to factor in unacknowledged variables, critics of glass recycling responded with more data to clarify their original claim. For instance, when a recycling specialist from Long Beach, California, objected that "here is a piece of the 'big picture' nobody has mentioned in this recent discussion of glass: energy costs/savings. While I don't have percentages handy on the energy used to produce virgin glass vs. recycled glass, it is my understanding that the difference is substantial" (Gates 2003), another poster responded with detailed statistics, saying that he had factored such costs and savings into his calculations (Reindl 2003a). Another recycling advocate objected that the statistics posted in the course of the discussion did not take into account upstream impacts from mining and production, but did not provide information of her own regarding what those aspects were (Hubbard 2003).

The defenders of glass recycling held the position that it should be maintained even if its benefits were not proven because abandoning it would be a step backward. This position was, in their view, political. Said one poster, "How far back you stand to look at this issue impacts the information you get. The reason you do or don't recycle impacts where you stand." In principle, she decried the fact that glass is not "looked at as a resource but rather as a garbage to collect off the street," concluding, "You can back up your own opinion easily. Seeing another viewpoint is more difficult" (Hubbard 2003). One warning summed up the notion that critique of the environmental or fiscal benefits of any form recycling is a slippery slope: "As of now, recycling is something that has the possibility of growing into something bigger than it is, with much economic import and environmental friendliness. Please don't douse the flame just yet, brothers!" (Kender 2003).

As of today, municipality after municipality struggles with glass. The question is how much they are willing to pay to recycle and for how long. In ongoing debates about the challenges of glass recycling to municipalities, applied-policy discourse casts the conundrum in apolitical terms of balancing "short-term program economics and long-term environmental impacts." In some cities, such as Boston, where, as this polite discourse puts it, "economics is paramount" and there are immediate goals of reducing costs in the short term, all glass is crushed into aggregate and used as alternative daily cover. In other jurisdictions, such as Binghamton, New York, whose surrounding county (Broome) has "made a commitment that they wanted to retain glass recycling, despite lower bids [by recycling processors] if the program excluded glass," funds are expended to presort glass before processing to use in municipal drainage and aggregate applications. Although Binghamton pays more for recycled aggregate than it would for virgin sand, it spends less money per ton than if it were to ship cullet to markets to make bottles and fiberglass (Clean Washington Center 2001, 1–4). A 2004 survey of municipal recycling programs, conducted by the National Recycling Coalition (NRC), notes that "cities throughout the U.S. are clearly devoting significant time and energy to the design of the glass collection and processing elements of their overall recycling program." Putting a positive spin on the "challenges" glass poses, the NRC wrote that "compared to other recyclable materials . . . most often glass is the material that garners the most attention and resources during program redesign" (2004, 3).

In the 2003 debate on the GreenYes listserv, one poster hopefully described new investments in cullet-cleaning technologies in Fayetteville,

Arkansas, that would prove that glass reuse as aggregate can save cities money. "Why not take advantage of all the troublesome properties of glass (heavy, color separation, bale contamination) and re-use it as an environmentally responsible substitute for gravel (which needs to stay in the streams/rivers/quarries from which they're currently extracted) in the application of a road base, fill material and/or sand for filters at biotic wastewater treatment plants?" wrote a former Fayetteville municipal employee. The city, she reported, had been

awarded a grant to purchase a glass pulverizer so that we may begin converting commercial glass waste streams into a money-saving gravel/fill alternative for our municipal street/parks departments. Before we applied for the grant, we conducted an in-house audit on how much we spend for gravel and sand. . . . [Y]ou would be amazed to know how much money (in our case, several thousand) your government is spending to extract/purchase a fill material (gravel/sand) while also paying to landfill a perfectly good base material. It's crazy. (Terry 2003)

I called Fayetteville in early 2008 and found that the project had not materialized. In the words of the city's recycling manager, buying the pulverizer was "putting the cart before the horse."[6] Fayetteville agencies would not switch to recycled aggregate. Their consumption of sand and gravel would far outweigh the amount of recycled substitute the city would produce, and they were hesitant about how the change in mix would affect their road-building activities. Moreover, because Fayetteville happens to be near a glass plant in Lubbock, Texas, and thus can sell its color-sorted glass for a price that covers some of the cost of transporting it there, cost savings to the city for using recycled glass locally in public works would have been "a wash," according to this manager. This case, like so many others, was chronicled in its nascent stage as something that "could work!" but quietly extinguished under the reality of market forces. Such iterative attempts to "make recycling work" in this case typify the past fifty years of municipal glass recycling.

In the GreenYes debate, as in all discussions of glass recycling, there is one point of agreement. Refilling, as opposed to recycling, of bottles has substantial, measurable environmental benefits (Saphire and Bluestone 1994; Platt and Rowe 2002). A return to refill systems of reclamation for bottles is, without dispute, by orders of magnitude more environmentally relevant than any form of recycling. Bottle refill saves substantial quantities of energy, eliminates impacts of bottle production, and forestalls truck emissions from municipal recycling collections. As the definitive study on the subject concludes, however, such a system would require a banning of nonrefillable bottles at a national scale in order not to implode under competition (Saphire and Bluestone 1994). Given the U.S. beverage industry's successful resistance of bottle bills (so that in the 10 out of 50 cases in which they have passed, glass is routed to recycling, not to refill), the reasons why refill is not mandatory national policy are obvious.

Although all environmental groups acknowledge the superiority of glass refill to glass recycling, they are hesitant to loosen their focus on the latter reclamation option for fear of losing overall momentum in the larger struggle for sustainable waste management. [7] In this view, even in bottle-bill states, environmental action is focused on preserving the role of glass in the municipal program and creating artificial market conditions in which glass recycling or reuse can be carried on at acceptable levels of state support. In addition, the environmental movement's preference for holding municipalities accountable for implementing curbside recycling is heavily focused on a metric that rewards one thing and one thing only: weight. For this reason alone, it behooves municipalities to keep glass recycling in their programs, even at considerable subsidy. Textiles, for their part, have quietly escalated as a fraction of municipal solid waste with the rapid increase in output of a globalized apparel industry. Inexpensive, short-life fashions are now the marketing model in the developed world. The thrift-shop sector, working with a still surviving scrap-textile trade, can absorb and reroute only a small fraction of the clothing and linens swirling through the economy, most of which still ends in refuse. Municipalities are hardly in a position to add textiles to their curbside collections (even though textiles' weight would help them earn points) because of textiles' unique qualities in the context of commingled collection. When textiles are collected with other materials, even relatively dry paper, moisture, contamination, and the resulting rot stand to destroy any market value they might have. At the same time, U.S. environmentalist voices that in past decades have forced municipalities to act in reducing municipal solid waste do not in the main concern themselves with this objective anyway.[8]

The environmental movement today constructs problems of municipal solid waste more amply than in the 1970s. Among risks, littered glass pales in comparison to global threats of ecosystem destruction, resource depletion, and pollution at stages of extraction, manufacture, and disposal. Yet the visibility of glass litter (or the memory thereof) and the momentum started toward municipal curbside collections at the prodding of the beverage and bottling industries continue to cast recycling managers into a pitched battle to defend and spend money on a relatively irrelevant activity, with voices in the environmental movement poised to cry foul at any suggestion that glass recycling doesn't pay.

Although the environmental movement and municipalities nod to the need for residents to donate used clothing and linens as part of waste-reduction policy, they do not do so with the same urgency that is focused on glass. Increasing masses of synthetic and natural-fiber materials go to disposal, and there are serious ecological and social implications to the mounting quantities of cheap, low-priced clothing made in the developing world, sent to developed markets to be worn for a few weeks, and then, at best, donated and sent back across the sea to different developing nations for ultimate consumption.

This outcome suggests that visibility is an important feature in the construction of municipal solid waste problems and solutions. Here, the visibility refers primarily to glass waste, whose appearance was symbolized in the "one way," but also to the relative invisibility of the scrap industry, which remained sidelined and faintly stigmatized despite its repeated efforts to professionalize over the course of the twentieth century and even to seek the embrace of the recycling movement. The recycling movement ignored the fact that "glass scrap" did not exist as a tradable commodity. More salient were the weight and presence of glass in the "avalanche" that hit in the 1960s. Textiles were not considered part of this avalanche, despite the rag's prominent place in U.S. household discards going back centuries. Textiles were not packaging; they were not disposables. And although the wasting of rags had been decried during both world wars, the 1960s movements failed to construct clothing waste as a problem. To the extent that old clothes were considered, the nation's network of thrift shops offered a readily acceptable and indeed quite utilized outlet. No one seemed to notice that this outlet failed to absorb roughly 85 percent of the textile waste that was being generated.

The whole point of recycling is to privilege ecological rationality over a purely economic calculus so as to spare human health, resource stocks, and ecosystems the physiochemical burden of a linear flow of materials through the human economy. Prior to this motivation for recycling, economic reasoning dictated the reclamation of rags, paper, and metal as inputs to new production and the reclamation of glass for refill, not recycling. When the latter model failed to sustain profits—leading to the generation of a largely new category of waste—the industry profiting from this industrial shift was the same one to help construct a diversionary, pseudo-alternative to refill: glass recycling. With a small investment in research and development and public relations, the GCMI was able to hand the recycling movement a ready-made solution, one premised on the model of scrap reclamation for a material that had never made sense to include as scrap. In this context, glass recycling as we know it is a manifestation of busy-ness when contrasted with the unpolitics of textile recovery.

The motivations for the scrap industry itself to "reach out" to the ecology movement of the 1970s were quite different from those for the glass bottling industry. Bottlers sought to deflect criticism and onerous bottle-bill legislation. The scrap industry sought to graft its existing profit model onto an emerging concern over sorted municipal discards. In the areas of metal and paper, the industry made some inroads—although its role would be challenged by the private waste-management industry in the 1980s and 1990s for the right to reclaim valuables from commingled municipal collections. But the struggling rag branch of the industry lacked a hand to reach out to among community recyclers. In the face of its relatively weak position at the time due to the proliferation of synthetics, the rag branch was hardly in a position to push ecological attention toward textile reclamation.

In the conclusion, I discuss some ways I believe we can reprioritize glass and textile diversion in a way that makes more ecological and social sense. Part of this project will require unraveling the tightly constructed set of institutions and practices we know today as curbside recycling, which are built on four pillars—paper, metal, glass, and plastic. How did these materials come to be collected in mixed form by most municipalities, spawning a vibrant industry organized around separating them through multiple stages of processing? In the next chapter, I investigate this history in the context of New York City, the nation's largest producer of urban waste.

2

Curbside Recycling Collection

In the previous chapter, I showed that the recycling movement was willing to accept uncritically the notion that glass should join metal and paper as materials worth collecting for recycling in cities. This acceptance entailed their acknowledgment of a certain amount of leadership by the glass container industry, which stepped into a new role to fill that of the nonexistent scrap-glass industry. Today, environmentalists and recycling managers are still struggling with the developments that followed from this confluence of events in the early 1970s. In 2001, Roger Guttentag, a recycling consultant and columnist for *Resource Recycling* magazine, addressed a post to the Grassroots Recycling Network community of activists amid an earlier round of discussion of the environmental benefits of glass recycling:

We are obligated to deliver environmentally beneficial services (such as recycling) in an economically efficient manner. As part of determining this, we often (or should) consider the impacts of sacrificing short-term gains for long-term gains as well as the reverse. What I believe hobbles our discussion of recycling programs' economics is that many municipal recycling professionals are loathe to admit that certain materials are not worth recycling due to their unfavorable short-term marginal cost/benefits out of fear of triggering a slippery slope descent into a world where only aluminum cans and newspapers are recovered. There is, furthermore, a smaller constituency who believes that recycling is always justified, regardless of the short-term economic costs, on the basis of estimated long-term social/environmental benefits and ethical/moral principles, as long as we can afford to pay these costs because we are obligated by these principles to pay them. . . . [T]he result is that, while we (meaning municipal recyclers) do talk about doing "more with less" we often never take the public lead in discussing where it may make sense to cut back on a program's scope. (2001)

Guttentag went on to discuss the wasted energy and public funds that are poured into defending glass recycling from attacks by right-wing interests "antithetical to municipal recycling," who use issues such as the irrationality of the present structure of glass reclamation to argue for "protecting the taxpayer's wallet." The desire to protect recycling from those who criticize it on purely economic grounds, he wrote, "places us in an unfavorable position of defending municipal recycling and making us appear as though we are more interested in protecting our sacred program cows and bureaucratic turf than doing what is right socially, economically and morally." Guttentag was here addressing those who work for local and state recycling programs. He called on them to "take the lead in managing the public dialogue on what works and what doesn't including identifying and explaining the reasons underlying either position" (2001).

Given the fact that an economically irrational and ecologically marginal practice (glass recycling) persists firmly within the core construction of recycling, it is important to understand in more detail how the recycling movement ended with so much at stake in the preservation of a system that even after forty years still diverts only one-third of all wastes from disposal and in many cities considerably less than that (U.S. EPA 2009b; *Waste News* 2010a). To this end, we need to look beyond glass per se and at the array of waste materials and program options that were considered and not considered as appropriate for environmentalist activism in both discourse and practice. This chapter focuses on New York City as a case study of various industry sectors' overt co-optation of important actors in the recycling movement. The lessons from this story, I argue, are relevant for the vast majority of cities, towns, and counties that collect recycling in mixed curbside setouts and route materials at considerable expense to large, private recycling plants for sorting and marketing.

Earth Day 1970, New York City

The nation's first Earth Day, April 22, 1970, was marked by celebrations in major cities across the country. In New York City, more than 100,000 people came together in Central Park to speak and listen about pollution, ecology, and the earth's future. Mayor John Lindsay closed midtown streets to traffic. Reynolds Aluminum set up a "trash-in" bounty station offering half a cent for each returned can. When Lindsay addressed the crowd, he compared the "deplorable state of the environment to the 'immoral' war in Vietnam" (qtd. in Corey 1994, 326).

The event was testimony to the widespread public concern over environmental issues. The *New York Times* described it as "an interlude of national contemplation of problems and man's deteriorating environment." In the eyes of the media, as indicated in this article, the gathering symbolized not only a "massive alert to public awareness but also as the dawn of a new era of 'ecological politics'" (Hill 1970, 36). This politics saw senators, congressional representatives, governors, mayors, and even corporate representatives walking side by side with protestors and environmentalists. Only the Nixon administration, whose "posture toward Earth Day formalities has been one of calculated or involuntary detachment," remained on the sidelines "(Hill 1970, 36).

Earth Day had been the brainchild of Wisconsin senator Gaylord Nelson, who donated money, raised funds, and organized a group in Washington, Environmental Action, to coordinate the event across the United States. Most of the organization's volunteer staff of college students returned to school after the event was over, but the chapter did not disband. On April 23, 1970, it changed its name to the Environmental Action Coalition (EAC) and issued its first official mission statement. Karen Dumont, its new executive director, promised a "campaign to recruit those millions who are daily victimized by pollution—New Yorkers." She urged "amateur ecologists in the five boroughs to volunteer for a rainbow of coalition projects to benefit the city and, ultimately, Mother Earth." Rallying for "soldiers for the war on pollution," she offered "an opportunity for people to translate their ecological zeal into effective action" (qtd in Loetterle 1970b, 6). The premier venue for such action would be a program to organize and fund community recycling centers throughout the city. Thus began New York City's first experience with recycling in the modern, ecological sense of the word.

The context was ripe for environmental action. In 1970, New York was in crisis on multiple fronts that converged on the issue of waste. Severe fiscal problems gripped the city, and New York was hit by the nationwide recession, which curtailed jobs and revenues even further (Mollenkopf 1992). At the same time, the city was contending with a staggering volume of garbage that had to be collected, trucked, and disposed of every day. An estimated 24,000 tons per day were moving through the city's system, increasing at a 4 percent rate annually—a rate higher than the national average (Melosi 1981). Population increase was only partly to blame. On a per capita basis, refuse generation increased 100 kilograms per capita annually between 1960 and 1970 (Walsh 2002).

Mounting volumes of garbage posed a crisis of disposal capacity. Unlike newer cities in the West and the South, the densely settled isle of

Manhattan and its surrounding boroughs had severely limited space for landfills. In 1967, a *New York Times* article depicted Sanitation Commissioner Samuel Kearing at wit's end: "'We're facing a real crisis,' he said, pointing to the isolated red shaded areas on a map in his office that indicate areas in the city where raw garbage can be dumped. 'Within ten years, at the outside, there will be none of these areas left'" (Bird 1967, 37). The alternative, to Kearing and to many municipal managers of the time, was clear. "Central incineration," said the commissioner, "is the only technology now available to solve our problems" (qtd. in Bird 1967, 37). But such a solution required incinerators, which had been neglected for decades as the city had unwisely come to rely almost completely on landfills. Waste planners had known for decades that landfill capacity, unlike that for incinerators, was finite, yet they had taken no steps to forestall the inevitable exhaustion of fill space (Corey 1994). The sense of waste crisis that gripped New York during this time was typical of the nation. By the mid-1960s, dim awareness was emerging in Washington that, as President Johnson stated, "better solutions to the disposal of solid waste" were needed (qtd. in Melosi 1981, 199). The federal Solid Waste Disposal Act, which was passed in 1965, broke ground in acknowledging that although "collection and disposal . . . should continue to be primarily the function of State, regional, and local agencies," the federal government had the duty to provide financial and technical assistance to localities to develop new methods to "reduce the amount of waste and unsalvageable materials and to provide proper and economical solid-waste disposal practices" (qtd. in Melosi 1981, 200). The act, however, did little more than enable the gathering of some basic information about the extent of the municipal solid waste crisis. In 1969, *New York Times* journalist Gladwin Hill noted that "while much valuable basic information has been amassed—(nobody knew anything about the national waste disposal picture before)—and a number of experimental projects launched, the program has not yet come up with any cure-alls." Hill warned, "An avalanche of waste and waste disposal problems is building up around the nation's major cities in an impending emergency that may parallel the existing crises in air and water pollution" (1969, C38). By and large, the prevailing wisdom among those involved in solid-waste management was that sanitary landfilling and incineration were the only ways to stem the crisis (Melosi 1981).

But outside the mainstream of public-works administration, a few voices advocated a different option. Hill's article, menacingly entitled "Major U.S. Cities Face Emergency Trash Disposal," also observed that "there is an often overlooked third possibility, and some scientists think it is the only one for the long run. That is to reclaim refuse—to break it down into its main constituents for reuse" (1969, C38).

The Environmental Action Coalition Steps In

On the day after Earth Day, April 23, 1970, the EAC began its work. Its success was rapid. The organization was able to raise funds quickly for a community recycling program called "Trash is Cash" that would provide start-up money, training, collection services, and transportation for community centers to collect scrap paper, metal, and glass. As one staffer described it in 1970, "At first the profits will go directly to the community groups running the collection-sites. . . . in a little while we will have payment schedules worked out so that we can pay the ordinary citizen cash for his trash" (Loetterle 1970a, 5). The EAC also pursued a vigorous public-education campaign, with much of its efforts focused on children. By the end of 1970, it had developed an elementary school curriculum, Don't Waste Waste, with an accompanying motivation film, and had begun to hold teacher workshops. *Eco-news*, EAC's illustrated newsletter, came out that same year, offering information and action projects for children on a number of environmental topics, including recycling, tree planting, and nature exploration. The EAC also pursued a long-term agenda of public institutionalization of curbside recycling. In its promotional literature, community volunteers were quoted again and again as saying that their "goal was to go out of business" (Koehler 1975b). The real aim of the program, said the EAC, was to make the city responsible for collection, processing, and eventual marketing of recyclables. As one EAC publication put it, "The transfer of operational responsibility from community-run projects to existing city services is essential. Herein lies the *necessary future* of broad-scale recycling" (EAC 1973, 2, emphasis added).

The EAC's success was remarkable. In the span of two years, more than 20 community redemption centers had been established, with modest tonnages of metal, glass, and paper redeemed each month. In a 1973 progress report, the group celebrated its strong ties with legislators in Albany and Washington. Executive Director Karen Dumont was named to the President's Environmental Advisory Committee. Then Congressman Ed Koch spoke in favor of the project in Congress in May 1971 (Koch 1971). Federal and state legislators often sent foreign visitors to tour EAC facilities (EAC 1973). The organization's relations with city government seemed good as well. In 1971, New York City

Environmental Protection Agency (NYC EPA) chief Jerome Kretchmer wrote a general letter of commendation for the EAC, stating that the relationship between the NYC EPA and the group was "one of continuing cooperation," and noting that the EAC staff "have used their available resources very well" (Kretchmer 1971).

Given the background of the NYC EPA and Jerome Kretchmer himself, municipal support of waste-reduction initiatives was not surprising. In 1968, Mayor Lindsay had taken a bold step in addressing the city's environmental problems by establishing the NYC EPA as a superagency governing the Department of Sanitation, the Department of Air Resources, and the Department of Water Resources. The metaorganization was established with a nod to ecological principles, "to coordinate environmental problems—so that solving one . . . problem would not inadvertently create another" (NYC EPA 1974). Mindful of a sanitation strike that had crippled the city in 1968 and the problems that entrenched bureaucrats posed for innovation, Lindsay staffed the agency with people very different from the civil-service norm of the time. Stephen Corey observes that the NYC EPA brought with it "a new layer of policy makers, lawyers, industrial engineers, and public relations experts [who] superseded the [Department of Sanitation's] traditional uniformed chain of command. Rather than experienced sanitation workers making decisions, a new breed of young, idealistic and often irreverent provisional EPA managers called the shots" (1994, 320).

Among the new breed was Jerome Kretchmer, whom Lindsay named EPA commissioner in 1969. A native New Yorker, Kretchmer had attended New York University and Columbia Law on scholarships and in 1960 became leader of a fledgling Democrat reform movement on Upper West Side. He soon after was elected district leader and in 1962 began four terms in the New York State Assembly. Kretchmer was known there as a "maverick backbencher" who alienated traditional Democrats with his support of divorce reform, addiction treatment, and low-income housing. This progressive stance gained him the support of Robert F. Kennedy and ultimately of Lindsay, whom Kretchmer helped to reelection in 1969 (Lichtenstein 1971). The environmental community in New York initially considered Kretchmer unqualified due to his lack of professional experience or education in waste issues. As a 1971 biography in the *New York Times Magazine* explained, however, he soon won them over: "As head of the EPA . . . he has waded into every environmental battle in sight, flailing at Con Edison's proposed power plant expansion in Astoria, [and] voting the city's GM stock in favor of a Ralph Nader group during that company's recent proxy battle" (Lichtenstein 1971, 31).

Kretchmer announced a goal of building a "constituency in the city for the environment," a move that "thrust the EPA with its 22,000 employees and $394 million annual expense budget into a political activist role it never had before" (Lichtenstein 1971, 31). Among his early accomplishments were to prohibit outdoor spraying of asbestos, establish an environmental court to handle pollution offense, and regularize trash pickups citywide. And Kretchmer outspokenly linked waste to social issues. In 1970, he described garbage as a "social and political question," noting that it had become an acute problem in low-income neighborhoods and a "surrogate" issue for other tensions in middle-class areas (Bird 1970b, 23). Kretchmer was in fact the first city official to call waste disposal an "environmental problem" (Bird 1970b, 23).

In 1970, Kretchmer was named acting sanitation commissioner in addition to role as EPA chief. He supported the EAC's 1971 project to test Department of Sanitation curbside collection of newspapers for recycling, and by 1973 EAC's efforts had resulted in fledgling curbside programs in parts of Brooklyn, Queens, and Staten Island. But Kretchmer's relationship with the group was complicated and would sour quickly. In hindsight, this tension sheds great light on the political and ideological meaning that recycling carried in New York City from the day it came to town.

Recycling and Corporate Activism

Key to the EAC's rapid success was its willingness to accept donations from sources then considered inimical to the environmentalist cause. As reported in a *New York Daily News* article in July 1970, "More than 200 companies—many of them prime targets for environmentalists—have pledged millions in dollars in cash, time, and services to a massive war on solid waste," spearheaded in New York City by the EAC (Loetterle 1970b, 4). According to the EAC's Robert Gale, the move was unprecedented. He remarked that "this is the first time industry has sat down with an environmental group and worked out wide-ranging plans for united action" (qtd. in Loetterle 1970b, 4). Among those on board was the National Petroleum Council, whose representative Walter J. Hickle, articulated his vision of the garbage crisis and the EAC's role:

We've got to clean up the garbage our advanced civilization produces in such quantities and in so many forms, but we don't have to and ought not to slow down industrial growth or progress in the process. The right to produce is not the right to pollute, [but] let's find new ways, better ways, of doing business so that our industries can prosper and our environment flourish at the same time. That philosophy jibes with the "Trash is Cash" movement being started by the EAC. . . . This is one of the wisest ways to attack the pollution problem, whereas faddists peddling quack cure-alls are worse than useless. (qtd. in Loetterle 1970b, 4)

The business community was enthusiastic about EAC executive director Karen Dumont. A former fund-raiser for Vassar College with a background in medical writing, she was profiled in November 1970 in a *Daily News* article entitled "Coalition Head Plans to Fight the Polluters." Who were the polluters? According to Dumont, they were "people." "It makes me furious," she said, "that people can be so indifferent about their natural resources. They create pollution wherever they go." Commented the article: "She is angry about what man is doing to his environment, and means to fight it by action." This action, however, was not to be in the form of protest or critique. "I don't believe you are really ever going to change things by standing on the outside and screaming," declared Dumont. "You have to get inside the system and turn it around" (*New York Daily News* 1970, 3).

Dumont's ideas of environmental reform and individual responsibility were well received in many quarters. The Upper East Side People's Environmental Program, one of the first EAC-funded centers, was profiled in *Manhattan East Community News* as "committed to cleaning up its street and reducing pollution" (Mottus 1970, 3). The paper's editor spoke warmly of Dumont:

Refreshingly, she places responsibility not just on the manufacturer but on the consumer as well. Consumer spending habits cast a deciding vote for improving our environment. Little things, such as refusing extra paper bags at the grocery store . . . all contribute to a better earth. It is within the realm of every individual to combat in some way all forms of pollution. . . . We must work together knowledgably and attempt to steer a safer course for the sake of our common destiny. (Mottus 1970, 3)

Just what were the faddist, quack cure-alls in play? Who was standing outside screaming, and why? Who sought to place responsibility "on the manufacturer"? These observations were in fact alluding to a decade of activism outside New York City for what in the early 1990s would come to be called "product stewardship" and in the late twentieth and early twenty-first centuries "extended producer responsibility"—that is, policies that targeted, to various degrees, producers of waste-generating commodities. At the time, the range of such policies included bans or taxes on producing or marketing products made of certain materials as well as mandatory deposits on reusable or recyclable commodities, mainly beverage containers. Other alternatives would be included later, as I discuss in subsequent chapters.

In the 1970s, however, the precedent for such initiatives was based on the resurrection of deposits on beverage containers, which were to be brought out of retirement in state-mandated form. As chapter 1 chronicled, the beverage industry itself had moved from refill to one-way containers in midcentury; it had no need for deposits once the decision not to refill had been made. In 1953, the state of Vermont had enacted the nation's first source-reduction measure with its ban on nonrefillable containers. Fierce industry opposition prevented the renewal of this bill upon its expiration four years later. It would not be until 1971 that another state bottle bill would pass, this time in Oregon. The Oregon law required the beverage industry to impose a five-cent deposit on beer and soft-drink containers and a two-cent deposit on liquor bottles. It established redemption centers at "state stores" (Oregon Liquor Control Commission outlets). Within a few weeks, return rates averaged 80 to 95 percent. Nonetheless, as soon as the law was enacted, the American Can Company brought suit, "claiming the . . . law would directly injure them and that it was unconstitutional in that it placed an undue burden on interstate commerce" (New York State Senate 1975, 28). The Oregon Circuit Court of Appeals rejected the suit. And, according to a series of Oregon state studies that followed, price increases were found to have little effect on the retail cost of drinks or on the success/failure of beverage manufacturers, distributors, or retailers (New York State Senate 1975).

Vermont quickly followed suit, enacting its own deposit law in 1973. In 1974, Oregon senator Mark Hatfield introduced the "Nonreturnable Beverage Container Prohibition Act" (S. 2-062) in the 93rd U.S. Congress. This act proposed to ban the interstate shipment and sale of nonreturnable beverage containers and ban "flip-top" cans. Despite strong support by such groups as the League of Women Voters and the National League of Cities–U.S. Conference of Mayors as well as many environmental organizations, the measure was defeated. Similar efforts in Congress would be blocked by producer activism over decades to come, up to present day (CRI 2008). Extensive pressure and lobbying by container and beverage manufacturers as well as by organized labor working in these sectors are credited with keeping this legislation down (Hays 1987, 81).

The stakeholders in fighting such legislation were clear. As a 1976 study by Stanford University Law School trenchantly put it,

Many forces have been responsible for the movement from a returnable/refillable system towards a throwaway system. Chief among these is the profit motive as it operates within the container industries. The more containers they sell, the more money they make. And more containers are sold (both cans and bottles) under a throwaway than under a refillable system. . . . It is these groups who have sold the idea of "convenience" to the consumer. Ultimately, however, it is the public who must pay for this "convenience" while the proponents of the non-returnable system profit. (Fenner and Gorin 1976, 5)

Industries as a whole feared the "slippery slope" of source-reduction measures that bottle bills might present. To follow might be other source-reduction measures such as bans or taxes on polluting or litter-causing products. As early as 1969, environmental groups had proposed disposal charges—often to be federally coordinated—on consumer products that would become waste within ten years of purchase or less (Bird 1969). Shortly before the first Earth Day, Gaylord Nelson had sought "legislation requiring industries to pay fees for product packaging materials that are not easily disposable and to establish a fund for fees collected to be passed on to local governments for waste disposal programs" (*New York Times* 1970c, 59). In 1969, New York businessman Leonard Wegman, a contractor with the Department of Sanitation on engineering and evaluation projects, set forth a plan to levy a one-cent disposal charge per pound on producers of nonfood items marketed in the city. This idea was met with interest by then NYC EPA commissioner Merril Eisenbud, who stated that it "deserves very serious consideration. . . . [B]y making the economics of disposal one of the factors in designing containers, we might be able to reduce the gross amount of discarded matter" (qtd. in Bird 1969, 42).

Despite these attempts, however, the disposal charge remained little more than an idea in activist policy circles. The Nixon administration opposed all such policies on the grounds that there was not sufficient information as to their effectiveness in reducing solid waste (*New York Times* 1970a, 27). In addition, industry was set to fight back. The *New York Times* reported that bottlers were gearing up for a nationwide campaign to convince the public to return old bottles voluntarily and to argue that "any significant breakthrough in recycling will have to come from devices that will separate collected mixed garbage after it arrives at a central depot" (Bird 1970a, 60).

The lines were drawn. According to the 1973 report *Cities and the Nation's Disposal Crisis*, "packaging standards are a spectre to the private sector" (qtd. in Kovach 1973, 1). Ironically, however, it would be the "environmental action" of recycling that would provide industry with the first and most institutionalized means to fight this specter.

The Business Environmental Action Coalition Committee
The years 1970 to 1973 saw the introduction of community recycling to New York City and the first consolidated efforts to involve municipal government in recycling collection and processing. This three-year period overlaps with the tenure of the Business Environmental Action Coalition Committee (BEACC), the EAC's funding arm. During that time, the organization received close to half of its funds through a committee of businessmen who volunteered to act as fund-raisers. The balance was supplied by a mix of government grants, foundation grants, private donations, and sale of materials. Among the most active members in the BEACC were Charles Millard of Coca-Cola; Samuel Goldsmith, executive vice president of the Aluminum Association; and Sidney Mudd, CEO of Seven-Up New York (EAC 1970–1988).

BEACC members solicited donations for the EAC from colleagues in a number of industries. An examination of EAC funders for 1973 shows supporters including aluminum, steel, glass, paper, and plastic trade associations; bottlers; container manufacturers; retailers and retail associations; beverage producers; beer distributors; and newspapers (EAC 1970–1988). BEACC members contacted colleagues in these fields with personalized pleas for EAC donations. In their letters, they made it clear that the intent of funding the EAC was to develop recycling as an alternative to source-reduction legislation. One form letter sent to the membership of the National Aluminum Association expressed the trade group's concerns about "drastic legislative proposals in the very near future": "During the last few weeks, a small group of soft drink and beer executives have [sic] been developing a program ['Trash is Cash'] which we believe has substantial promise to help all concerned cope with the very real threat of irresponsible 'ecological' legislation in New York City. Our concern has not been limited to our own industries, but has extended across the entire range of industries which are under the gun" (Goldsmith 1971).

The explicit intent of pushing voluntary alternatives was to deflect citizen interest in passing producer legislation. In May 1973, Irving

Mendelson, president of Good-O-Beverages, wrote to Charles Pickering of Airco Industrial Glass:

As you know our industry has been under attach [*sic*] by governmental bodies on all levels across the country because of the packing devices utilized. These attacks have gone to the extremes of attempting to enact legislation to either ban one way containers or to tax them. If enacted, these measures would have been extremely harmful to all concerned—you, us, and the public. In New York we have been indeed fortunate to have had the good services of Karen M. Dumont and her Environmental Action Coalition. They have helped immeasurably in this fight to preserve our way of doing business. Their "Trash is Cash" recycling program, educational efforts, continued research, Eco-News and public relations, are but a few of their many efforts. I firmly believe that no punitive legislation has been enacted in the State of New York largely because of these efforts. No question but this all costs money. When Karen or an E.A.C. board member calls you, please see fit to pledge financial support. (Mendelson 1973)

Karen Dumont was active in articulating this message among industry groups as well. In an undated draft letter to potential funders of a motivational film celebrating the "Trash is Cash" program, she wrote:

There are brush fires starting up all over the state (and for all I know all over the country) of legislation to ban non-returnable beverage containers and to tax containers in general. The need is great to get out the message of community involvement in self-determination of answers to the solid waste problem. Environmental group support for such legislation is being sought and gained. A credible alternative to legislation must be found. (Dumont n.d.)

One of the most threatening precedents to such "brush fires" was the Oregon experience in bottle-bill legislation. Said Dumont at a BEACC meeting, "The Oregon 'laboratory' is an unusual one. Oregon has a history of extreme environmental interests. . . . I will not try to tell you what you know already and probably better than I—the kind of effect a well-educated public has on the senseless band aids for environmental problems" (Dumont 1971a).

The EAC's focus in instituting the "Trash is Cash" program was on teaching by doing. Acknowledging the support of the U.S. Brewers Association for EAC's "education of the general (if you will) voting populace about problems, complexities, and solutions to the solid waste problem," Dumont noted that "a well informed and experienced public is better equipped to make decisions on matters of legislation or advocacy than those dealing with the problem on an uninformed, emotional level. We believe it will be the natural conclusion of this public that the solid waste problem must be attacked by changes in municipal handling procedures and that the totality of the refuse must be processed for reuse" (Dumont 1971b).

I quote EAC statements at length here to show a process of tactical but also ideological development that was under way. The EAC and its industrial funders promoted a strategy that ended up combating or preempting bottle-bill legislation through its support of voluntary recycling by volunteer consumers and eventually municipal governments. But that was not all that was going on. EAC as an environmental organization was working up the social meaning of ecological citizenship through recycling, with lines being drawn between rationality and emotion, personal and systemic responsibility, education and regulation. In the meantime, the men behind the curtain remained clear-sighted as to what was at stake. A letter from the chair of the U.S. Brewers Association to John Cashin, a business student researching corporate attitudes toward recycling, summed up the philosophy behind the EAC's efforts in this regard:

The official policy of the [U.S. Brewers Association] is to support voluntary programs for reclamation and recycling of packaging materials where and when such programs appear feasible. It is only fair to state that we, as an association, do not believe such programs will provide any significant or lasting solutions to problems of solid waste management. Such solutions, we think, can only result from major changes in the collection and disposal techniques presently employed in most American municipalities. (U.S. Brewers Association 1972)

The Brewers Association's words are similar to those of the Glass Packaging Institute discussed in chapter 1. "Major changes" meant publicly funded, commingled collection and processing of postconsumer recyclables from the curb. "Major changes" decidedly did not mean the array of producer-responsibility laws that Kretchmer and others would fight for and usually lose on in the decades to come.

Kretchmer's Source-Reduction Plan

By 1972, Kretchmer, despite his early warm relations with the EAC, mounted a direct challenge to the municipal curbside model of recycling that the EAC had put forward as the "necessary future of broad-scale recycling." His efforts to implement fees, taxes, and other surcharges to force costs and material back onto producers followed those had been introduced in other parts of the country in the late 1960s and in 1970. There had been precedent within New York City as well. In 1970, for instance, New York's City Club had proposed a plan for a disposal fee of two cents per pound to be levied on most nonfood items. It estimated that the fee paid by retailers or their suppliers would average only $15 a year per resident but would raise $125 million for the city (Burks 1970, 45). Shortly before Earth Day 1970, President John DeLury of the New York City Uniformed Sanitationmen's Association stated that, "according to his rough calculations, Sunday editions of the *Daily News* and *NY Times* alone cost the city $13,260,000 yearly to dispose of, and make up 7.8% of the Sanitation budget." In his view, "those who contribute to the burdens should pay part of the costs" (qtd. in Montgomery 1970, 40). And in September 1970, Kretchmer himself hinted at what by 1972 would turn into a multifaceted, local, source-reduction initiative. Telling *New York Times* reporters, "Packaging is the most visible and most unnecessary contribution to the nation's garbage output. It costs the city about 30 cents to collect each can or bottle discarded as litter," he alerted journalists that the mayor's administration would soon be sending the New York City Council a plan that would address problems of non-returnable bottles and cans, mixed metal containers, beer can tabs, odd-size containers, and even candy wrappers (*New York Times* 1970b, 37).

With these plans under debate, in 1971 Lindsay signed into law a supplemental tax that included a levy of two cents on all nonfood plastic containers. The law was struck down by the New York Supreme Court after the Society of the Plastics Industry objected on grounds of equal protection, due process, and interstate commerce (Dumont 1971b). In a speech to the Citizens' Council on Environmental Quality in 1971, Dumont attacked Lindsay's measure as well as "several taxes [that] have been proposed by city and state officials." She stated, "My personal reaction to this is that taxing should be the last recourse and that it is more desirable to prepare people emotionally and intellectually to make changes than try to force legislation. . . . Real progress will be seen when an environmentally aware public demands changes in . . . collection and disposal of their household refuse and are really ready to sacrifice for it" (Dumont 1971c).

A December 1971 article in the environmental newspaper *Our Daily Planet* captured the tension between Kretchmer and the EAC that was brewing at the time. Kretchmer was invited to an EAC meeting to announce a $275,000 pledge of support for the EAC from a coalition of 43 companies, 31 of which were involved in the sale of soft drinks. The mood was tense:

Because of the recent controversy over the merits of recycling versus the merits of legislation discouraging excess packaging and non-reusable containers, Jerome Kretchmer, Administrator of NYC's Environmental Protection Administration and a participant in the press conference, expressed only limited praise for the cooperative venture [saying] "This joint effort . . . is a welcome interim step but should not be looked upon as the final solution to the solid waste problems of the city. . . . [T]he real need is to reduce packaging at its source. (*Our Daily Planet* 1971, 1)

By April 1972, Kretchmer's plan was ready to go before the city council. It included a five-cent deposit on soda and beer containers, a one- to three-cent packaging tax for food containers, with an exemption for bottles, cans, and other receptacles that contained at least 30 percent recycled content. According to Kretchmer, this initiative would generate close to $30 million dollars, almost all the amount needed to cover the $35–40 million per year that the Department of Sanitation spent collecting and disposing of cans and bottles. Kretchmer sent a letter to 54 of the state's leading beer and soft-drink companies urging them to "dissociate themselves from the deceptive advertising and narrow self-serving and obstructionist lobbying against the proposed city container tax." And he defended allegations that his plan was simply a "revenue seeking measure," saying it was "totally avoidable if companies . . . simply adjust their purchasing policies to favor recycled materials" (qtd. in *New York Times* 1972, 33).

In testimony before the city council in May 1972, Dumont forcefully expressed EAC's opposition to Kretchmer's 1972 efforts to tax nonreturnable containers: "This is not a recycling incentive tax. It is nothing more than a revenue measure. . . . The tax is discriminatory. It taxes only a portion of materials which make up our solid waste stream. . . . [T]he definition [of] 'recycled material' is too vague and leaves loopholes which can do nothing to help the solid waste with which New York City deals every day." She concluded that "The law . . . will not cut down on New York's solid waste problems to any significant degree, and it will create an administration for the policing of the tax which will decrease the actual income from the tax. . . . It is obvious that retailers will pass the tax on to the consumer. . . . I hear every day about mismanagement of our government's money." Dumont advocated instead what she called a "comprehensive approach to the problem" that included the EAC's "Trash is Cash" and Department of Sanitation collection programs as well as possible privatization of sanitation functions. She predicted that if the city were to "turn over collection and disposal of garbage to private carting and let the free enterprise system 'take it away,' I'll bet . . . that within four years . . . industry would come up with a way to get recyclable material out of city garbage" (Dumont 1972).

Kretchmer's plan failed to pass the council under what the *New York Times* called "very heavy pressure from bottlers and canners" (Bird 1972, 62). These forces would continue to squelch most such initiatives in individual states over the next two decades. At the federal level, presidential opposition to source-reduction policies was relentless. Kretchmer nevertheless persevered. In November 1972, he spoke before the American Management Association Industry Conference, stating that the city had received "no cooperation from bottlers, canners, and packers," who, he said, "have added an 'extraordinary mess' to the solid-waste problem, accounting for 43% of what is discarded in the city's MSW [municipal solid waste]." According to one article, "Kretchmer held these groups responsible for the nation's MSW crisis and termed industrial efforts at recycling a form of tokenism." He singled out the plastics industry in particular, saying that "the plastic bottle was being extensively tested for such things as durability and sales appeal but there was no concern on the part of industry about the bottle's effect on the environment once it was discarded" (Bird 1972, 62).

By 1973, Kretchmer would step down from the NYC EPA when Abraham Beam ousted Lindsay from office. There is evidence to suggest that until then the BEACC was aware of and quite concerned about Kretchmer's producer-focused initiatives. Notes taken at a November 19, 1971, meeting between Karen Dumont and the BEACC quote a member concerned that "Kretchmer may be working with Washington" (EAC 1970–1988). A letter to Allan Rothstein of the Economic Development Administration in 1972 from Sidney P. Mudd, the head of Seven-Up and a BEACC chair, warned against the "disaster of Mr. Kretchmer's ill-advised legislation" (Mudd 1972). Yet amid this controversy, the EAC itself appears not to have come under criticism in New York's environmental community. Articles about the group in local newspapers were laudatory. Between 1970 and 1973, the EAC participated in other environmental initiatives with some of the city's major environmental groups, many of whom had testified in favor of Kretchmer's plan and vigorously promoted state bottle bills. Working with the NRDC, the EDF, the Citizens for Clean Air, and the Clean Air Coalition, the EAC opposed increased public-transportation fares and the expansion of a Con Ed plant in Astoria, Queens. It later participated in organized opposition to the Super Sonic Transport, a highly noise-polluting airplane. And, most remarkably, the group would change its position the year after Kretchmer left office and begin to support a New York State bottle bill. By then, however, it had already set the ball rolling for curbside recycling.

Ideological Turnaround

Although the EAC records do not explain why, the BEACC disbanded in December 1973. It does not appear that this move was unplanned because it is alluded to in BEACC correspondence in March 1973, with Seven-Up's Sidney Mudd writing to Dumont that "the broadening financial commitments of industry in the total field of solid waste management and resource recovery would make it highly unlikely that our committee as such could support EAC beyond the present year of 1973" (Mudd 1973).

Dumont was aware that the dissolution of the BEACC would leave a "financial gap" and that "with the energy crisis and the economic crunch, money is becoming tighter and tighter." But she appeared confident that she would be able to raise funds from "corporations and foundations in order to broaden our base," saying, "this isn't the first time we've had our backs to the monetary wall" (Dumont 1973a). In a 1973 fundraising letter to Norman Alexander, president of Sun Chemical, Dumont wrote:

In the past, EAC has largely depended . . . on a relatively small number of corporate donors, mostly companies engaged in the production or direct use of recyclable materials. . . . Because of a feeling that a broader base of support would allow EAC greater independence (though all support in the past has been on a "no strings" basis) and because of hints that some of EAC's present contributors may be planning to reduce their levels of support in the future, the Coalition has instituted a broadly based search for sources of additional funding. (Dumont 1973b)

The year 1974 would signal major changes for the EAC as well as in the local and national climate surrounding waste management. In late 1973, conservative Abraham Beame defeated John Lindsay. He took office in early January of the next year. Beame installed a new EPA commissioner, Robert Low, and cuts to the Department of Sanitation budget followed, with 47 percent of street sweepers laid off. A *New York Times* article entitled "City Environmental Body Is in Turmoil under Beame" quoted the new sanitation commissioner, Robert Groh, as saying, "He now gets only 'vague reports' on progress toward new methods of solving the city's increasingly pressing problem of what to do with garbage in the face of rapidly dwindling dump space" (Bird 1974a, 1). And that year it became apparent that the city and the nation faced an energy crisis. This meant new concerns for environmentalists and citizens, new hopes for waste-to-energy incineration, and budgetary hardships all around. To compound these problems, New York City was entering its deepest period of fiscal crisis. Recession meant a plummet in the price of recycled materials, making recycling unprofitable and leading in some cases to the dumping of bottles, cans, and paper that had been conscientiously collected at community centers (Bird 1974b). The Department of Sanitation's newspaper-collection program was called off due more to lack of markets for recycled paper than to budget cuts.

In 1974, the EAC experienced a change in leadership that coincided with a full turnaround on deposit legislation. For the first time since 1971, there was correspondence between the EAC and the NYC EPA. Low wrote to Dumont that he looked forward to "working with the EAC on the solution to the [solid-waste] problem" and that he welcomed her "suggestions and assistance" (Low 1974). Dumont's memos to staff indicate that as 1974 progressed, she spent increasing amounts of time fund-raising in order to fill the gap left by the withdrawal of much, though not all, funding from bottlers and beverage distributors (EAC 1970–1988). At this point, it appears that the EAC's stance against deposit legislation was beginning to weaken. Although at a February 1974 hearing before the New York State Council of Environmental Advisors Dumont rearticulated the warning not to follow "radical" Oregon's example, the EAC's anti-bottle-bill stance was on its way out, along with Dumont herself (Dumont 1974). In October 1974, Sherry Koehler took over as executive director. The circumstances of the change in leadership are not documented in the EAC archives, but the shift clearly coincided with a change in stance on packaging-waste policy. At a Women's City Club dinner in November, Koehler looked back approvingly to Kretchmer's efforts, noting that during the Lindsay administration, the NYC EPA

attempted for at least two years . . . to effectively reduce the packaging components of our solid waste by submitting to the City Council container deposit legislation and a tax earned at the wholesale level on packaging materials. The legislation failed. Many states, however, are now considering beverage container legislation . . . but beverage containers are only a part of the packaging problem. Beside packaging and container legislation, guidelines could be set for products that would ultimately reduce garbage. These include specifications for efficient product design and durability, reparability and ease of material recovery. (Koehler 1974)

In 1975, Koehler came out even more forcefully against the antideposit arguments that once had characterized the EAC's position. Staff meeting notes from early that year indicate that the EAC had met with the recently formed New Yorkers for Returnable Containers, which sought a ban on one-way bottles. In response, noted the minutes for a February 1975 meeting, "EAC has adopted a general position in favor of the reduction of solid waste at the source. . . . [T]he coalition [will] develop a more definite position on excess packaging and two way container legislation" (Koehler 1975c, 3).

From then on, the EAC formally endorsed both federal and state container legislation, supporting a moderate version that covered "traditional" containers and imposed low deposits, as opposed to more far-reaching options advocated by other groups. Koehler's 1975 testimony before the New York State Assembly Committee on Commerce, Industry, and Economic Development shows the extent of the ideological shift in the EAC's position: "Some would have us believe that resource recovery [i.e., curbside recycling] is a panacea, the answer to all our solid waste problems. They tell us that container legislation and resource recovery are incompatible. That is simply not true! The industry argument that removing beverage containers from the solid waste stream will make resource recovery uneconomical is unfounded" (Koehler 1975a).

At the same time, however, the organization's position on community and curbside recycling remained. Wrote one staffer, "'Trash is Cash' has and will continue to play a significant role in encouraging national, state, and municipal recycling policy. The very existence of these groups and their obvious commitment to recycling and resource conservation is a sure sign of public interest and willingness to move in this area. Citizen recycling projects are a first step in changing a national life-style that has been foolishly wasteful" (Popp 1975).

Despite the EAC's turnaround on state and federal bottle bills, industry opposition kept these measures from going forward in the late 1970s and into the early 1980s. Complicating the waste-management picture during this period was growing interest in waste-to-energy incineration as a way to meet disposal needs and lessen American dependence on foreign oil, which was especially worrisome to the public and policymakers during the energy crisis of the mid- to late 1970s. In this period, EAC's position regarding waste-to-energy was complex. On the one hand, it supported this technology as part of a comprehensive "materials utilization and conservation policy at all private and public levels" (EAC 1970–1988). At the same time, the group was concerned that enthusiasm for waste-to-energy would detract from the development of recycling and source-reduction policies. In late 1975, EAC staffer Walter Popp noted in public testimony that newsprint was currently worth more as fuel than as paper, which, in his view, set a dangerous precedent: "There is a psychology growing, we fear, which views solid waste as a valuable commodity in itself because of the energy inherent in it. This psychology is fostered by the obstacles that have been thrown in the way of source reduction, source separation, and materials recycling measures" (Popp 1975). The years 1976–1981 saw the EAC pursuing a comprehensive agenda of education, support of community recycling centers, and advocacy for source reduction and recycling as methods of combating the municipal solid waste problem. Fluctuating secondary materials markets had made it such that most centers were accepting recyclables on a voluntary basis only, paying residents nothing. Groups like the People's Environmental Program, Neighborhood Ecology, and the Village Green Recycling Team operated drop-off centers and conducted environmental education and advocacy at the community level. The EAC continued to fund these enterprises as examples of community action and as organizing points for environmental education.

Thereafter, the EAC advocated drop-off and curbside recycling at the same time as it supported source reduction through "planned local programs, tax incentives, and legislative action such as passage of a mandatory returnable beverage container bill" (Citizen's Solid Waste Advisory Council 1976). This change in approach coincided with a change in the political climate in New York City around waste. Unlike the progressive Lindsay–Kretchmer era, inaction on solid waste characterized the Beame administration more than anything else. Beame dismantled the EPA superagency entirely and returned the Department of Sanitation to independent status. In 1977, Sherry Koehler resigned from the EAC and was succeeded by Seymour Josephson, a longtime EAC board member, but there was no apparent shift in the group's message. "Trash is Cash," educational literature, and lobbying for government involvement in both source reduction and recycling at local, state, regional, and federal levels continued. From that point forward, the EAC presented a public position of favoring most source-reduction and recycling programs and policies regardless of whether the burden fell on citizens, municipal funds and operations, or producers. And the EAC remained a driving force behind the institutionalization of recycling in New York City.

Aftermath: The 1980s and the Institutionalization of Recycling

The 1980s were a complicated decade for waste management in New York City. On the one hand, a statewide bottle bill finally passed in 1982 imposing five-cent deposits on soft drink and beer containers. Seven years later the EAC saw its goal realized as the city council ordered the Department of Sanitation to organize, implement, and enforce a mandatory, curbside, postconsumer recycling program throughout the city. Modern recycling was institutionalized in New York at two different and long-sought levels.

On the other hand, in the 1980s the city experienced new pressures over what to do with mounting volumes of garbage. Over the decade, most of the city's existing incinerators were closed for failing to meet air-quality standards. In-city landfill space was dwindling as well. In 1984, the city's second-to-last landfill in Canarsie, Brooklyn, closed under order by the U.S. EPA. The reaction of a local councilwoman reflected the political mood of the time. Said Brooklyn's Priscilla Wooten, "We are tired of being dumped on in East New York. I am delighted the Federal Government [closed] it down" (qtd. in *New York Times* 1984, 18).

Citizen activism of the two prior decades, in particular the community uprising against toxic contamination at Love Canal, New York, in 1978, had set precedent for effective local opposition to waste facilities. In New York City, this opposition was manifested in fierce resistance to both new and existing landfills and incinerators. Any project having to do with waste was opposed by increasingly sophisticated groups who had learned from activists upstate how to organize resistance to "locally unwanted land uses," or LULUs (Gandy 2002). Over and above the strains of a growing waste stream and increased costs for disposal, resistance to facilities at home further reduced New York City's "ability to implement a solution to the city's growing garbage crisis" (Corey 1994, 328).

Between 1970 and 1980, municipal solid waste generation in the United States had grown from 3.3 to 3.6 pounds per capita per day. By 1986, residents and businesses were throwing away 4.3 pounds a day (U.S. EPA 2009b). Community recycling drop-off centers and deposit systems in a few states hardly made a dent in this growth as packaging materials and paper in particular proliferated in the waste stream. In 1980, the costs of handling municipal wastes in the United States exceeded $4 billion annually, up from $300 million in 1940 and $1 billion in 1960 in real dollars (Melosi 1981, 198). In the decade that followed, public alarm both intensified and changed form. The focus of the waste crisis had previously been litter in the streets and the costs of managing growing tonnages of waste; now there was the added prediction that the United States would "run out of landfill space" very soon.

This forecast—sounded by environmental groups, some municipal spokespersons, and the media—was based on what turned out ultimately to be erroneous data (Ackerman 1997b; Miller 2000). Nevertheless, the specter of "nowhere to put the garbage" held great currency in the preoccupations of city managers and environmentalists alike.

Alarm over the garbage crisis reached its peak in 1987, the year of the high-profile voyage of the Mobro 4000, a barge filled with waste from Islip, Long Island, that sailed around the Western Hemisphere for months in search of a dumpsite. Protracted political negotiations, backroom deals, and public posturing surrounded this media event. The reason the barge was unable to rid itself of its contents had more to do with public relations than with any lack of landfill capacity nationally or globally (Miller 2000). It was good press for a local politician to stand at his city's dock and order the stigmatized barge away, even if other barges like it would arrive and be accepted days later in the quiet commerce of waste transport and disposal that had slowly taken shape throughout the United States in the 1980s. In fact, the steady increase in garbage, paired with a lack of federal and in many cases state support to the municipalities that managed these streams, had created ripe market conditions for growth and consolidation of the private waste industry. Over the 1980s, several multinational "waste giants" formed, the product of mergers among regional carters (Crooks 1983, 1993). These megacarters established collection, transport, and disposal networks that spanned the East and the Midwest and capitalized on cheap, accessible land in poor rural areas for landfill and incinerator siting. Noted *Business Week*, "Garbage is big business today. With fiscal crises facing the cities and the federal government mandating more stringent disposal standards, private garbage-handling companies such as Waste Management, Inc. are reaping a bonanza" (1978, 102).

The simultaneous growth in (1) the volume of waste, (2) concern over waste, and (3) the private waste sector took place against a backdrop of changing environmental politics and activism. Historians of modern American environmentalism generally agree that by the end of the 1970s ecological concern among the general public was mellowing. In 1976, *U.S. News & World Report* wrote that the U.S. EPA "no longer rides the crest of a nationwide ground swell for a cleaner environment" (52). The article ascribed the waning of popular environmentalism to people's new concerns over job losses from the national recession and the energy crisis. According to E. B. Speer, chairman of the board at U.S. Steel, "the lifeblood of America's economic strength was being undermined by the

Clean Air Act of 1970" (qtd. in *U.S. News & World Report* 1976, 52). This comment was typical of the business community's new approach to responding to the environmentalist message. Samuel Hays writes:

The strategies institutional leaders used to bring [the environmental movement] under control were reactive rather than expressive. During the first two periods of environmental politics, 1957–65 and 1965–72, they could do little but try to hold back the tide. By 1972 they began to launch counterattacks, and by the mid 70's the political climate shifted in their favor. Energy issues provided a major opportunity to check environmentalists. (1987, 60)

In 1980, the election of Ronald Reagan cemented this trend of retrenchment. Reagan ran on a deregulationist platform of small government, tax relief, cuts in social spending, and militarism that accorded well with the economic concerns of business at the time. As Frank Ackerman observes, "Any stirrings of environmental activism in the federal government were brought to a halt in 1981; crisis-oriented efforts to clean up hazardous wastes were virtually the only EPA activities that moved forward during the Reagan administration" (1997b, 17). Antienvironmentalists Anne Gorsuch and James Watt were put in charge of the EPA and the Department of Interior, respectively. They, like Reagan, made no secret of their disdain for environmental protection and pollution-control policy.

Federal retrenchment meant little progress in new legislation, funding of state and local programs, or even enforcement of existing regulations. At the same time, however, Reagan's agenda is widely credited with having regalvanized the environmental movement. Contributions to environmental organizations grew, and large groups such as the NRDC and the EDF mobilized a new tactic for combating polluting industries outside the framework of the EPA and other regulatory agencies: the lawsuit (Dowie 1995). The scandal of Love Canal, which culminated in the federal designation of much of an upstate New York town as a "disaster area" due to heavy chemical contamination from improper industrial-waste disposal in the 1950s and 1960s, brought community opposition to siting and contamination to the forefront as a tactic as well (Szasz 1994; Colten and Skinner 1996).

These events led to complicated outcomes in the area of solid-waste policy. On the one hand, environmental organizations were now providing legal and scientific expertise to citizens in their struggle against siting of what were perceived (often rightly so) as toxic facilities in their neighborhood (Gould, Schnaiberg, and Weinberg 1996; Tesh 2000). At the same time, environmental groups that focused on promoting recycling rather than on opposing LULUs increasingly approached questions of recycling and its connection to corporate municipal solid waste disposal in an apolitical fashion. "Rather than campaign against corporations or trying to 'break their grip,'" Benjamin Miller writes, "the movement's current goal seemed simply to be producing laws and regulations that would 'level the playing field' between the corporate exploitation of 'virgin' and 'secondary' resources." Among environmental groups and state agencies, "the shared goal now seemed to be 're-engineering of the corporation' and 'reinventing government'" to encourage sustainable production (2000, 263).

This new agenda was especially apparent in the area of source reduction. Ideas for product bans, recycled content requirements, and disposal taxes receded in environmentalist discourse by the late 1980s. As discussed in chapter 5, they would not be reinvigorated until the turn of the next century. What was left on the table was the issue of deposits on soda and beer containers, which were now the law in Oregon and eight other states. The leading proponent of deposit legislation in New York State, Manhattan assemblyman G. Oliver Koppel, would introduce a bottle bill to the state legislature once a year. Each year the EAC and other groups such as the League of Women Voters, the New York Public Interest Research Group (NYPIRG), and the Regional Planners Network would make their case for deposits in front of committees in Albany. Each year lobbyists from container industries fought back by blocking legislation. The environmental groups then went back to New York City to spend the rest of the year working on promoting voluntary, postconsumer recycling and weighing in on the question of incineration, the administration's last hope for disposal.

The New York State Bottle Bill

In 1980, the "brush fires" that Dumont had warned about ten years earlier were flaring up. Thirty separate state legislatures were sponsoring bills mandating container deposits. In Maine and Michigan that year, bottle bills had just passed overwhelmingly by referendum. In New York State, the now 10-year-old fight to pass this bill had been, in the words of *New York Times* reporter Josh Barbanel, subject to the "most intense lobbying efforts in recent memory" (1982c, A1). In 1980, legislators from Nassau and Suffolk counties once again introduced a five-cent deposit bill in Albany, arguing that for taxpayers to continue to pour more and more money into collecting and disposing of these containers amounted to a public subsidy of waste pollution (Mitchell 1980).

When the bill again failed to pass, Long Island for the first time began debating county-level action on its own. In April 1981, Suffolk County broke ground and enacted a local five-cent deposit on soda and beverage containers. Such a move at the county level was unprecedented and posed serious questions of economic competitiveness among local jurisdictions—an unwelcome prospect for proponents of local and regional development. Long Island legislators, as a consequence, focused their attentions on Mayor Ed Koch, urging him to follow suit. But since his election in 1977, Koch had taken a business-as-usual approach to waste collection and disposal that focused on landfills and increasingly on new incinerators. As opposed to the Lindsay era, in which source-reduction measures were regularly considered in debates over municipal policy, waste reduction under Koch was largely the nonissue it had been under Beame.

In the 1980s, Koch's stance became more and more probusiness as his early alliances with the city's minority leaders deteriorated and his Democratic administration drifted to the right. It was not surprising, then, that Koch opposed the bottle bill. According to him, the bill would harm industry, eliminate skilled jobs, inconvenience storekeepers, and raise beverage prices. After Long Island's move, however, Department of Sanitation commissioner Norman Steisel strongly urged the mayor to follow suit, publicly estimating that it would achieve a daily municipal solid waste reduction of 700 tons. Koch finally agreed and reversed his position in April 1981. Calling deposit legislation "an idea whose time has come," he gave it support, but provided that it include a "sunset" clause of two years to test economic and waste impacts (*New York Times* 1981, 30). Industry fought back in its usual fashion. In Albany, a coalition of trade groups proposed an alternative bill that would impose a small tax on producers of glass, aluminum, and plastic containers. When the scheme failed, Steisel called the measure "such a sham that everybody could see through it," noting that it was a clear case of trying "to deflect public opinion" (Barbanel 1982b, 28)

The year 1982 proved decisive for the bottle bill. Public support of the bill was very high throughout the state (Barbanel 1982a). It was an election year, with terms in the legislature due to expire and reapportionment of assembly districts set to unseat at least five incumbent members of the state Senate. Koch himself was considering a bid for governor in the midst of his second term in the mayoralty. Momentum from his change of stance and Long Island's local law drew more and more legislators into support of the bill. Industry backlash intensified. Bottlers spent hundreds of thousands of dollars adorning their products with "neck hangers" that read, "the bottle bill will make this package MORE EXPENSIVE" (qtd. in Barbanel 1982a, B1, caps in original).

During this period, Governor Hugh Carey maintained his longstanding opposition to the deposit law, citing fears of layoffs and water pollution from washing refillable bottles and threatening to veto any measure that came across his desk. But in March a study from his own office concluded that these eventualities were unlikely and that "many of the arguments advanced by the beverage industry against the bill were unfounded" (qtd. in Barbanel 1982d, 1B). After careful cost-benefit analysis, his staff found no evidence that deposits would bring about job loss or impact corporate profitability. Industry was, according to the report, well able to absorb the capital costs that a bottle bill would entail. The report predicted a reduction in municipal solid waste of 5 to 7 percent and a savings of $25 million per year for New York State localities.

In April 1982, NYPIRG mobilized a march from Long Island to Albany in support of the measure, with sympathetic legislators joining activists once they reached the capital. Allied with what the president of the New York State Food Merchants Association called "ragtag college kids carrying signs" was none other than the city's own Department of Sanitation (Barbanel 1982a). In what a Department of Sanitation spokesman called the department's "first campaign directed at a legislative issue," the agency placed placards on 2,000 garbage trucks in support of the bill, urging residents to "Write Your Legislature Now!" (qtd. in Barbanel 1982a, B1). Pepsi called the department's activism nothing short of socialism, stating that it was "a pernicious invasion of rights in a free enterprise system by a government body" and warning Americans to "look at what happened in Russia, Germany, and Cuba when governments had too much control" (qtd. in Barbanel 1982a, B1). But the message on New York City's sanitation trucks made its point as activists marched through New York City on their way upstate.

New York finally enacted a bottle bill in June 1982, joining Oregon, Vermont, Connecticut, Massachusetts, Maine, Michigan, Iowa, and Delaware. The legislation placed a five-cent deposit on plastic, metal, and glass containers for soft drinks, mineral water, beer, and other malt beverages. Sidney Mudd, former BEACC chairman and now president of Joyce Beverages, called the bill an "awful, cruel, hoax" (qtd. in Barbanel 1982c, A1). But New York would be the third-to-last state in the union to enact such a bill. Only California and Hawaii followed suit, leaving most of the United States without beverage-container deposits, a situation that continues to this day. In New York State, the bill was an instant success, though, with redemption rates measured in 1984 in excess of 90 percent and a estimated 15 to 16 percent reduction in litter in New York City (Steisel 1984). According to Sanitation commissioner Steisel, the daily tonnage going to landfills was cut by 550 tons per day. Unfortunately, this amount was a drop in the bucket of the nearly 14,000 tons a day that the city still had to dispose of.

Incinerator Battles in New York City

In New York City, the 1980s were characterized by round after round of protests, negotiations, plans, and stallings concerning the siting and construction of a waste incinerator at the Brooklyn Navy Yard. Early in the decade, the New York State Senate gave initial approval for a facility that would convert the heat from waste combustion to steam. The plan was that the city would build the incinerator under contract with a private concern, which would in turn share "eventual profits" (Raab 1980, B10). As soon as the plan was announced, however, community opposition mounted swiftly and intensely. Environmental and neighborhood advocates used state and local permitting and planning requirements to delay progress on the project. Legal environmental groups such as the EDF and the NRDC effectively mobilized lawsuits and injunctions to prevent the siting process from going through. These efforts were paired with public demonstrations and vociferous participation in public-review meetings against the project. A coalition of Latino and Hasidic groups in Brooklyn neighborhoods took to the streets in protest (Gandy 2002).

Meanwhile, the mainstream New York City recycling movement, as represented by the EAC, NRDC, EDF, and NYPIRG began to voice the need for long-term, comprehensive alternatives to disposal and incineration for managing waste. With regard to the role of waste-to-energy, however, mainstream groups fell into two distinct and conflicting camps. NYPIRG, the same group that had organized the "rag-tag college kids" to march for the bottle bill, joined citizen-activists of Greenpoint and Williamsburg Brooklyn to oppose the siting of any kind of incinerator in New York City. They were joined in this effort by Dr. Barry Commoner, biology professor at Queens College and longtime New York City environmental activist. Since he had moved his Center for Natural Systems from St. Louis to New York in 1982, Commoner had actively critiqued New York City's waste-management policy. Now he made headlines citing the dangers of dioxin emissions from the incineration of chlorinated plastics and other waste materials.

In a separate camp were well-established environmental groups such as the NRDC and the EDF as well as the by now relatively low-profile EAC. Their position was to offer limited support for waste-to-energy incineration, albeit with heavy environmental controls, if the city promised to institutionalize recycling "on a full equivalent basis" (Miller 2000, 247). Despite these rifts, what both camps unambiguously supported was a system "in which the city's citizens would be called upon to participate in managing their own wastes. The alternative they advocated was called 'source-separation recycling'" (Miller 2000, 243). This system was none other than the curbside collection program, which in the 1970s the EAC had seen as the "necessary future" of recycling.

In 1985, the EDF released an eighty-page study claiming that a curbside recycling program could be cost competitive with and as efficient as a waste-to-energy facility, given a recycling rate of 40 percent. With the mayoral primary soon at hand, Koch was willing to promise equal consideration of recycling if waste-to-energy moved forward. In 1985, the city signed a contract with Signal Environmental Systems to build and operate the waste-to-energy plant. This firm would receive $46 million in state construction grants and tax benefits and would share in 20 percent of the eventual revenue from electricity production. But the incinerator was not to be. The project would continue to be opposed by community and some environmental groups until 1996, when then Mayor Rudolph Giuliani announced that no new incinerators would be built in the city. This announcement was timed with his decision to close Fresh Kills, the city's last active landfill. Well before that point, however, the political battle around the incinerator finally forced the city's commitment to institute a curbside recycling program.

In June 1985, after negotiations with the environmental and citizen groups opposing the incinerator, the city announced that it would implement a voluntary recycling pilot program in five residential sections of New York City. Residents would be asked to separate newspaper, glass, and metal and place them in recycling bins at curbside for biweekly collection. The Department of Sanitation would contract with the EAC for technical advice and pilot studies of apartment recycling. The EDF called the pilot program a "step in the right direction" but advocated a much more aggressive plan, predicting that the city could save "hundreds of millions of dollars" in avoided incinerator costs if it implemented curbside recycling citywide (Purnick 1985, B3).

The Department of Sanitation's response to its new charge was luke-warm. Steisel had considered the EDF's predictions of 40 percent recycling within three years wildly out of line. As he put it, "You have to learn to crawl before you can walk, and before you run. . . . They [the EDF] are not talking about running, they are talking about flying—without the benefit of wings" (qtd. in Barbanel 1985, 39). Recycling 15 percent of the city's waste was the best, he estimated, that could be achieved after full implementation of the program and a learning period. Nevertheless, Steisel grudgingly if vaguely conceded that recycling could in the long run "help the city" (qtd. in Purnick 1985, B3).

Foes of the Navy Yard waste-to-energy facility increasingly reformulated their argument about the relationship of recycling and incineration. Whereas reform groups had previously called for equal consideration of the two options (in terms of funding and planning), and activist groups had focused on hazards in their opposition to facility siting, elements of both camps now began to argue that recycling could be a substitute for incineration. In 1986, NYPIRG released a report stating that incinerators might have potentially devastating health consequences on New York City residents and advocating "total recycling" as the alternative. Its message hit home as increasing numbers of citizens and local politicians sought hope in curbside programs as a way out of the waste crisis. The state issued a Comprehensive Solid Waste Management Plan in 1988 that put priority on the waste-reduction hierarchy of prevention, reuse, and recycling before disposal. The *New York Times* reported that some in the New York Assembly were beginning to "side with environmentalists, who argue that the state should devote its limited resources to reaching its stated goal of 50 percent recycling. These legislators argue that the incinerators, which are a potential source of hazardous air and water pollution, are being built at the expense of recycling" (Kolbert 1988, B1). In vain did Department of Sanitation officials point out that "recycling is a feasible waste-management alternative only for that fraction of municipal solid wastes that can be reused in the manufacture of new products" (qtd. in Miller 2000, 12). Even with the 40 percent recycling imagined in EDF's early optimistic proposals, nearly 8,000 tons of garbage per day would still have to be disposed of somehow and somewhere. Without incineration, one landfill (Fresh Kills) would have to absorb this tonnage indefinitely. It was knowledge of this fact that led Deputy Commissioner Paul Caslowitz of the Department of Sanitation to say bluntly, "Anybody who feels that they can avoid making tough decisions by hiding behind recycling is crazy" (qtd. in Carmody 1986,

4). Nevertheless, total recycling became the environmental community's voiced alternative to incineration. Miller trenchantly comments on the lack of empirical grounding for such a position:

Accepting these premises left no logical alternative but to recycle everything the city's 7.4 million residents threw away. Despite the fact that no community in the country—from the smallest New Age commune in California to the most environmentally conscious suburb of Massachusetts—had ever managed to recycle more than a third of its refuse, despite the fact that [moderate environmentalists] thought the 25% target in their mandatory recycling law near the limit of what was realistically achievable for New York . . . incinerator opponents unrolled their Panglossian new campaign slogan: "Total Recycling." (2000, 261)

In 1987, NYPIRG activism and research had finally convinced state environmental officials that the city's incinerator plan was environmentally deficient. Department of Environmental Conservation commissioner Thomas Jorling refused to grant the city a permit to build, forcing Koch to reopen public hearings on the matter. The city council by that point was fully behind a citywide recycling program and had introduced a bill outlining a mandatory system to be phased in over five years. The Department of Sanitation's pilot efforts had come under increasing criticism since they started in 1985. A year later, the department was embarrassed by the Uniformed Sanitationmen's Association's opposition to efforts to rein in the very high costs of recycling collection by reducing men in the field. For about a week in 1986, the union threatened to strike if recycling trucks were manned by one rather than two men even though lighter loads and shorter routes argued in favor of a reduction in manpower (Barbanel 1986). Calling the city's efforts to implement recycling "woefully inadequate," Queens councilman Sheldon Leffler complained that "the Koch administration had not given recycling enough financial or political support" and that the Department of Sanitation had "dragged its feet because it has not received the direction from the top that it might have or should have" (qtd. in *New York Times* 1988, 3).

In 1988, New York State passed its first Solid Waste Management Plan, which set a 40 percent recycling goal for New York localities statewide. In New York City, support was gathering in the city council to pass a law mandating recycling that would hold the Department of Sanitation accountable for meeting certain annual tonnage targets for recycling. In March 1989, with Koch up for reelection and struggling against fellow Democrat David Dinkins for nomination, the council passed Local Law 19. The law mandated 4,250 tons of recycling collections per day by 1994. The department would be responsible for achieving this rate by designing a citywide program of curbside collection of marketable materials from the waste and was directed to implement a range of research and experimental programs in voluntary citizen composting and waste prevention.

For the first time since World War II, the city required residents to set out separated materials at the curb. The city resumed its role of old, taking responsibility for collection of useable waste products, turning them over to private firms, and paying them a "processing fee," with the hope—if markets were good—of recouping some of the costs through the sale of paper and metal, certain plastics, but not glass. And for the first time ever, municipal sanitation policy would be "environmental" policy. Participating in recycling would, for residents, no longer be just a matter of good citizenship or obeying the law; it would be a way, in the words of one Department of Sanitation poster, to "be Earth's friend." If 1970 was the year recycling came to New York, 1989 marked its settling down—at least for a while.

Recycling beyond New York City

Access to the EAC archives—its internal meeting minutes, BEACC letters, and rosters of funders—has enabled me to make a pointed case that in the 1970s industrial interests crafted an explicit policy of diversion via cooptation through an environmental organization that presented its face to the public as one focused on community and ecology. Cities and towns throughout the nation followed trajectories similar to New York's, even if their local grassroots recycling groups were not as explicitly manipulated. Celebratory histories of post-1970s recycling tell a story of mobilization of grassroots, community-based action as local centers staffed with volunteer labor established themselves as a drop-off depot for newspapers, glass bottles, and cans (NRDC 2002; Bell 2004; Berkeley Ecology Center 2008). The fact that few such centers (Berkeley being a notable exception) still handle some or all of municipal recycling suggests that most lacked the marketing expertise, reliable labor, and in particular the scale to sustain recycling in more than a token form (Weinberg, Pellow, and Schnaiberg 2000; Eureka Recycling 2008). These centers' brief lives were useful, but not primarily as a model for grassroots action (as their histories today proclaim them to be). Throughout the 1970s, Reynolds Aluminum, Coca-Cola, and the Glass Packaging Institute, among other industry groups, sought to forestall bottle bills nationwide, promoting what they knew to be at best symbolic and at worst doomed citizen drop-off efforts with one hand as they lobbied against legislation with the other (*New York Times* 1970a). These same industries went on to become enthusiastic and outspoken supporters of curbside recycling programs in the 1980s and 1990s. They were joined at that point by firms within the nation's waste-disposal industry who stood to benefit from municipal contracts to collect and process commingled curbside recyclables (U.S. Senate 1991a; Gould, Schnaiberg, and Weinberg 1996). It was just a matter of time until municipalities and counties, pushed by both civil society and industry, stepped in to take over recycling as a function of municipal service.

Except in very rural situations, drop-off centers run by municipalities were never able to garner more than a tiny fraction of recyclables in the waste stream. Environmental groups called for curbside collection; municipalities provided it in order to collect effectively what was being generated as recyclable residential discards. But for municipally organized curbside collection to work fiscally, materials had to be collected in commingled form, which meant they would have to be sorted out post-collection. Once up and running, this structure of reclamation was self-reinforcing. A private recycling industry heavily subsidized by public funds was supported by an environmental movement that called for, if anything, more of this model even as they pushed for alternative forms of producer-focused legislation (NRC 2001).

The impetus behind the environmentalist strategy was then and still is today not corporate agenda making, but genuine environmental concern. The Container Recycling Institute (CRI), a nonprofit organization organized around support of legislation proposed at the national level as well as in 18 states (12 without bottle bills, and 4 in which expansion is being sought), is anything but a front group for industry; its lobbying is in direct conflict with beverage producers and bottlers who still vehemently oppose expansion of existing bottle bills or imposition of new ones. Yet the CRI makes a point of arguing generally that "bottle bills Complement Curbside Recycling Programs," even as it concedes that "specific impacts of a deposit program on an existing curbside program will vary depending on the particular local economies of the curbside program" (2008). In fact, as the CRI quietly notes, bottle bills do rob municipal curbside programs of high-value plastic and aluminum (2008). This inconvenient truth has been borne out by my own research in the case of New York City, in which I have found, moreover, that the problems with recycling that glass so markedly manifests are intensified by the dual bottle-bill/curbside strategy endorsed by environmental groups locally, in particular NYPIRG. Statistics on the material composition of New York City's refuse, curbside recycling, and bottle-bill redemptions strongly suggest that glass is redeemed by consumers and scavengers at much lower rates than certain plastics or aluminum because of its weight (imagine bringing a bag of glass bottles back to the store) (NYC DS 2008b). Bottle bills consequently leave municipal collections heavy in broken glass, without the benefit of lighter, more valuable recyclables to counter the costs of collection and processing. This is not at all an argument against bottle bills, but one that invites reconsideration of the interaction between them and mixed curbside models heavily reliant on maximizing revenues from sold collections.

The Costs of Curbside Collection

The tension between bottle bills and curbside recycling today highlights important material and social implications for the political economy of waste diversion. Industry initially pushed curbside recycling as a means of forestalling bottle bills and other Kretchmeresque forms of producer-focused waste policy. The rapid growth in curbside recycling programs in the 1980s and 1990s, in comparison to the far more modest progress of bottle bills in only 10 states, suggests that this strategy was largely but not wholly successful. This finding is not in and of itself new. Several authors have described the role that the nonprofit organization Keep America Beautiful played in the 1970s era to reconstruct litter as an individual failing and to encourage state policies such as fining litterers and voluntary citizen clean-up programs as a direct strategy to forestall the passage of bottle bills (Rathje and Murphy 1992; Rogers 2005). In their studies of the recycling movement in the national and in Chicago, Kenneth Gould, Allan Schnaiberg, and Adam Weinberg have also observed that in the early 1970s environmental movements promoted "somewhat more benign forms of waste reduction," but that "through the efforts of trade association and their coalitions with local and national citizen-worker groups . . . much of this environmental protection strategy was deflected into a more exclusive focus on post-consumer waste recy-cling" (1996, 127).

What is brought to light in the case of New York is the extent to which the environmental movement was a big, cooperative part of this deflection despite its ongoing advocacy for bottle bills and associated forms of producer-focused legislation. This perspective can be summa-rized as "If some recycling is good, more recycling is better!" without regard to the interaction of the two structures of reclamation materially or socially. At the material level, bottle bills and curbside programs siphon tonnage from one another, making each weaker and less viable than it would have been had the other not existed. Had bottle bills been the only structure for the reclamation of beverage containers, if they had existed in all 50 states, and most of all if they had been organized via one federal act of legislation, far larger quantities of clean, sorted material flowing back to bottlers might well have enabled structural change in processes of beverage production and distribution that would result in more refill, less downcycling, and diminished vehicular impacts as backhaul supplanted municipal collections. At the very least, they would have been more successful at diverting tonnages from disposal because their high rates of recovery in comparison to curbside recycling are well established and not contested (CRI 2008). For reasons discussed in chapter 1, the benefits of a deposit system over curbside collection are particularly true in the case of glass (I argue in chapter 5 that this same reasoning applies to plastic containers of all kinds). Conversely and ironically, if industrial victory had been complete and no bottle bills had been passed, municipalities forced into curbside collection would have been in a marginally better position fiscally than they are today, especially again with regard to glass. The pursuit of both goals simultaneously by the environmental movement was the most counterproductive outcome from the standpoint of sustainability—both ecological and fiscal.

Even more important is the social fact demonstrated by the recycling movement's uncritical embrace of curbside recycling. First and foremost, municipal curbside recycling was an explicit strategy on the part of producers of certain container and paper commodities to keep the costs of negative externalities squarely on the public. The fact that curbside recycling continues to be so vehemently defended today, even by groups actively involved in fighting for producer legislation, suggests that its role in diversionary weakening has not been fully grappled with by activists concerned with problems of solid waste. Second, the story of the emergence of curbside recycling was an effective test run for a model of corporate response to environmental pressure that, I argue in the rest of this book, has proven effective again and again as the history of U.S. solid-waste problems and solutions has progressed. The story starts with volunteer efforts to organize material reclamation at the community level and to integrate this function with ecological education and community building. The story then goes that municipalities and states see the wisdom and potential of the grassroots effort and concede to its institutionalization. Here, for example, is the EAC's 2002 history of itself:

In 1970, a diverse group of educators, business people, and grassroots community leaders came together to organize New York's first Earth Day. The event was a success and the group decided to carry on the Earth Day spirit as a full-time, uniquely urban environmental organization. Since then, Environmental Action Coalition (EAC) has worked to make New York more livable . . . pioneering efforts in recycling. Seeing what works persuades decision-makers to adopt these models. (EAC 2002)

With state-organized structures of reclamation up and running, there is the impression that progress is being made. In a sense, progress is indeed being made; it is just that this progress is one of state program building and associated economic activity, not material progress in reducing waste or social progress in making the burdens and benefits of waste disposal/diversion more equitable. Tonnages of certain marketable commodities are being diverted from disposal at significant public expense, but as the national diversion rate of 33 percent existing today shows (U.S. EPA 2009b; see also appendix I), and even more saliently as the continued growth in materials flow through the U.S. and global economies confirms (WRI 2001; Rogich 2008), this diversion is at best marginally relevant to the ecosystemic additions and withdrawals associated with solid waste. And if, as it is so often countered, one should not critique recycling as presently organized because it is "a start," this argument begs the question, "A start of what?" A structure of reclamation based on a federal bottle bill and additional Kretchmeresque provisions, similarly applied nationwide, would also be just "a start" from the standpoint of tonnage due to the fact that municipal solid waste is only a small fraction of the nation's overall solid-waste burden (more on this in chapter 3). But it would be a start premised on a model that does not integrate contradiction into its core structure.

Front Groups, Co-optation, and Hegemony

In 1977, Laurie Davidson Cummings authored an article entitled "Voluntary Strategies in the Environmental Movement: Recycling as Cooptation." Identifying voluntary recycling as a "major focus of public interest in the environment" around Earth Day, Cummings drew attention to the fact that "campaigns involving voluntary recycling were more of a cooptive strategy on the part of business than they were an effective strategy for mobilizing partisans in the environmental movement" (153). In this article, Cummings considered the role of voluntarism in social reform, acknowledging it as an entry point for reform in a pluralistic system, but also [as] "a tool with which to blunt the capacity for change" (153). At the same time, she noted the environmental movement's hesitancy to engage in critique of the latter tendency for fear of losing momentum, writing that "in efforts to get a social movement going, any support appears to contribute to consciousness-raising about an issue" (153). Citing Mancur Olsen's seminal work on the logic of collective action, she noted that "whenever a voluntary strategy is adopted to deal with a collective problem, the status quo prospers" (159).

The dynamic to which Cummings referred in 1976 is still alive, well, and much richer today than it was in the years after the first Earth Day. It is also complicated by the momentum that decades of curbside recycling has accumulated symbolically, economically, and institutionally. It counterposes not only voluntarism, but also social and material action organized at the level of consumption, the individual, and the locality against producer-focused initiatives involving regulation of firms' autonomy to make and market products. Environmental groups are key actors in the renegotiation of strong contradictory positions such that they are made complementary and weaker. "Inconvenient truths" about the physiochemical and economic properties of glass bottles, for example, are only partially discussed and under conditions of great tension.

Various social scientists have drawn attention to the contemporary construction of recycling as having dangerous implications for meaningful environmental change. Timothy Luke says of recycling that "core supply-side changelessness is preserved by enveloping it in a demand-side mobilization for marginal change" (1997, 132). Allan Schnaiberg states that "socially progressive words about recycling continue to mask socially regressive deeds, alas" (1997, 239). Nina Eliasoph describes a larger social process currently under way in the United States in which the structure of voluntarism gets volunteers "to convince themselves that regular citizens 'really can make a difference' without addressing issues that they would consider 'political'" (1998, 13). These authors, along with Cummings, are describing a common social fact that is approximated but not adequately described by the word *co-optation*. This term implies an active strategy of containment and absorption of a potential foe. Antonio Gramsci's notion of cultural hegemony comes closer. The interests of those in power become perceived as the interests of society as a whole, even those who lose in the end.

Defense of curbside recycling today (Hershkowtiz 1998) is complicated by a need for pragmatism that requires stepping down from a lofty position rooted in conflict (e.g., taxes on packaging products) to search for solutions that seem to work in a material sense (curbside collection). As the years since 1970 have passed and curbside recycling as the structure of municipal reclamation has been cemented into the fabric of the city, the need for such pragmatism has intensified, reflecting the power of inertia (Becker 1995). As Cummings warned, and as Peter Spendelow (2002) courageously noted, there is a justifiable fear of losing ground already gained. This fear sometimes translates to a version of censorship when troubling questions of material efficacy are debated (as in the case of glass). It leads to the cry, "As of now, recycling is something that has the possibility of growing into something bigger than it is, with much economic import and environmental friendliness. Please don't douse the flame just yet, brothers!" (Kender 2003). In the remainder of this book, I continue to question the material efficacy of recycling as we know it, investigating additional perspectives on the contradictory social approach to waste problems that are under debate and contention today. In the next chapter, I look at a case of "unpolitics," in particular the little-studied fact that the municipal solid waste is only a tiny fraction of all solid waste generated in the United States.

3

Tonnage and Toxicity: The Nonissue of Nonhazardous Industrial Waste

I have spent my adult life studying and working in one way or another with garbage. As a result, I have spent a great deal of time looking at data on waste quantities and composition—how much municipal solid waste is produced in a city, state, or country; what materials make up different waste flows; how much is disposed and how much goes to recycling, composting, or another alternative. The U.S. EPA publishes biennial data on this subject for the United States as a whole, detailing the composition of municipal solid waste by material as well as by product type. States, counties, and cities all over the country also compile and report data on municipal solid waste generation and composition, as do several trade publications (see, e.g., *Waste News* 2007; *BioCycle* 2008). Combined, these sources paint a detailed picture of what is in U.S. municipal solid waste and how much there is of it over time. The EPA data, which as of 2008 reported the total annual U.S. municipal solid waste generation at about 250 million tons annually (U.S. EPA 2009b), is the basis for what has become a frequently cited statistic, often quoted to shock and shame: "The average American throws out 4.3 pounds of garbage . . . per day—1.6 more pounds than 30 years ago" (Royte 2005, 11).

Like many Americans, I had come to consider the hundreds of millions of tons of municipal solid waste produced annually as an indicator of the "throwaway society." Then, ten years into my study of solid waste, I stumbled on a waste statistic quietly put out by the EPA in a document called *Guide for Industrial Waste Management* (U.S. EPA 1999). This technical manual, meant to provide tips to factory managers for handling waste at their plants, noted, without further comment, that manufacturing industries were generating some 7.6 billion tons a year of solid waste. Some digging on my part uncovered an older, unpublished report that was the source of this estimate as well as two follow-up government documents that cited other industrial, mining, extractive, and agricultural operations as bringing the total industrial waste tonnage generated in the United States up to around 12 billion tons (U.S. EPA 1987, 1988; OTA 1992). These amounts were an order of magnitude greater than the tonnage of municipal solid waste that every book, volunteer effort, government program, or household conversation about trash and its problems seemed to focus on. Yet very little had been published about this far larger quantity.

Where and what is the shadowy, massive fraction of solid waste that environmental business consultant and journalist Joel Makower has called the "gross national trash" (2009)? It certainly is not garbage as we know it. Instead, this massive stream represents solid waste disposed of as unintended consequences of industrial processes: it consists of the discards of the factory itself, excluding recycled or reused materials (for which there are simply no comprehensive national data). As I discuss in this chapter, we know very little about what materials are in it or where it is being disposed. And despite the EPA's classification of manufacturing wastes as "nonhazardous," there are reasons to be concerned about its toxicity. As the Congressional Research Service observed in 1994,

In general, [nonhazardous] industrial waste presents a number of causes for concern. There is a large number of facilities, nearly 28,000 industrial land disposal units . . . which the EPA estimates have 125,000 surface impoundments (ponds) in which liquid wastes are disposed. Many of these facilities handle wastes with the same characteristics as hazardous waste. There is also a growing recognition that non-hazardous waste can contaminate groundwater. . . . Many states do not require permits for on-site disposal of industrial waste. . . . Few facilities have adequate safeguards to protect groundwater. (McCarthy 1994, CRS-11)

Nonhazardous industrial wastes in this context do not include wastes that the EPA has explicitly deemed hazardous. Nor do they include coal ash, the subject of much current focus due to a massive structural failure in a Tennessee holding pond in December 2008 that spilled 5.4 million cubic yards of sludge over 300 acres of land, damaging homes and threatening groundwater quality (Hall 2008). The residue from coal-fired electrical plants, coal ash is classified among other wastes called "special" in that they fall outside the EPA's relatively robust regulatory structure governing hazardous industrial waste. Special wastes include "mining waste; oil and gas drilling muds and oil production brines; phosphate rock mining, beneficiation, and processing waste; uranium waste," and other utility wastes from fossil fuel combustion (U.S. EPA 2009d). Special wastes are arguably even more important than nonhazardous industrial wastes from a standpoint of risk and toxicity. They clearly stem from precursors to manufacturing—the production of energy and the extraction of raw materials. Nonetheless, in this chapter I focus on the roughly 7.6 billion tons of what the EPA specifically calls "nonhazardous industrial wastes" and what I abbreviate simply as **manufacturing wastes** (understanding that it excludes the smaller tonnage of specifically identified hazardous wastes generated in the manufacturing process and refers to solid wastes and not wastewaters or airborne emissions). (See appendix I.)

I focus on manufacturing wastes because of their close connections to the garbage we live with and worry so much about. If products and packaging are the subject of our concern over a life cycle from cradle to grave, then manufacturing wastes are their parents. These wastes arise from the production of glass, plastic, metal, paper, textiles, processed food, chemicals, electronics, machines, and many other goods we consume. Yet despite this direct relation, so much more is known about municipal solid waste than about manufacturing wastes that it is hard to exaggerate the gap. Most interesting to me as a sociologist, the existence of the 7.6 billion tonnage, which has crept into discourse over solid-waste problems only in the past few years, is still understood by those in the recycling movement and by members of the public concerned about garbage as a consequence of wasteful *personal* consumption. This chapter takes the reader through some rather dry but necessary information on the state of manufacturing-waste data and policy today, concluding with some surprising findings on the degree to which the existence of manufacturing wastes are erroneously linked to personal choice in the home and community.

Data and Governance for U.S. Solid-Waste Streams

Municipal solid waste is a small subset of all solid waste but enjoys rich structures of governance. National-level regulation is organized under the Resource Conservation Recovery Act (RCRA), which passed in 1976 and was substantially amended in 1980 and 1984. The EPA's regulatory responsibilities with regard to municipal solid waste are spelled out in "Subtitle D" of the act. They entail setting standards for construction and operation of municipal solid waste landfills and incinerators and approving of state plans for municipal solid waste management. Unlike in the European Union, in the United States there are no national mandates or targets for municipal solid waste diversion. At most, federal involvement in municipal solid waste management has involved grants and other subsidies to localities, nonprofits, and firms for research and development, demonstration projects, and some market development through federal purchasing requirements. Municipal solid waste diversion via recycling, composting, and other methods is instead coordinated under a wide array of state and municipal laws and programs. As detailed in prior chapters, the municipal and state role in municipal solid waste diversion is extensive throughout the United States.

Subtitle C of the RCRA applies to solid wastes emanating from manufacturing that have been classified as hazardous on the basis of ignitability, corrosivity, reactivity, or toxicity or that have been listed as such on several preestablished inventories (U.S. EPA 2008a). As with municipal solid waste, there is a great deal of federally organized information gathering and reporting on disposed tonnages of hazardous industrial wastes, although this involvement takes a different form. RCRA's Subtitle C sets guidelines that require firms generating more than a certain annual tonnage of hazardous waste and those engaged in transport, treatment, and disposal of any hazardous industrial quantities to track movements, quantities, and constituents (U.S. EPA 1997). Methods to contain, haul, recycle, or otherwise "beneficially use" or dispose of hazardous wastes must adhere to RCRA safety requirements. In most cases, individual states implement RCRA Subtitle C provisions, with each state required to meet minimum national standards (Scicchitano and Hedge 1993). A few states, such as California, have expanded requirements that go beyond RCRA requirements for the safe handling of hazardous industrial wastes (National Research Council 1999).

Under RCRA and other federal environmental laws, the EPA not only gathers and disseminates tonnage data on hazardous industrial wastes, but also enables public access to geographic information about the sites that generate or handle hazardous substances, including solids regulated under the RCRA and other chemicals not classified as solid waste. The EPA's Toxics Release Inventory was enacted with the express purpose of providing geographical information system and other spatial data resources to citizens so that they can participate in decisions about sited hazards around them. Despite imperfections, the Toxics Release Inventory remains a potent resource for civil society (Hamilton 2005; Kocha and Ashford 2006). With some research, a concerned citizen is able to map and monitor emissions of toxics in the neighborhood, and Toxics Release Inventory data have been used extensively within the realm of environmental justice activism to demonstrate and contest risky facility sitings (Morello-Frosch, Pastor, Porras, et al. 2002).

In contrast, the lack of information on manufacturing wastes classified "nonhazardous," which also fall under Subtitle D of RCRA, can scarcely be exaggerated. An EPA research study conducted in 1987 constitutes the sum total of knowledge about manufacturing-waste tonnages and disposal practices for the United States as whole (see U.S. EPA 1987 and 1988). This study continues to act as reference to this day. Go to the EPA Web site today, and you will find the 7.6 billion ton estimate of annual manufacturing-waste tonnage still reported (U.S. EPA 2010b). This statistic has been and continues to be repeated throughout the scant and desultory discussion of this waste stream that has taken place since 1987, appearing in publications by the EPA, in congressional testimony, in the academic literature, and in the rare contemplation of manufacturing waste in environmental popular discourse. No data are currently collected or reported on waste generation, recovery, or disposal practices for U.S. industries as a whole, nor do voluntary statistics put out by industry trade groups enable an across-the-board examination of manufacturing-waste flows and disposal sites.

Matthew Eckelman and Marian Chertow (2009) have conducted the only twenty-first-century study of manufacturing wastes in the United States, using data from Pennsylvania, the only state to comprehensively monitor generation of such discards, which it terms "residual wastes." Their research suggests that the gap between municipal solid waste and manufacturing wastes, in terms of tonnage, may recently be narrowing, at least in Pennsylvania. In 2001, the state's Department of Environmental Protection reported an estimated 40 million tons of residual waste as compared to 9.2 million tons of municipal solid waste (PA DEP 2001). Eckelman and Chertow's research found that in 2004 this tonnage was down to 20 million metric tons for residual wastes and up slightly to 10 million tons for municipal solid waste. Nonetheless, the authors note that "while often overshadowed by municipal solid waste (MSW) in policy debates and research, nonhazardous industrial waste is the dominant waste stream of modern societies" (2009, 2551). Their research, which is based on Pennsylvania's exceptional reporting requirements for disposed residual waste, supports the state's finding of a wide range of heterogeneous constituents to this waste stream, including

linoleum, detergents and cleaners, filters, rubber, contaminated soil, fertilizers, glass, ceramics, pesticides, gypsum board, leather, pharmaceutical waste, pumps, textiles, photographic film and paper, piping, industrial equipment, asbestos-, oil- and PCB-bearing wastes, storage tanks, electronics, metal-bearing wastes (e.g., foundry sands, slags, grindings and shavings), residues such as sludge (from the treatment of public water supplies, emission control, lime-stabilized pickle liquor, paints, electroplating, and waste from the manufacture of lime and cement). (PA DEP 2001)

Eckelman and Chertow's research indicates substantial untapped potential to divert substances from residual waste disposal to beneficial use. Using voluntarily self-reported data from Pennsylvania industries on reuse and recycling of residual wastes, they estimate that the substitution of recycled residual discards for virgin production can potentially save the equivalent of almost one percent of Pennsylvania's annual total energy use as well as diminish sulfur dioxide and nitrous oxide emissions (2009, 2550). Pennsylvania's data reporting is exceptional. Few states mention manufacturing waste as a category to be considered as part of the state's overall solid-waste generation. And no other state reports manufacturing-waste tonnages in total. It should be noted that the reuse or recycling of some manufacturing discards does in fact take place to varying degrees in states across the nation. State-level criteria for deeming an application of manufacturing discards "beneficial," defined as "use either in a manufacturing process to make a product or as a substitute for a raw material or product provided such use of the solid waste does not adversely impact human health or the environment" (ASTSWMO 2007, 3), is the subject of study and reporting by state agencies as well as by the Association of State and Territorial Solid Waste Management Officials. Throughout the country, problems of "sham recycling," in which manufacturing wastes have been applied to land, burned for energy, or otherwise used in an unsafe manner, have required a complex regulatory structure for "beneficial use determinations," and the association's work documents the administrative and procedural variation across states in issuing these determinations. Nonetheless, neither the association nor any other governmental or nongovernmental organization compiles information on the generation or composition of manufacturing wastes disposed, reused, recycled, or otherwise beneficially used on a national scale, as is done every two years for municipal solid waste in intricate detail. Looking at the evolution of the RCRA sheds light on this starkly disparate treatment.

The Evolution of the Resource Conservation Recovery Act

Although deliberation over the RCRA's initial scope included regulation of production to prevent waste and the development of a national policy to conserve materials, its industrial regulatory focus in practice has been confined largely to the control of hazardous wastes post-generation (Szasz 1994; Geiser 2001). The 1979 uprising over soil contamination at Love Canal, New York, and a case in Times Beach, Missouri, in the early 1980s (in which dioxin-laden waste oil that was sprayed on city streets for dust suppression sickened hundreds of residents—a case of sham recycling if there ever was one) brought intense focus on risks from hazardous industrial waste nationwide (Szasz 1994). At that time, the EPA was already under fierce criticism from Congress, the Washington environmental lobby, and even some of its own disaffected employees over the agency's failure to promulgate regulations to protect the public from hazardous wastes (Norland and Friedman 1979). Love Canal and Times Beach galvanized public opinion and demanded federal response. The RCRA was amended in 1980 and 1984 to address extensive delays in implementing Subtitle C protections.

The 1980 amendments required the EPA to conduct a series of studies on extractive and manufacturing wastes not covered under Subtitle C and report them to Congress. The EPA's report to Congress was issued eight years later, debuting the statistic of 7.6 billion tons of manufacturing waste that would be repeated for the next thirty years. In that same year, the RCRA came up for reauthorization and with it an opportunity to expand its regulatory reach—a goal described as one of Congress's top priorities that year (Keane 1992). Reeling from the Reagan administration's assault on environmental regulation, the Democrat-led Congress began a six-year effort to expand the RCRA's regulatory purview. Between 1988 and 1994, more than 100 bills were proposed in Congress to reauthorize RCRA. Most included provisions focused on municipal solid waste—improving regulations on incinerator and landfill operations; addressing the effect of interstate commerce in municipal solid waste; and supporting secondary-materials markets for recycled fractions of municipal solid waste. But some of the bills—notably the Waste Materials Management Act of 1989 (proposed by Rep. Charlie Luken, D–Ohio), the Waste Minimization and Control Act of 1989 (proposed by Sen. Max Baucus, D–Mont., also called the Baucus bill), and the Municipal Solid Waste Source Reduction and Recycling Act of 1989 (proposed by Sen. Lincoln Chafee, R–R.I.)—also included provisions to comprehensively gather and publish data on manufacturing-waste generation as well as to set federal standards for disposal of manufacturing waste at the same level of stringency as applied to municipal solid waste disposal.

Testimony on these bills and their successors in the early 1990s show manufacturers unsurprisingly opposing any manufacturing-waste regulation, including the requirement of mandatory annual reporting of tonnages disposed and diverted. Their argument was that manufacturing wastes were best addressed through gradual and voluntary process changes in production operations, which were, in the industry's opinion, already under way. In 1991, the Virginia Manufacturers Association testified that source reduction, reuse, and recycling have become "fully a mainstream corporate environmental interest." There was concern among its members that "during the upcoming RCRA debate, several issues of particular importance to . . . manufacturers are likely to surface. . . . [W]e urge this subcommittee to consider the importance of voluntary waste minimization options in the management of industrial waste" (U.S. House of Representative 1991b, 24–25). Manufacturers held that rather than regulate Subtitle D industrial waste, "Federal and State regulatory programs should serve to encourage the development of successful implementation of workable waste management strategies. These include a well-defined role for voluntary programs. Such strategies must be flexible . . . private sector voluntary initiatives" (U.S. House of Representatives 1991b, 24–25).

Consumers were also encouraged to realize their part in demanding products that meant the creation of manufacturing waste. In 1987 oversight hearings leading up to the Baucus bill, representatives from Mobil made clear that they favored "public education as a fundamental requirement that must be achieved if our good nation is to gain optimum management of this critical national problem. Individuals create an important and central ingredient in this effort. [The industry must] educate the public that the goods and comforts consumers want and enjoy produce waste" (U.S. Senate 1987, 40).

In these debates, Washington-based environmental groups' position on manufacturing waste regulation was present but weak. The NRDC and the EDF had been active in the battle to amend RCRA earlier in the 1980s. During RCRA amendment hearings in that period, both organizations had critiqued the EPA's failure to promulgate municipal solid waste landfill regulations, its deferral of reporting requirements, its delay on imposing regulations governing hazardous-waste storage impoundments and incinerators, and other requirements under the law. In subsequent debates over RCRA reauthorization, the NRDC supported imposing standards for disposal of manufacturing waste in on-site surface impoundments but did not feature attention to data gathering in its policy advocacy. It, along with the EDF, focused the bulk of its testimony on supporting other aspects of reauthorization bills focused on municipal solid waste. Both organizations urged legislative measures that would boost alternatives to municipal solid waste disposal, such as establishing national packaging standards and imposing a national bottle bill, using federal procurement and grant funding to strengthen secondary-materials markets for recycled commodities, and strengthening siting and operational requirements for municipal solid waste landfills and incinerators (U.S. Senate 1987).

The most eloquent and direct statements in favor of regulating manufacturing waste during this period of debate came surprisingly not from elected officials or Washington environmental lobbying groups, but from the National Solid Wastes Management Association (NSWMA), the trade group representing the private municipal solid waste hauling and disposal industry. As one spokesman stated, "The EPA has taken no steps to lay the groundwork for adequate regulation of waste from oil and gas production, municipal sludges or from agricultural, industrial, construction and demolition activities. Apparently, EPA has not even created the obvious data-gathering mechanisms that would allow such steps to be taken" (U.S. Senate 1987, 553). Support for expanded programs to mitigate hazards and increase reduction and recycling of manufacturing waste came not only from NSWMA, but also from the Institute of Scrap Recycling Industries and municipal solid waste collection and disposal giants such as Waste Management, Inc. Both sectors saw further business potential from the increased regulation of more categories of waste, especially if such waste would be required to be moved off site for disposal in permitted landfills and incinerators, or the source of materials for reclamation as scrap.[1]

Work between 1988 and 1992 to pass an RCRA reauthorization failed to yield a bill acceptable to both houses of Congress. In 1991, the George H. W. Bush administration "surprised Congress by opposing the Senate reauthorization plans" on the grounds that any expansion of the RCRA would unnecessarily expand "the federal government's role in solid waste management" (Davis 1991, 47). In 1990, Congress passed several other federal laws to address hazards, including the cross-media Pollution Prevention Act, which made process redesign, phase-out of toxic chemicals, and other waste-preventing changes a "national priority," albeit a voluntary one. The Pollution Prevention Act has been critiqued for the yawning gap between its stated mission and the results from its implementation (Geiser 2004; Bayrakal 2006). Its impact on manufacturing-waste tonnages can only be guessed at. A 2006 report on its accomplishments lists a total reduction in materials and waste of

2.5 million tons between 2004 and 2006. Of these wastes, "solid wastes other than RCRA hazardous wastes" were estimated to be reduced by 900,000 tons over three years, involving municipal solid waste and manufacturing waste wastes as well as industrial, commercial, and residential processes that require material inputs (National Pollution Prevention Roundtable 2008, 27).

In 1993, President Bill Clinton responded to calls from the recycling industry, states, and localities for a federal role in strengthening secondary-materials markets when he issued an executive order mandating federal procurement of products with recycled content paper and urging agencies to undertake other waste-prevention and recycling measures. After that, there was "no further serious proposal to amend RCRA in any succeeding Congress," and as of today "the EPA remains without enforcement and permitting tools that presumably it would need to implement a regulatory program under RCRA Subtitle D" for manufacturing waste (Barringer 2003, 192).

The failure to enact manufacturing-waste provisions in the RCRA can to a degree be attributed to a federal antiregulatory stance that dominated federal environmental policymaking during the debates over RCRA reauthorization (Szasz 1994). This stance certainly existed under Reagan and both Bushes, but was also a feature of the Clinton's "kinder, gentler" antiregulatory politics as well (Holifield 2004). Nonetheless, the RCRA was amended with respect to Subtitle C during the most antienvironmental period of the Reagan tenure. During that period and through the 1990s, antitoxics and environmental justice activism was increasingly and successfully contesting the siting of facilities known—through experienced illness or published data—to pose risk, including facilities handling hazardous industrial waste and municipal solid waste. But whether manufacturing waste was actually risky or not as well as where manufacturing waste was being disposed were simply not known. As such, these matters did not constitute a nexus of concern for grassroots groups focused on sited hazards.

The failure to regulate manufacturing waste at the federal level also reflected its nonissue status within the recycling movement, including the increasingly participatory recycling public. During the 1980s and 1990s, the recycling public was growing rapidly in response to the enactment of curbside programs. In the mid-1990s, it was first stated that more Americans recycled than voted (*Consumer Reports* 1994). Calling manufacturing-waste tonnages a "huge amount of wasted energy and material" that is not likely to be permanently contained by any technology,

John Dernbach, a legal scholar and former Pennsylvania waste administrator, suggested that "municipal waste issues dominate the public consciousness so intensely that industrial waste is not likely to be fully and thoughtfully addressed unless all substantive aspects of industrial waste management are dealt with in a separate part of legislation" (Dernbach 1990, 10290). Municipal solid waste absorbed all the attention of those concerned not just about health, but also the squandering of resources.

The exclusion of manufacturing waste from the concern of the recycling movement is, I argue, more puzzling than its exclusion from antitoxics or environmental justice activism. The sited nature of manufacturing-waste disposal, it turns out, was and is quite different than that of landfills and incinerators because the bulk of manufacturing waste is disposed of without permit or public knowledge on the industrial property where it was generated. In many cases, these properties are located far from communities (Atlas 2002). And although manufacturing waste is potentially hazardous, it is not acutely so; thus, health effects that slowly alert the community through groundwater contamination and other forms of pollution in the case of hazardous wastes (as in what happened at Love Canal) are unlikely to surface to the degree needed to mobilize local activism.

What is less understandable is the recycling movement's absence of concern regarding manufacturing wastes. Its focus has traditionally been on the environmental consequences of consumption and on methods for diverting discards toward remanufacture, reflecting a concern over not just risks from municipal-solid-waste disposal sites, but also the question of environmental impacts of flows of materials through stages of manufacture (Hershkowitz 1998). Since 1987, published statistics on manufacturing-waste tonnages, albeit not tremendously accessible or updated, have been available to the recycling movement. From time to time, scholars have brought the comparison between these tonnages and municipal solid waste generation to light, but no one within the recycling movement seems to be interested.

(Lack of) Public Consciousness

Throughout the 1990s, discourses of environmental concern about waste generally treated the subject of manufacturing waste by omission. Manufacturing waste did not feature in the understanding of municipal solid waste as a "staggering garbage crisis" to cities (Shabecoff 1988). This crisis was symbolized in the aimless voyage of the garbage barge and the ultimately unfounded conclusion that the nation was running out of landfill space (Miller 2000). Landfill space was in fact abundant, but it was increasingly distant and expensive due to both the victories of local urban resistance movements and increased federal regulation of landfill construction and operation under the 1984 RCRA amendments. If municipal officials were, as indicated in chapter 2, at wit's end about waste, the reasons had to do with the difficulty of collecting and moving it out of urban territory. All this was happening in the wake of a massive urban deindustrialization that took place throughout the Fordist period (Gordon 1978). Stated crudely, manufacturing waste was not a part of the garbage crisis for cities because heavy manufacturing industries were not by and large in cities anymore (Gandy 2002).

But concern over municipal solid waste and enthusiasm for recycling as a municipal solid waste–oriented solution among environmentally conscious publics went beyond the practical difficulties of urban waste management. Within environmental discourse, addressing problems of municipal solid waste was intimately tied to protection of the planet's natural wealth and health. As municipal recycling proliferated in the 1980s and 1990s, hundreds of thousands of pamphlets, vision statements, how-to books, and other forms of popular literature celebrated the transformative potential of citizen participation to save resources and diminish pollution beyond city limits. In this context, recycling was portrayed as an individual activity with world-changing potential, as in the 1990 *Recycler's Handbook*, which stated: "We can no longer afford to treat the Earth, and its resources, as if they were disposable. Recycling is a fundamental way of affirming this. Literally, we save parts of the planet" (Earthworks Group 1990, 6).

If mentioned at all in such discourses, manufacturing waste was relegated to a footnote. The World Wildlife Fund's 1991 *Getting to the Source* sums up the marginalization of the topic. Opening with a warning to citizens that "despite the success of recycling, Americans are producing too much garbage* . . . some of which is causing increasingly serious problems in the environment," the authors advocated a solution rooted in "remarkable partnerships of people—in both public and private sectors—who are working together to achieve progress" in new, innovative forms of municipal solid waste reduction. The asterisk next to "garbage" referred to the following in fine print: "*Municipal solid waste or 'garbage' generally refers to solid wastes from residential, commercial, institutional, and certain industrial sources. The term typically excludes . . . *industrial process wastes*" (xi, emphasis added).

Within academic policy studies of the time, the fact of the 7.6 billion tonnage of industrial waste was similarly footnoted. A rich literature on municipal solid waste problems grew, analyzing the effect of product changes (particularly in packaging) on the quantity and quality of municipal solid waste, elaborating the dangers and inequities of landfills and incineration as well as the inability of traditional curbside recycling to address municipal solid waste problems completely, and questioning local and state jurisdiction over the shipping of garbage for disposal (Blumberg and Gottlieb 1989; Ackerman 1997b; Chertow 1998). Between 1989 and 1995, a few sources within the engineering and legal scholarship did directly address manufacturing waste's vast tonnage and potential toxicity. In 1996, a pair of chemists noted of manufacturing waste that "the common designation of 'nonhazardous' is misleading because these wastes often contain the same toxic and carcinogenic compounds found in [EPA-designated] 'hazardous industrial wastes'" (Schaeffer and Bailey 1996, 245). During this same period, Dernbach was a lone voice insisting that ignoring manufacturing waste was, as the title of his article suggested, "saving the worst for last." He wrote, "There exists a widespread perception that Subtitle D, or nonhazardous waste, is mostly municipal waste. This perception is reinforced by news reports highlighting disposal capacity, ash barges, recycling, and the anticipated publication of the EPA's final municipal waste regulation. However, this perception is wrong" (1990, 10283).

In the mid-1990s, whatever scant attention was given to manufacturing waste as a problem, which had taken place almost entirely within the context of congressional hearings and legal scholarship, ceased with the failure of RCRA reauthorizations to pass. Since then, there has been a continued lack of direct engagement within any literature or discourse on the vexing questions of how much manufacturing waste there is in total; how much is potentially hazardous; where dump sites are; and to what degree recycling or diversion is taking place or needs to take place for the nation or even most U.S. states in total. The rare instances in which the disparity between manufacturing waste and municipal solid waste tonnages is directly discussed within the environmental community today provide clues to why manufacturing wastes stay hidden.

Stationary, Watery, and Unsexy

As mentioned in chapter 1, GreenYes is a listerv maintained by the progressive Grassroots Recycling Network. Its archives, which begin in

1997, contain tens of thousands of exchanges, ranging from the practical to the philosophic, on a broad range of subjects related to the prevention, reuse, recycling, composting, and disposal of solid waste. During the long period in which GreenYes has been active, however, the discrepancy between manufacturing waste and municipal solid waste tonnages has come up very rarely.

In 2002, an individual representing Spectrum Recycling, a nonprofit social services agency in Iowa that operates recycling drop-off centers, posted the following question:

A few years ago I read something which compared municipal solid waste to "all the waste generated in the U.S." including mining and logging wastes, air pollution, water pollution, manufacturing wastes. MSW [municipal solid waste] was described as being just (approx.) 2% of that total waste amount. The point of the statement was to point out how relatively minimal the impact of recycling can be in conserving energy and materials, especially if our national recycling rate is somewhere around 26, 27%. The greater benefit, then would come upstream from recycling, at the extraction and manufacturing stages. I wonder if anyone can help me verify the accuracy of this 2% MSW figure. Is there a waste characterization study which lumps MSW with all these other waste categories? (Swets 2002)

One response came from recycling/solid-waste consultant and author Roger Guttentag, the courageous questioner of the goals of municipal recycling cited in chapter 2. He cautioned the poster not to overinterpret these statistics.

It appears, at first blush, that the total annual generated MSW is indeed about 3% of total industrial waste production. But wait a moment, we need to look at this issue a little more. According to the Introduction to the EPA's *Guide for Industrial Waste Management*, "about 7.6 billion tons of industrial solid waste are generated and managed on-site at industrial facilities each year. Almost 97 percent is wastewater managed in surface impoundments; the remainder is managed in landfills, waste piles, and land application units. Most of these wastewaters are treated and ultimately discharged into surface waters under Clean Water Act permits issued by EPA or state governments (National Pollutant Discharge Elimination System or NPDES permits)." My interpretation of the above statement is that about 3% of the total non-hazardous industrial waste or 228 million tons, could be considered a solid type waste. Therefore it appears that the total size of the industrial solid waste and municipal solid waste streams appear to be comparable in terms of annual generated weight. (2002)

Another response from a recycling specialist with the Oregon Department of Environmental Quality was similarly reassuring about the lack of significance in the discrepancy:

Much of the "waste" being referred to is not solid waste as you or I know it. Most of it is wastewater—not just the solids in the waste water, but all of the industrial waste water. As such, it is a very misleading statistic to imply that industrial waste is so much greater than municipal waste. . . . I think a better comparison is to look at the solid waste generated that actually ends up in land-fills and other disposal units. Oregon has data on this. . . . [T]he tons of municipal waste disposed in all types of landfills and other disposal facilities is [*sic*] larger than the tons of industrial waste disposed. The total for all industrial and other wastes was only 1,031,826 tons in 1999, or only 27% of the total Oregon solid waste disposed that year. MSW made up the other 73% of the disposed waste. (Spendelow 2002)

Both responses suggested that the disparity in tonnages was not as stark as a comparison of EPA statistics would suggest. After discounting the fraction of water in manufacturing waste and focusing on manufacturing waste "that actually end[s] up in landfills and other disposal units," the questioner's colleagues steered her away from a "very misleading statistic [that implies] that industrial waste is so much greater than municipal waste." And, in fact, the EPA's 1987 research on manufacturing waste did find that 97 percent of manufacturing waste was disposed of on the site where it was generated, largely in surface impoundments, which are watery lagoons in which solid waste is deposited (OTA 1992). But this fact, far from contextualizing manufacturing waste into irrelevance, turns out to be crucial in interpreting manufacturing waste's nonissue status.

As the Oregon official noted, disposal of manufacturing waste in off-site landfills and incinerators that accept manufacturing-waste deliveries does count in some states' waste-tonnage statistics. Nationally, 3 percent of manufacturing waste is not disposed of on site, but rather transported to off-site disposal. After leaving the site of generation, this small percentage of manufacturing waste joins municipal solid waste in landfills and incinerators permitted to receive Subtitle D wastes (the RCRA designation for solid wastes not regulated as hazardous under Subtitle C), and only then is it counted and acknowledged. Another state with this approach is California, one of the most progressively thorough states in regulating solid-waste management. It excludes the bulk of manufacturing waste from its regulatory oversight, focusing only on that small fraction of manufacturing waste that is transported off the site of generation for disposal (CIWMB Waste Line 2008).

In sum, on-site disposal practices fall outside existing solid-waste-monitoring structures because there is no transport involved. The vast majority of manufacturing waste is stationary, contrasting sharply with municipal solid waste, which, by its very nature, must be collected and delivered to an intermediate or final point. Municipal solid waste's mobility guarantees its visibility at levels of governance and experiential knowledge (Tesh 2000). Citizens see trucks on the road and feel the effects on traffic and air quality. "Tipping" fees are assessed for each ton delivered; as a consequence, municipalities and private waste haulers monitor truck weights for oversight and fiscal purposes. Deliveries must ultimately be accepted at Subtitle D landfills and incinerators, which (unlike on-site disposal points) are regulated by the EPA and often require additional permits at the state and local level as well. Permits impose reporting requirements on tonnage and composition of wastes received. They also require citizen participation in approval and alert communities to the existence of such outlets.

The EPA's regulation of hazardous industrial waste is also organized around movements in space. The "cradle to grave" manifest system imposed by the EPA means that hazardous industrial-waste tonnages must "check in" periodically as they move from point of generation through transport and final destination. As the EPA explains, "A manifest must accompany every waste shipment. The resulting paper trail documents the waste's progress through treatment, storage, and disposal. A missing form alerts the generator to investigate, which may mean calling in the state agency or EPA" (1997, 18). When on-site disposal of hazardous industrial waste does take place, the same reporting requirements apply.

Complementing the uniquely stationary status of manufacturing waste is its aqueous nature, as referred to in both responses to the GreenYes posting. Wastewater that is discharged from "point sources" (i.e., pipes, outfalls) is regulated separately and stringently under the Clean Water Act. What the GreenYes posting refers to as wastewater in the case of manufacturing waste is instead the mix or slurry of solids and liquids that is deposited in surface impoundments. Estimates of the fraction of disposed manufacturing-waste tonnage that is in aqueous form vary. Early EPA studies set it at 70 percent (OTA 1992). Today, the EPA's published 97 percent statistic, which in fact refers to the 1987 estimate of the percentage of manufacturing waste disposed of on site in surface impoundments, is often misinterpreted (as in the GreenYes interchange) as meaning that 97 percent of the 7.6 billion tons of manufacturing waste, or 7.37 million tons, is water, leaving a total manufacturing-waste annual tonnage of 228 million dry tons as comparable to 250 million tonnages of municipal solid waste. But none of the percentages cited above in fact leads to such a calculation; they only estimate how much manufacturing waste makes its way into watery surface impoundments on site as opposed to other disposal outlets (such as landfills or incinerators). The percentages do not convey information about how much of these manufacturing-waste tonnages is water and how much is solids.

Moreover, although it is clear that some if not much of the tonnage discrepancy between tonnages of manufacturing waste and municipal solid waste can be explained by the weight of water, this fact does not exempt manufacturing waste as a waste stream of concern. The presence of water in fact compounds the potentially toxic nature of manufacturing waste in a manner not comparable to the much drier municipal solid waste. In the 2002 GreenYes exchange, one poster quoted the EPA as reassuring the public that "most of . . . manufacturing waste wastewaters are treated and ultimately discharged into surface waters under Clean Water Act permits issued by EPA or state governments (National Pollutant Discharge Elimination System or NPDES permits)." The current version of the EPA source he cited has subsequently eliminated this reassurance, nor have my interviews with EPA officials extended it (U.S. EPA 2003). The treatment of "most" aqueous manufacturing waste before permitted discharge is in fact far from evident.[2] Independent (although dated) research suggests that only 29 percent of industrial surface impoundments have discharge permits that require the treatment of liquid waste before release into surface waters under the federal National Pollutant Discharge Elimination System (Dernbach 1990). In sum, although it would be convenient to diminish the importance of manufacturing waste as a problem by extracting the weight of the water therein or to treat only manufacturing waste that is deposited in a landfill or incinerator as a waste flow, the fact remains that there is really no way of knowing what the actual tonnage of manufacturing wastes is, how much of this tonnage is or is not water, or how hazardous such wastes might be.

The 2002 exchange on GreenYes quoted earlier was a rare one, notable in that seasoned recycling professionals lacked basic knowledge about a large and important fraction of U.S. solid waste and that respondents sought to minimize its importance by using features that help explain its invisibility and riskiness. And not much has been learned since then. In 2009, Joel Makower published an article discussing the disparity between municipal solid waste and manufacturing tonnages, concluding provocatively that "our purchases of green-labeled goods may be lulling us into assuming that companies are on the case—that we can, as I posited 20 years ago, have a positive impact on the environment without significantly compromising our way of life. It turned out to be a false hope: that we could shop our way to environmental health" (2009). This article, which calls for "demanding accountability and transparency" in industrial data reported, sparked a brief reprise of the 2002 conversation on the GreenYes listserv, again with caution urged in comparing watery industrial tonnages to relatively drier tons of municipal solid waste.

A clue to the dissatisfying and lingering lack of resolution with respect to a now more than 30-year-old question can be found in a final post to the initial question in 2002. A noted waste-policy researcher used an odd word in regard to the lacuna in understanding. Responding to the initial question, she wrote, "If you get more info please post—industrial waste is not sexy!!" (Raymond 2002). The same term, *sexy*, was used in 1997 in an article in the trade journal *BioCycle*, which observed that manufacturing waste was "not as sexy an item as its municipal cousin" (Glenn 1997, 54). Manufacturing waste's lack of issue status was, in this author's opinion, attributable to the fact that municipal solid waste and its recycling had taken hold in the public imagination because of its closeness to everyday life. "Everyone could relate to what was thrown out in their trash bag. But industries—who knew what they were throwing out?" The author called manufacturing waste "something of a last frontier, which is strange given that in many cases, there is such a volume of material with similar characteristics in one place. Supply-side waste reduction methodology suggests that industrial waste would be the first location to start recovering resources" (54).

The question "Industries—who knew what they were throwing out?" has still not been answered. The needed data have not been gathered because of the structure of existing public policy, and this public policy reflects and is reflected in public consciousness. Citizens worry greatly about the toxicity of wastes around them and look to themselves for the restorative action (recycling in the default sense) that will stem the loss of resources, wealth, and opportunity that landfilled garbage conveys. But manufacturing waste has not entered into this calculation—at least until recently.

In the upswing of environmental concern that has accompanied the growing consensus on the reality of global climate change, mention of the disparity between industrial and municipal waste is making a comeback in formal policy and environmentalist popular discourse. And the way it is making a comeback is interesting because the topic of manufacturing waste is addressed quite differently that it was in the late 1980s and early 1990s. On the one hand, governments at all scales are advancing a flexible, industry-specific, and often voluntary approach to encouraging the minimization of waste in the industrial sector, whether this waste is process waste disposed of on site and counted in the 7.6 billion statistic or waste entering the realm of municipal solid waste through certain products of industry (this distinction is frequently blurred). On the other hand, the recycling movement has begun to negotiate the disparity between producer and consumer wastes by linking them, through policy or philosophy, to the realm of municipal solid waste.

Voluntary Success Stories and Industrial-Materials Recycling: The Resource-Conservation Challenge

Despite the failed attempts to reauthorize the RCRA and to incorporate manufacturing-waste tracking and disposal regulations into its mandate, the EPA today does acknowledge that "management and recycling of industrial products and materials are key priority areas. While typically not seen by the general public or part of most of our daily lives, these wastes are often generated in large volumes" (U.S. EPA 2009f). Since 2002, the agency has administered an initiative to "provide renewed urgency to EPA's message of reducing, reusing, and recycling valuable materials habitually discarded by American industry," called the Resource Conservation Challenge (U.S. EPA 2008c, 2). The challenge is nonregulatory. It is a nonbinding program that, among other goals, targets three industrial sectors (construction and demolition debris, coal combustion by-products [ash], and foundry sand) with technical assistance in the area of waste reduction.

The three industrial sectors targeted by the Resource Conservation Challenge correspond only in part to the manufacturing-waste classifications used in the development of the 7.6 billion ton estimate. Coal ash, as mentioned earlier, falls into the "special waste" category that exists alongside the EPA's "nonhazardous industrial waste" definition. In the EPA's 1992 update to the 1987 report, waste from electric power generation via coal burning was estimated at 1 billion tons annually over and above the 7.6 billion tons of manufacturing wastes (OTA 1992). In 1992, the EPA reported that most such waste was disposed of in on-site landfills and surface impoundments (OTA 1992). Today the EPA reports that coal ash is generated at a rate of 128 million tons annually. Out of this total, 47 percent is recycled in the making of concrete, which the EPA estimates has saved "80 trillion BTUs [British thermal units] of energy—equivalent to the annual energy consumption of more than 420,000 households" (2008c, 15). It is difficult to tell how much of the increase in coal ash recycling is due to the work of the Resource Conservation Challenge because the EPA's performance indicators require but lack data on a baseline upon which to measure this achievement (U.S. EPA 2007b). Nonetheless, the recycling of some 60 million tons of coal ash in concrete production is a measurable indicator of the diversion of some of the unknown contemporary total of industrial waste in existence.

Data are lacking on progress in the second area of manufacturing waste targeted under the Resource Conservation Challenge, foundry sands, which result from metal-fabrication processes and fall into the definition of "nonhazardous industrial waste." The EPA's unpublished 1987 report estimated that primary iron and steel manufacturing (not mining) accounted for 1.2 billion annual tons of manufacturing waste, although it did not break foundry sand waste out of that total (C-8). As explained by the EPA today, "Less than 15 percent of the 6–10 million tons of spent foundry sands generated annually are recycled. The Agency believes a greater percentage of spent foundry sand can be safely and economically recycled" (2007a). A range of 6–10 million tons is therefore the estimate of the manufacturing-waste stream composed of foundry sands today. The Resource Conservation Challenge has yet to achieve measurable reductions in this tonnage due to lack of data. Writes the EPA, "As seen in the 6–10 million ton range referenced above, we do not have solid data on the amount of foundry sand produced and recycled. To rectify this situation, our trade association partner the American Foundry Society is surveying their members. Once we establish baseline data with AFS, we will work with them to develop recycling goals" (2007a).

The third area that the Resource Conservation Challenge targeted as an industrial waste for minimization is not a solid-waste category that was counted in the 7.6 billion ton manufacturing-waste estimate either. Construction and demolition waste, an output of private- and public-sector building and road-construction activities, totals around 330 million tons annually (U.S. EPA 2007b, II-102). In public-sector planning and policy, construction and demolition waste is generally treated as a parallel waste stream to municipal solid waste in that its collection, disposal, or recycling is managed at the urban scale under through local governance and with a similar range of private carters, disposers, and recycling. Like municipal solid waste, construction and demolition waste is set out on the curb in dumpsters and collected or travels to landfills or is diverted to beneficial use via secondary-materials markets. This process has been going on as long as construction and demolition waste has been generated. Although a somewhat new structure of socially and ecologically minded reclamation is emerging in the form of building deconstruction (the rescuing of reusable building materials prior to demolition), rates of recycling for construction and demolition waste have always been relatively high. A large portion of construction and demolition waste is valuable scrap metal that is easily separated for sale within the private scrap-reclamation industry, and the bulk of the waste consists of inert materials (fill, rubble) that can easily find safe outlets for application in road building, site remediation, and other earth-work projects.[3] The EPA's fiscal year 2007 performance report announces that "we estimate that approximately 40 percent of building materials and 88 percent of road surface materials are currently being recycled. This translates into an industrial materials recycling rate of nearly 65 percent" (U.S. EPA 2007b, II-101). This is not a Resource Conservation Challenge achievement, however. Footnotes reveal that the construction and demolition waste–recycling rate cited was in fact the rate already under way in fiscal year 2003, when the Resource Conservation Challenge was launched.

A final claim of achievement of the Resource Conservation Challenge's activities in industrial-materials recycling is conveyed in statistics on waste tires, a waste stream also not included in the 7.6 billion figure or in the stated targets of the Resource Conservation Challenge announced in 2002. Nonetheless, the program's achievements list the fact that "in 2005, more than 73 percent of scrap tires were diverted from landfills" (U.S. EPA 2008c, 17). And, indeed, scrap-tire reclamation and recycling, funded without federal mandates and aided through tire-deposit systems and retailer take-back laws enacted at the state level, are one of the more successful areas of waste reclamation. But tires have never been considered part of manufacturing waste.

Careful reading of the Resource Conservation Challenge progress documents suggests that a total of 54 million annual tons of coal ash recycled into concrete is the Resource Conservation Challenge's only industrial waste–relevant achievement (albeit one targeting "special" wastes, not manufacturing wastes as I have identified them). For anyone other than a solid-waste expert, the context in which Resource Conservation Challenge achievements can be evaluated is inaccessible. The absence of accountability is highlighted in an interchange between

Congresswoman Lois Capps (D–Calif.) and then–EPA administrator Matthew Hale in the 2004 Resource Conservation Challenge oversight hearings:

Capps: Is the Resource Conservation Challenge keeping track of the various recycling rates, and if not, is there an area within the Office of Solid Waste that is keeping track, not only of the numbers, but also of the trend in the way that Americans are recycling?

Hale: We keep track of recycling rates, particularly within the municipal solid waste area, the plastic bags and so forth, through a report that we put out every year. Within other areas, as part of the RCC [Resource Conservation Challenge], we are working with trade associations and other industry sources, other sources for more specialized waste streams called combustion ash, foundry sand, tires, categories of waste like that. (U.S. House of Representatives 2004, 18)

What is far easier to read are the many general statements of celebration by the EPA in its Resource Conservation Challenge documents, such as: "We are helping develop public–private partnerships to conserve resources in key areas. We collaborate with our partners in innovative, non-regulatory efforts to minimize the amount of waste generated and promote recycling to recover materials and energy. Through programs like our Resource Conservation Challenge, we promote opportunities for converting waste to economically viable products, thereby conserving resources" (2007b, II-81).

Short on numbers in context, the Resource Conservation Challenge documents are liberally peppered with success stories (U.S. EPA 2008c). This form of data is far and away the favored means of reporting program achievements with regard to waste prevention and reduction outside the realm of municipal solid waste (Geiser 2004). Publications on the Resource Conservation Challenge and a second, older EPA partnership program, Wastewise, feature various ways in which pounds or tons of materials—some inherent to the production process itself, others emanating from offices and employee lunchrooms on factory properties—are prevented from going to disposal (U.S. EPA 2008d). Unlike case study methodology in the social sciences, however, such stories do not contain common indicators upon which comparisons can be made, nor do they enable aggregate statistics to be calculated.

Compare the success-story approach to the approach John Dernbach advocated in 1990, when RCRA reauthorization was under consideration.

Congress should require each generator, transporter and industrial waste treatment, storage or disposal facility operator to send notice to the state identifying its activity, its location, and the kind and amount of industrial waste produced. . . . States should collect and organize these data and make them public. The notice would provide useful information to government officials, the public, and industry manager. The notice would also encourage industry to improve waste management and waste generation . . . and . . . would probably provide more information than a study conducted solely by the EPA. . . . This notice should be required on a biannual basis to provide baseline and progress report on waste minimization across the country within specific industries. This notice could also be tied to waste reduction planning requirement for industrial waste generators, based on Oregon's law. Data collected from this program would help measure the effectiveness of the industrial waste program. (1990, 10292–10293)

The EPA's failure to address manufacturing waste comprehensively in the fashion described here or in a manner that simply enables data access continues to this day. The benefits of voluntary, case-specific federal initiatives such as the Resource Conservation Challenge are obvious to waste-generating industries and the elected officials advancing their interests—something can be said to be "in the works" without much accountability. This approach to industrial-waste minimization has thus far made the reporting of comprehensive, verifiable, aggregable data across industries voluntary and massively untabulated. But there is more to the story. In Lukesian terms, there is more than the first- and second-dimensional power exertion going on. To the extent that the contemporary recycling movement considers problems of industrial solid-waste generation, it draws on three distinct frameworks for thinking about solutions: industrial ecology, extended producer responsibility and personal responsibility. As I argue, each framework has serious deficiencies with respect to the large task of bringing about change in industrial practice across sectors of waste-producing manufacturing activities, yet each is being embraced to some degree as a way to address manufacturing wastes. These deficiencies have in common an underappreciation of producers' exigency always to be manufacturing more.

The Unpolitics of Industrial Ecology

In the EPA's report to Congress in 2004, Administrator Hale outlined the future of the RCRA and the role of the Resource Conservation Challenge: "We must maintain the cradle-to-grave system that is protecting and cleaning up our land. This approach, however, is inefficient when considering resource conservation, but it is and will always be the critical foundation to a cradle-to-cradle system of efficient materials management" (U.S. House of Representatives 2004, 4). William McDonough and Michael Braungart titled their influential 2002 book *Cradle to Cradle*, laying out a compelling vision of healing environmental problems through the reinvention and redefinition of economy. McDonough and Braungart's blueprint is radical in that it envisions material by-products of production as not just recycled but designed so as to support and reconstruct, instead of harm, natural complexity. For the authors, "clean" or "efficient" production is less the goal than "effective" production that designs the destructiveness out of capitalism and guides its creativity such that its effluents clean and nurture their conditions of production, yielding abundant and delightful products engaged in constant cyclicity. McDonough and Braungart's ideas are premised in industrial ecology, a discipline organized around a systemic-theoretical study of the cycles of natural and human-mediated materials (Frosch and Gallopoulous 1992; Ayres 1996). Industrial ecology's intellectual heritage dates to the 1950s, and today it is, if not yet fully in the mainstream, "progressing with unprecedented vigour" within environmental policy discourse (Erkman 1997, 1).

The problem with cradle-to-cradlism as a framework in which to consider the problem of manufacturing waste is its implicit voluntarism. It assumes that industries will design waste out of manufacturing processes as they progress in an overall course of enlightened corporate evolution. This view does not accord well with the history of industrial development or with the active efforts by industries as an interest group to defend themselves from checks and controls on their greening. John Dryzek and James Lester (1995) use the term *reform ecology* to describe the work of industrial ecologists and their peers in natural science and engineering who seek a transformation of human political economy. Although appreciating reform ecology's use of principles and data from chemistry and biology and in particular its application of these fields of knowledge to product/process design and life-cycle analysis, they highlight its pervasive inattentiveness to the structure of social, economic, and political institutions and contexts. *Cradle to Cradle*, despite its widespread influence in environmentalist thought, suffers from this inattentiveness, displaying a disarming naïveté to questions of power and history. In this book, the current "ecological crisis" is said to have resulted from the development of civilization without thought or organization to consider natural limits. The history put forth is simplified: "cyclical-cradle to cradle biological systems have nourished a planet of thriving, diverse abundance for millions of years. . . . [T]hen came industry, which altered the natural equilibrium of materials on the planet"

(McDonough and Braungart 2002, 92). The trajectory of this history can be bent back to natural equilibrium by social processes of focusing of attention where attention has lacked. Through redesign, the authors argue, profitable industry can be reinvented so as to work with and not against natural systems. To the extent that this approach, like others falling under the umbrella term *ecological modernization*, implies a social theory, it is an implicit one, holding that, as sociologist Fred Buttel puts it, "while the most challenging environmental problems of this century and the next have (or will have) been caused by modernization and industrialization, their solutions must necessarily lie in more—rather than less—modernization and 'superindustrialization'" (Buttel 2000, 61).

Arthur Mol, ecological modernization's leading scholar, sees the necessary evolution in environmental policy as a move "from centralized to decentralized wherever possible, and from domineering, over-regulated environmental policy to a policy which creates favorable conditions and contexts for environmentally sound practices and behavior on the part of producers and consumers" (1995, 46). The expectation is that industrial ecosystems will green themselves by maximizing the market's efficiency in guiding decisions, leaving the state the role of simply stimulating "self-regulation" through market mechanisms (Mol 1995). For McDonough and Braungart, even market-based state policy is unnecessary:

We do not mean to lambaste those who are working with good intentions to create and enforce laws meant to protect the public good. In a world where designs are unintelligent and destructive, regulations can reduce immediate deleterious effects. But ultimately regulation is a signal of design failure. In fact, it is what we call a license to harm: a permit issued by government to an industry so that it may dispense sickness, destruction and death at an "acceptable" rate. But as we shall see, good design can require no regulation at all. (2002, 61)

As the recycling movement considers perspectives with which to grapple with the problem of manufacturing waste, there is a danger in overfocusing on design and process change, effected through smart consideration of the factory's metabolism, as the unpolitical mechanism that will bring about reductions in tonnage and toxicity. This approach to industrial greening, notes geographer Ray Hudson, is "grounded in an undersocialized conception of production based on biological analogy and a naturalistic view of markets," reducing social processes to market transactions between buyer and seller, with regulation appropriate only in cases of market failure through adjustments of prices. He writes, "There is scant recognition of the possible role of state regulatory mechanisms that do not rely upon manipulating market pricing and little recognition that such forms . . . may be necessary in relation to at least some aspects of the natural world (for example, via imposing maximum legally permissible limits or outright prohibition, or by regulatory approaches that compel companies to produce in less polluting ways" (2001, 293).

In Mol's Europe, ecological modernization as a social theory *has* in practice been integrated into structures of supranational governance, few entailing direct regulation, but all entailing some degree of final accountability for the delivery of voluntaristically promised results (Janicke 2006). In the United States, voluntarism is, well, voluntary. Corporations undergoing design and process change may voluntarily provide some data, but accountability is massively lacking (King and Lenox 2000; Delmas and Keller 2005). We are left to guess and hope that, overall, industries are moving in the right direction, with green processes and materials driving nongreen ones out of existence over time through competition, but we don't really know. With no baseline, no state-by-state, industry-by-industry, or national-aggregate statistics to monitor and compare, the recycling movement and the public at large are utterly beholden to the good intentions of all industries, not just green ones, to do the right thing. The framework of industrial ecology, interpreted within an American form of ecological modernization that champions voluntary change behind factory gates, offers an elegant but insufficient solution.

Extended Responsibility for End-of-Life Products

The second new form in which the problem of manufacturing waste and industrial waste in general is being negotiated has to do with the notion of responsibility. Several environmental organizations, including the Product Policy Institute, the Product Stewardship Institute, INFORM, Inc., and the Institute for Local Self Reliance, are working to foster state and local laws and extended producer responsibility programs for end-of-life products, in particular those containing toxic components such as electronics and batteries. I discuss these developments in more detail in chapter 5, but for the moment I ask that you keep in mind that the core concept underlying extended producer responsibility is that a portion of the financial or operational burden of revalorizing or managing discards falls on the producer of the product in question.

The range of extended producer responsibility laws and practices in place or under consideration in the United States runs the gamut from those organized with extraordinary producer–state–civil society collaboration to those that evoke hostile push-back from producers along the lines of the still fierce fights against bottle bills. In either form, extended producer responsibility policies are notable in that they target producers, including manufacturers, forcing or requesting them to play a role in reducing solid waste. These instruments are, as I argue in chapter 5, potentially quite powerful for increasing recovery rates of certain products in municipal solid waste. But does extended producer responsibility represent a means to address producer wastes that are by-products of manufacturing? The title of one report, INFORM's *Extended Producer Responsibility: A Materials Policy for the 21st Century*, would suggest that it does, noting that

> recycling rates commonly quoted are deceptive, since they usually are for municipal solid wastes only. Although many American communities are now recycling 25 to 50 percent of the trash they collect, other kinds of wastes are recycled much less and are produced in greater quantities. All told, an estimated 23 billion tons of waste (excluding water) are produced in the United States each year. Of this, less than 2 percent is actually recycled, most of it paper, glass, and metals. (Fishbein, Ehrenfeld, and Young 2000, 36)

The authors of this report do not engage further with the 23 billion tonnage cited, leaving a gap that mirrors the gap in knowledge and policy regarding manufacturing waste in general. A more general work of contemporary recycling policy advocacy, *Wasting and Recycling in the United States 2000*, a joint publication of the Grassroots Recycling Network and the Institute for Local Self Reliance, takes up the issue more directly. The authors observe that "few studies have documented how much manufacturing, mining, and energy related wasting could actually be eliminated for every ton of municipally generated discards reduced or recovered" (Platt and Seldman 2000, 3). It's clear not only that data are lacking, but that, at the moment at least, extended producer responsibility cannot really be said to be "contemporary materials policy" because its policies don't target manufacturing waste. As another publication puts it, extended producer responsibility "has mostly been used to describe . . . producer responsibility for the 'post-consumer' stage of products, after they have been discarded at the end of their useful life" (Fishbein, Ehrenfeld, and Young 2000, 60).

This quality need not be permanent for extended producer responsibility, but it does bear stating explicitly. As these policies develop, there is a crucial need to build mechanisms for large-scale industrial data gathering into laws and programs that promote responsible stewardship of end-of life products. As Fishbein, Eherenfeld, and Young note:

Materials use is rarely tracked and rarely the subject of public debate. Few of those who make decisions about individual projects and broader development strategies—engineers, architects, designers, financiers, insurers, manufacturers, politicians—are conscious of the materials-use implications of what they do, or perceive any reason to do things differently. For most Americans and those who aspire to the American way of life, environmental damage from unchecked materials consumption is viewed simply as a necessary cost of prosperity. There is a critical need to track materials consumption at the national, regional, and local levels, as well as by industry, much as it has now become common to track energy use. Such data will help create benchmarks against which progress in resource efficiency can be measured. (2000, 60)

There clearly is consensus among those active in contemporary recycling-policy advocacy that more information on producer activities is needed and that we should "broaden focus of waste reduction efforts beyond municipal solid waste to encompass other types of wasted materials, which need to be part of the waste reduction agenda" (Platt and Seldman 2000, 51). How other types of waste will be "encompassed" in this agenda is at the moment an open question, and here claims made about the connection of municipal solid waste to its manufacturing waste parent suggest that the direction of that connection starts with *us,* the public. Write Brenda Platt and Neil Seldman, "We do know that for every ton of consumer products and packaging recycled 'downstream,' we eliminate wasting of many more tons of materials 'upstream'" (2000, 3). In this publication, municipal solid waste is likened to a canary in a coal mine. "Wasting municipal discards is a symptom of a much larger problem—our overconsumption and inefficient use of resources and materials" (2). Will reduction of manufacturing and other upstream wastes be achieved through recycling and not through wasting downstream? This backward connection from grave to cradle bears closer examination because it is potent ideologically, but it may in the end deliver little in material results.

Extended Personal Responsibility

With regard to even the end-of-life products that extended producer responsibility targets, the notion of responsibility over solid waste is highly contested. Producers, such as Mobil cited earlier in this chapter, firmly prefer to transfer responsibility from the corporation to consumer, from the industry to the individual. This preference is eminently rational given producers' imperative to maximize profits. What is not as rational is that in this endeavor they are abetted by a recycling movement that contradictorily welcomes such transfer even as it struggles to push back against industry. The welcome is expressed in concerns of recycling public's everyday life. Despite INFORM's observation on the apathy of "most Americans" with regard to the "environmental damage from unchecked materials consumption" (including, presumably, producer consumption of raw and intermediary materials), high rates of participation in and support for recycling as well as a flourishing discourse in popular online and print media on matters of consumption and its relation to environmental problems suggest that apathy does not fully characterize the American public.

Annie Leonard's short documentary *The Story of Stuff* (2008) is a well-known and extremely popular example of such popular discourse. Using cartoon drawings and accessible language, Leonard critically examines the U.S. role in a global economy predicated on inequities in consumption, speaks about the consequences of production in political and economic contexts, and pays attention to issues of labor. It is in this ample context that Leonard states, "We should all recycle. But recycling is not enough. Recycling will never be enough." She continues: "The waste coming out of our houses is just the tip of the iceberg. For every one garbage can of waste you put out on the curb, 70 garbage cans of waste were made upstream just to make the junk in that one garbage can you put out on the curb. So even if we could recycle 100 percent of the waste coming out of our households, it doesn't get to the core of the problem." Leonard calls for a coalescing of small and large social movements, individual and institutional actions, into a critical mass that will change the material economy enough to effect systemic social and ecological change. In her compelling 20-minute video, she takes viewers through each stage of the materials cycle, discusses the relationship of the state to producer interests, the developed world to the developing world, the employee to the treadmill of consumption. Concluding with hope, she states: "There are people working here on saving forests and here on clean production. People working on labor rights and fair trade and conscious consuming and blocking landfills and incinerators and, very importantly, on taking back our government so it is really is by the people for the people."

In its most optimistic interpretation, Leonard's list of ongoing actions suggests a mutually constitutive whole of reform and resistance akin to the vision laid out by Paul Hawken in *Blessed Unrest* (2007) with regard

the environmental and social justice movement. Yet in the ongoing construction of responses to solid-waste problems in the twenty-first century
United States, certain actions on Leonard's list are emphasized over
others. "Blocking landfills and incinerators," as discussed in prior chapters, has effectively curtailed municipal solid waste combustion as a
disposal option and succeeded in moving municipal solid waste landfills
away from sites of collective consumption (Walsh, Warland, and Smith
1997). At the same time, the state and producers are consensually
advancing "clean production" in a particular form emphasizing voluntarism (also described earlier). Present but much less emphasized in the
recycling movement imagination are goals of "labor rights, fair trade,
and taking back our government," and the personal role of driving the
material cycle via "conscious consumption" is coming more and more
to be associated with recycling and by extension "saving forests." Here
at last is our link to manufacturing waste, and I argue that this link is
largely mythical. In this mythology, conscious consumption defines an
important role for individuals in diminishing manufacturing waste; this
role is achieved through the mechanism of the demand signal. The EAC
taught this to schoolchildren in 1992: "Waste is generated at every step
of a product's lifecycle, including mining, processing, manufacturing,
packaging, use, and disposal. Thus, our purchase of consumer products
creates waste that we don't see or deal with directly. Our consumer habits
directly affect the amount of industrial and agricultural waste generated
in this country and abroad" (1992, 4).

This is a story that the environmental movement tells itself, and I
invite readers to reconsider its factual basis. In this story, the contemporary negotiation of manufacturing waste by the recycling movement and
publics concerned about problems of solid waste is not supposed to take
place primarily via political action that demands industrial accountability. Like curbside recycling of municipal solid waste, it is to take place
in the achievable realms of home and shopping trip. Few contemporary
treatments of solid-waste problems have examined the struggle to reduce
solid waste in daily life in as much depth as Elizabeth Royte's *Garbage
Land* (2005). The author weighs and quantifies her own garbage, worries
over it, explores feelings of guilt and shame, struggles to follow it to
transfer station, landfill, and recycling plant. In the midst of this project,
she is dismayed to learn of the manufacturing waste/municipal solid
waste discrepancy. Considering whether "it would have been far more
radical for me to opt out of recycling: to throw everything into one sack
and set it at the curb," she nonetheless concludes that

the disparity between my personal waste and the waste it took to produce my waste shocked me, but it didn't mean that the tiny fraction in my cans was inconsequential. . . . [T]he 2 percent is not unrelated to the 98 percent, which has everything to do with the back end of our upwardly mobile lifestyles. . . . If a single barrel of waste on my Park Slope curb was indicative of thirty-two barrels of manufacturing waste, then by halving my garbage I could eliminate sixteen barrels up the line. (2005, 283)

Royte's perspective suggests an implicit social theory. The concerned citizen's agency depends on the mechanism of consumer sovereignty, but in reverse. Through choices and actions within the realm of the home and the shop not to consume and or to recycle, there is an assumed multiplier effect that reaches back behind factory gates, where regulation does not currently go, to slow or stop production of products and hence production of manufacturing waste by means of diminished demand. This notion is making its way into popular recycling (or in this case waste-reduction) discourse. Take, for example, the 2007 posting on cnviromom.com entitled "Upstream versus Downstream Waste": "Upstream waste is all the harvesting of raw materials, manufacturing processes and transportation of stuff that happens before it gets to you. Downstream waste is what happens to the stuff once you get rid of it. The upstream impacts are significantly worse for the environment than downstream. So, if you buy less stuff, less stuff will be manufactured" (Heather 2007). It all sounds intuitively true. But is it true?

Treadmills Rebounding

Allan Schnaiberg (1980; Gould, Pellow, and Schnaiberg 2004) uses the metaphor of a treadmill to describe the requirement of material production under capitalism to grow and expand at ever-increasing rates. Under Fordism, the substitution of technology for labor to enable mass production entailed intensified use of energy and natural resources at scales not experienced in previous periods of industrialization. At the same time during this period, as real wages fell, the workday intensified such that workers were left with less free time, and increased consumption substituted for the phenomenon Juliet Schor (1991) has identified as the "overworked American." The result? More and more stuff produced, traded, marketed, and consumed at faster and faster rates. So why wouldn't buying less stuff mean conversely that less stuff will be manufactured? Understanding why this reverse logic doesn't apply starts with restating the uncontroversial defining characteristics of capitalism. A capitalist system is one in which the means of production are privately owned, work is organized through a system of wage labor, and decisions about what, where, why, how, and how much to produce are driven primarily by the motive for profit, realized through exchange—and only secondarily in correspondence to social needs as expressed through demand. With these defining characteristics, other characteristics follow. Capitalism is marked by constant competition among producers, which can be effected through innovation, substitution of technology for labor, lowered wages, or increased output. And the availability/scarcity of inputs to production is communicated through one means only: prices.

Within this framework, firms respond to reduced demand by slowing or shutting down production only in cases of recession or depression, as seen in the last years of the 2000s. Demand reduction in such a situation reflects a decline in wages, a rise in unemployment, and a decline in the value of investments, all of which limit producers' ability to respond to demand reduction as they otherwise would—by innovating or marketing existing products to new markets or marketing new products to existing markets or doing all three. Marketing—a complex activity that includes claims making in the symbolic realm (advertising), geographic shifts, and the creation of demand through the alteration of physical and social structures of work and reproduction (highway systems, telecommunications)—focuses vast amounts of knowledge, creativity, and power on the goal of encouraging consumers to buy more stuff (Sack 1992).

The emancipatory hope of "buying less"—known in its most organized form as the voluntary simplicity movement, but in practice widely encouraged among all ecologically minded citizens today—is that consumers will be able to resist marketing such that there is a net decrease in consumption and production in total; there are no new types of products (or, if there are, they are not material products), and old types of products are not sold to new markets. Thus, the adherents of "buying less" assume the best of all potential outcomes in which competition for the green consumer market results in a dematerialization of production in toto such that profits are sustained, and we avoid the serious distributional consequences of a reduction in overall material demand (in particular the social impacts of the decline in wages that would result in the United States and more severely in the developing world).

In a neoclassical economic perspective of abstract buyers and sellers, distributional consequences—in other words, who remains poor and who prospers—are at best an afterthought. What this perspective looks at is the push and pull of supply and demand.

So it's fair to say that the social theory—implicit in many of the discussions I've quoted—that consumer choice will drive reduction in manufacturing waste is one rooted in neoclassical economic perspective. Yet even when tested empirically by neoclassical economists, the efficacy of green consumerism to change production patterns is at best equivocal. Clas Eriksson, for example, considers a model in which two theoretical industries manufacture products, one identifiable as truly "green" and the other "not green," to consumers. Eriksson asks whether green products eclipse nongreen ones in response to preferences exerted by green consumers. His findings are that both types of production thrive in competition with one another (2004, 282). Werner Antweiler and Kathryn Harrison examine the empirical effect of green consumerism on industrial pollution when its wastes or "releases" are made known to consumers via a Toxics Release Inventory–type information system. Their work, the "first to investigate the effectiveness of green consumerism empirically on a national level," finds that "companies respond most strongly to consumer pressures by reducing their releases to air and transfers of wastes off site, but also by increasing less visible releases to subsoil via underground injection" (2003, 496). Companies branding themselves as less polluting will actually pollute less only in cases where outside measurement and data dissemination make public what they are doing. These two examples point to a growing area of research within the neoclassical economic literature. Overall, the study of green consumer choice as a mechanism to draw out sustained, nonexceptional change in production practices is still in its infancy. A priori reasoning suggests that green consumption will work only in tandem with supply-side regulations that ensure the substitution of bad goods with good ones and, moreover, that guarantee the claims of green production via unified standards and labels, backed up through audit. Nonetheless, it is theoretically possible that consumer choice alone may be, as so many "buy less, recycle more" discourses imply, a strong enough lever to tip the balance of production toward overall sustainability. The question is not so much whether this can ever happen, but what a reflexive embrace of the market mechanism alone (à la Royte and "Heather", the Enviromom) means for the recycling movement as a feature of American environmentalism.

The Waste behind Factory Gates

Where does this leave us, then, with regard to the massive tonnages and uncertain toxicity of manufacturing wastes in the United States? From one perspective, the lack of political discussion of an issue of great material importance is pretty unremarkable—municipal solid waste has always been more visible than manufacturing wastes. Since the mid–twentieth century, the local state has been hard at work trying to manage increased products in municipal discards; it had no direct relation to manufacturing waste because manufacturing waste was not an urban material phenomenon. In the case of hazardous industrial waste, a series of disastrous outcomes mobilized antitoxics activism and was translated into political representation in Congress so that federal regulation was put in place. But manufacturing waste wasn't killing anyone or at least wasn't doing so in any way that would garner attention. A happy coincidence of spatial waste qualities (fixedness at the site of generation, remove from public gaze behind factory gates, existence outside the sphere of the lifeworld) allowed and still allows manufacturing waste to hide. The few timid inquiries into how much there was, what was in it, where it was, and whether it should be regulated, when voiced in the context of legislative reauthorization, were easily drowned out by more pressing concerns over hazardous industrial waste and municipal solid waste articulated by representatives of the environmental movement. The stakes for producers were clear: it was always their interest to operate free of restriction and regulation, and it behooved them to have nothing known about what they were doing. Aided by a series of administrations that at every opportunity rejected regulation, in particular environmental regulation, producer interests easily won this particular fight, played out in the formal arena of Congress. In this case, the first dimension of power was exercised.

On the other hand the story of the unpolitics of manufacturing waste requires more careful consideration. It is easy to say that manufacturing waste was and is "less visible" than other forms of waste. And if the visibility of waste were defined as its epidemiologically demonstrated health effects, its blight as litter, its nuisance as curbside matter requiring pickup, or even its stigma, then perhaps that would be the end of the story. But the social problem of waste is and has been since the 1970s constructed far more amply to address the unwanted consequences of materials cycling through economies organized at multiple scales. "Save the Planet" is extremely vague, but it still references the planet. Interconnectedness of all natural things is a trope constantly invoked by the environmental movement, and the recycling movement is no exception. These movements rightly point to the multiplicity of consequences that a small item of trash in hand signifies.

What is worrisome is that the exertion of political pressure to regulate manufacturing waste directly has never been part of the recycling movement's goals. Such direct regulation need not be the out-of-fashion command-and-control, end-of-pipe form that consensus from right, left, and center now seems to agree doesn't work (Sinclair 1997). It might merely be the compilation of accessible data to enable national monitoring of tonnages, toxicity, diversion rates, and disposal rates, which would entail some basic reporting by industries and field auditing by EPA regulators. Neither the recycling movement nor the environmental movement in general made this demand. At first, there simply was no demand with regard to manufacturing waste. Although the Resource Conservation Challenge's industrial waste focus solicited input from a few environmental groups, it appears not to have resulted from environmental activism but instead to have been a creation of the EPA as an economic development tool, with nods to industrial ecology as a new green form of market economy.[4] As the recycling movement matured and looked up from the garbage, bottles, cans, and newspaper on its doorstep to consider the context of material environmental problems, the demands it did articulate with respect to producers were for extended producer responsibility—but it does not address by-products of manufacturing. It addresses commodities that would otherwise end up in municipal solid waste, forcing them back to the producers that made them (directly or via economic mechanisms). When extended producer responsibility is advocated (albeit indirectly) as an industrial-waste policy, as it has been in the leading U.S. waste-policy statements of the recycling movement today (Fishbein, Ehrenfeld, and Young 2000; Platt and Seldman 2000), there is an incipient blurring of realms of responsibility. The realm of consumption (in which municipal solid waste is experienced) takes greater prominence than it merits on material grounds. The realm of production recedes into the mist, reachable only through our sending back items from our daily life. What goes on beyond the mist is still unknown. This fiction is reinforced and exaggerated by the unreasonably optimistic assumptions implicit in conscious consuming. Here we do not even send the item back; we signal that we want it produced in a certain way through our personal buying actions.

In the end, what we have for producers is freedom: freedom to be green or semigreen or not green, freedom to do what is in their best interests, without strife or inconvenience. What we have for citizens are (1) a definition of their scope of political action as not just personal behavior, but the purchase transaction, and (2) an utter lack of knowledge needed to reenter the realm of the political and to advocate for regulatory change. In the unpolitics of manufacturing waste, we have a clear case of what Kenneth Gould, Allan Schnaiberg, and Adam Weinberg have noted with regard to their own studies of municipal solid waste recycling in Chicago: "Illusions about the efficacy of particular environmental strategies are easy to develop. . . . In the absence of extralocal knowledge about both the economics and ecological impact of postconsumer wastes, citizen-workers are drawn into making erroneous connections between stated environmental goals and actual ecological consequences" (1996, 127).

When I present the statistics on the discrepancy between manufacturing waste and municipal solid waste to public audiences, they often conclude that I am suggesting that they trash the recyclable fractions of their personal waste in protest. The argument I have made in this chapter is taken to be cynical, as arguing, "What the hell, it all doesn't matter in the first place because there is so much more manufacturing waste than municipal solid waste" (see Royte 2005). This response, however, demonstrates in my view the degree to which personal action in the realm of consumption has been overconstructed along lines that can only be described as naive to the politics and economics of materials usage in the United States. Disappointed that their own contribution to urban recycling is not "making a difference" at a level of national and transnational materiality, people experience the reflex to be destructive in the personal realm rather than to organize in the political realm or merely (as I do) to stay still for a period to contemplate what this particular contradiction means in terms of social response to environmental problems. The frequent trash-tantrum reaction I encounter (and Royte is not the only example) suggests that, as Nina Eliasoph has noted in the context of U.S. civic engagement in general, "some citizens have had no practice in connecting their lives to politics. . . . [M]any citizens have already trimmed their aspirations before voicing them publicly—like impoverished people who, when asked what they would do with a million dollars, can imagine only as far as buying a warm winter coat" (1998, 260).

In fact, I continue to recycle for two reasons. First, recycling has modest benefits in terms of diminishing resource use and pollution; moreover, opting out of recycling in areas that run curbside programs is detrimental to the general local budget that funds schools, parks, and other essential services. Given the fact that recycling has been institutionalized into structures of urban life, it behooves residents, as taxpayers, to continue to do it while remaining clear-eyed (and dry-eyed) about its modest benefits, open to changing recycling practice in favor of more effective measures (such as bottle bills and other forms of extended producer responsibility) should they come along, and flexible enough to consider extralocal—in particular federal— forms of waste governance. Second, as I argue in the conclusion, there is a role for the separation of solid wastes in the home for curbside collection and reclamation that can improve the life of the city, but this role needs to turn away from inorganic (especially plastic) discards and toward the leavings of social reproduction at a more intimate level—organic wastes. Before turning to this consideration of alternative futures, I return to the urban scale to examine the actually existing political and economic activities being carried out by the most contemporary and progressive form of the recycling movement, the Zero Waste movement.

4

Scale and Sufficiency: Zero Waste and the Quest for Environmental Justice

In 2008, U.S. cities sent about 33 percent of their urban discards off to be made something new rather than dumping them (U.S. EPA 2009b; see also appendix I). In total, almost 83 million tons of material were routed back into the economy. This outcome is weighty. It may be true that despite thirty years of serious, if not concerted, efforts to cultivate methods of municipal diversion by government, corporate, and civil-society sectors, two-thirds of municipal solid waste still goes to disposal. It may also be true that municipal solid waste tonnages in total are far, far smaller than tonnages of manufacturing and other industrial wastes. Nonetheless, the sheer mass of active, ongoing diversion of urban dis-cards offers not just hope, but precedent for doing more. At the same time, the existence of this same flowing tonnage also raises crucial ques-tions about future practice. It is not enough simply to do more. The challenge is to do more *justly*, so that the health and communities of some people are not ruined to advance the material well-being or moral comfort of others.

The recycling movement that I have chronicled at work to promote diversion since the 1970s has consisted largely of white people, whereas those who work up waste into objects of use have historically been of color and continue to be so (Pellow 2002; Zimring 2005). And although ecology centers, thrift shops, and community gardens dot neighborhoods of all kinds in cities across the country, industrial zones—the only suit-able spots for large-scale processing of recycling as well as garbage transfer, disposal, and incineration—are overwhelmingly near the homes of people of color and sometimes working-class white people (Pastor, Sadd, and Hipp 2001; Pellow 2002; Sze 2007). As many scholars have argued, the spatial distribution of waste infrastructure and the organiza-tion of work inside that infrastructure both reflects and reproduces a racism and a classism deeply rooted in the American way of doing business and living in communities (Bullard 2000; Pellow 2002; Gandy 2002; Maantay 2002; Saha and Mohai 2005). This arrangement has, in addition to serious health and economic impacts on host communities, its own type of convenience. It enables both waste disposal and recycling as we know it to proceed in tandem such that among mainstream recycling publics and in studies of the recycling economy it can be hailed as "working" even if in need of more of a push (NRC 2001; Bell 2004).

At the same time, a progressive and visionary branch of the waste-focused environmental movement today is currently working up and articulating another vision: the Zero Waste movement. The Zero Waste movement has taken a courageous stance for more socially just models of recovery in its mission to transform economies so that discarded materials are always or nearly always treated as resources instead of as trash (Ciplet 2008). Although the Zero Waste movement's rhetoric is generally neither class nor race specific, it does acknowledge in a more than superficial way the historical fact of injustice inscribed in waste-related infrastructure upon urban landscapes. The Zero Waste movement explicitly allies itself with environmental justice activism, whose goals it includes in its own (Dimino and Warren 2004). It supports community struggles to force combustion (also known as waste-to-energy) off the menu of policy options for waste-management consideration and to oppose other waste-related sited hazards (Loundsbury, Ventresca, and Hirsch 2003). In contrast to the private recycling industry or to highly technocratic approaches to ecological modernization of waste management, the Zero Waste movement fully understands what environmental justice is and why it is important (Ciplet 2008).

Among other characteristics that distinguish the Zero Waste movement from now generalized support of recycling as we know it is its focus on reuse as a method of diversion of discards. Reuse—for example, by selling used clothing, salvaging building materials, repairing appliances, or refilling bottles—stands in contrast to the crushing, shredding, and refabrication that sustains the traditional model upon which curbside collection of cans, bottles, and papers is based. You don't need a complex life-cycle analysis to tell you that, ton for ton, reuse is vastly superior to recycling in terms of energy usage, material conservation, or emissions (Platt 1997). Entire circuits of processing and remanufacture are skipped as a working object is remobilized from a distribution center.[1]

The Zero Waste approach is furthermore bound up with priorities of social justice in a way that mainstream support of recycling is not. The movement's emphasis includes the cultivation of good, green jobs in repair, building deconstruction, and remanufacture using recycled input materials. These jobs are social enterprises often located in low-income communities historically overburdened with waste and other polluting industrial facilities siting (Gonzalez 2008). In such cases, Zero Waste projects seek to redress generations of harm wrought by waste-disposal industries and allied governments on populations who have had no other choice but to live and work amid waste and waste facilities (Gandy 2002). In the past twenty years, residents of such urban zones have forged a vibrant movement that not only challenges waste facilities and their trucks, but highlights the very premises of racial inequality and class domination inherent in U.S. society that have enabled the affluent to dump their trash on the poor (Freilla 2005). The environmental justice movement, with its overt critique of the growth economy and the domination of some groups by others, would seem quite resistant to busy-ness. Its willingness to call practices unsafe and unfair and to challenge "expert" epidemiology that denies risk where people are sick (Brown and Mikkelsen 1990) makes it one of the most politically relevant forms of environmentalism today (Dowie 1995; Bullard and Johnson 2000).

Nonetheless, as I follow measures of tonnage, I find uncomfortable contradictions between the model that Zero Waste offers for the advancement of environmental justice and this model's actual material outcome. Not only is it true that most urban trash is still moving through manifestly unjust channels that include consolidation at transfer stations, long-haul truck and rail transfer to rural landfills, and disposal in rural low-income communities, but the majority of recycling takes place under conditions that are, from a standpoint of domestic and global environmental justice, not much better. I am not the first person to make this point. David Pellow in *Garbage Wars* (2002) conducted extensive research with workers in some of the most dangerous kinds of materials-recovery facilities where recyclables are sorted out of raw garbage[2] and in otherwise progressive, community-based recycling centers. Although conditions in the former were clearly worse physically and constitutionally than the latter, both were hard, harsh jobs with little future potential.

In his study, Pellow highlights instances in which activists involved in environmental justice struggles unintentionally acted against their own interest by welcoming seemingly but in fact not really "greener" industrial facilities (recycling plants and even incinerators) to their neighborhoods in a quest for jobs and local economic development. Pellow interprets this tendency as but one iteration of the dynamics underlying colonization. He writes, "Throughout history, one of the most effective ways of controlling a colony was to create hierarchies (or intensify existing ones) between social classes and/or ethnic groups, so that each would have incentive to focus its energy on the others rather than on the colonizer" (2002, 80). The phenomenon Pellow is describing shares some characteristics with what I call "busy-ness" in that those in power recognize the utility of directing the energy of groups who would challenge that power into time-consuming, counterproductive outlets. In subsequent works, Pellow and his colleagues call for a critical approach to environmental justice studies that pays attention to such divisive strategies and does not flinch from asking the "larger question of whether this movement has the efficacy or the capacity to achieve its stated goals" (Pellow and Brulle 2005, 17). My aim in this chapter is not to evaluate the environmental justice movement in this regard, but to turn the same critical eye toward contemporary Zero Waste solutions that are being embraced by those inside and outside urban environmental justice movements today. At issue is the currently celebrated model of the community-based, reuse enterprise (and of similarly socially progressive forms of "waste to wealth" premised in community composting and locally coordinated industrial symbiosis). Such enterprises rightly take place with others focused on gardening, landscaping, and energy-efficient retrofitting in that they foster clean, safe, green urban communities and jobs (Lee 2005). As models of urban sustainable waste management, however, they are—as currently configured—deeply insufficient to address the problems of solid waste, its disparate effects on people of color and white working people, and the stated goals of recycling in terms of dealing with resource depletion and climate change. Even as I celebrate the Zero Waste enterprise model as a form of local economic activity and human endeavor, I see in it the potential to stand as the locus of a new, more elaborate, and even less socially apparent manifestation of busy-ness. Understanding this potential begins with a trip to an actually existing (not ideal-typical) local materials recovery facility, to which your, my, and most everyone else's waste for recycling is sent every week across the United States.

The Materials Recovery Facility and Its Neighbors

Like the glass-beneficiation facility I described in chapter 1, I find materials recovery facilities fascinating and impressive for the ingenuity with which they rapidly disentangle what decades of well-intentioned recycling activism and municipal imperatives for efficiency have demanded be mixed together. As a waste professional, I have toured materials recovery facilities across the United States and Europe and have been allowed close access to machinery and workers not usually afforded the public at large. What I describe here is common to most materials recovery facilities, which today give tours to schoolchildren and interested citizens from a safe, windowed vantage point. From above, visitors can watch the complex industrial process that teases apart loads of mixed metal, glass, plastic, and paper that residents have dutifully put out for recycling. The mix of technology and manual labor employed at materials recovery facilities across the country varies but follows the same general model. Throughout the day, diesel-fueled trucks bearing loads of compacted, commingled recyclables arrive and dump their contents onto the ground, or "tipping floor," of the plant. Workers with rakes may pull out large metal items of value or big contaminants such as tires or televisions that don't belong. What remains is loaded onto a conveyor belt that passes over a series of shifting, shaking screens called "trommel screens." Items under a certain size, often two inches in diameter, fall through the trommel and are routed into a pile of "unders"—consisting of broken glass, bottle caps, and other small bits of material. This muck may go to a glass-beneficiation facility for further sorting and cleaning, or it may be screened again to produce a low-grade glass aggregate for use in road building (see chapter 1). Medium-size materials continue along the belt. Steel and iron are the easiest substances to extract as the mix passes under strong magnets. Electrical currents react with aluminum and other nonferrous metals to send them springing off the belt and into designated hoppers. At this point, most of what is left is plastic and paper. Some materials recovery facilities use centrifugal separators to whirl off the paper (a marketable commodity) and plastic shopping bags (a troublesome contaminant that jams equipment) from the heavier plastic containers. After this, optical sorters may be used to identify and differentiate plastics by molecular structure or polymer—a sorting function that is crucial to plastics recycling. At its most automated, a materials recovery facility can do a great deal of teasing apart of commingled recyclables without a human hand.

But manual labor is always part of the mix. In even the most high-tech facilities, rows of workers, masked, gloved, and wearing protective eyewear, stand along the belts at various points and pick off assigned materials that mechanical separation methods miss or cannot yet extract systematically. Some materials recovery facilities are little more than conveyor belts with people sorting everything manually; others use older technologies (magnets, eddy currents, trommel screens) but don't yet find it worth it to invest in optical sorters. Materials recovery facilities are usually privately owned, but some may be public or in rare cases non-profit entities. Working conditions vary from execrable to good. But all materials recovery facilities are loud, dusty, dirty, monotonous, and often dangerous workplaces that pay low wages to pickers on the line. The submanagerial work involved is simple drudgery. As collection trucks arrive and long-haul trailers leave throughout the day, the materials recovery facility's driving imperative becomes clear—to move large quantities of mixed, urban discards continuously, to sort them out as quickly and efficiently as possible, and to produce semisorted bales of material that are ready for the next step in a long and elaborate journey whose destination to "remanufacture," the creation of something new, will require further sorting and a possible trip across the sea to a foreign land.

The materials recovery facility as a workplace and industrial process is interesting to compare to several other models of waste management operating at the urban scale, which are usually its neighbors. The mission of the materials recovery facility's seeming antithesis, the garbage transfer station, is to ready urban materials for a journey to a very different, far more despised, but always U.S.-based ultimate destination—disposal in a landfill or incinerator. As at the materials recovery facilities, diesel-fueled collection trucks arrive at the transfer station over the course of the day and deposit their loads onto a tipping floor. Long-haul tractor trailers (or sometimes rail cars) transport the material back out of the facility. Unlike at the materials recovery facilities, at the transfer station there is no sorting. A few well-paid skilled operators of front-end loaders scoop up the tipped material and deposit it into intermodal containers, seated high above the mess below. A low-wage employee usually sweeps and shovels. The transfer station's equipment and labor requirements are simple compared to the materials recovery facility's.

Possibly in the zoned industrial area at which both the materials recovery facility and the transfer station prepare their throughput for the trip out of town, different types of enterprises are at work. These enterprises may be taking in and repairing anything from just-out-of-date PCs to bicycles; they may be making decorative tile out of cleaned, color-sorted recycled glass or furniture out of discarded wooden pallets; they may be scavenging reusable materials from the garbage transfer station, or going into buildings before deconstruction to carefully disassemble fixtures, doors, and other building materials. The work in these enterprises is hard but more interesting than a pick line; the atmosphere is cleaner and safer; and the outputs of refurbishment, reshaping, restoration, rescue, and repair will not be traveling far. Whether explicitly for profit or not for profit, such enterprises are bound up with a model of social entrepreneurship. They will likely employ locally and thus will be drawing from a pool of people who live in the waste-zoned neighborhood.

The hope and the plan of Zero Waste are that the type of enterprises just described will come to eclipse materials recovery facilities and transfer stations as appropriately scaled, safe facilities take on more and more reusable, recyclable, and compostable discards and transform them into products of use with fair, rewarding labor. Given the current existence of a much different type of infrastructure handling most municipal solid waste today, we have to ask how this fundamental change will happen at a materially and socially significant scale so that "Zero Waste or darn close" (the Zero Waste movement's motto) is achieved. Is this task attainable through an incremental process in which small social enterprises coalesce to form indigenous, healing, alternative circuits to absorb waste, leaving big, dying waste giants—starved of waste—to fade away? I have argued in previous chapters that small-scale projects that are "a start" offer rich ground for cultivation by producers seeking to maintain the status quo on large scales. Might this possibly be happening with the Zero Waste enterprise as well? Here is a danger that must be uncovered and investigated.

American Zero Waste in Practice

The Grassroots Recycling Network defines Zero Waste as "a philosophy and a design principle for the 21st Century [that] includes 'recycling' but goes beyond recycling by taking a 'whole system' approach to the vast flow of resources and waste through human society. Zero Waste maximizes recycling, minimizes waste, reduces consumption and ensures that products are made to be reused, repaired or recycled back into nature or the marketplace" (2008). One Zero Waste leader describes it as a movement that

has grown steadily over the last decade, thanks again to the social activism from a growing number of mission-driven, social change organizations. Zero Waste as a resource conservation strategy goes beyond recycling in a few significant ways, including its focus "upstream," at the source of the waste stream, before a product is created, rather than simply collecting materials "downstream." Emphasis is placed on the industrial design of products and packaging, on redirecting the government regulations and subsidies that currently provide hidden support for the status quo (landfill and incinerator industries), and on the purchasing behavior that is fueling the wasting behaviors in American society. Of course, Zero Waste also calls for the adoption of "downstream" goals and social policies that will gradually lead to a reuse/recycling/composting rate of over 90 percent of society's discards. (Lombardi and Rogers 2007)

The Zero Waste vision did not originate in the United States. Conceived of in New Zealand, the practice now has adherents throughout the North, particularly in the United Kingdom and Australia. Robin Murray, an industrial economist and consultant to Greenpeace U.K., is a well-known advocate and author on the subject. He describes Zero Waste broadly as a "new way of seeing" that conceives of all discards as resources and seeks to restore "pre-industrial circuits—the biological circuit of organic materials and the technical circuit inorganic ones—using post-industrial means" (2002, 29). In his 2002 treatment of the subject, he identifies Zero Waste as both trend in progress and blueprint for a sustainable future. Zero Waste is the framework in which to envision and practice a new form of economy in which recycling goes beyond the default meaning to encompass multiple circuits of organic materials through decomposition and inorganic materials through cycles of recovery and remobilization, with strict controls on those hazardous substances that are absolutely necessary for society. Although there is room for state regulation in this vision, the state's role is limited to synthesis. Markets, recaptured for social purposes, are seen as the drivers of what will be an economic transformation (Murray 2002).

In terms of practical, on-the-ground solutions, U.S. Zero Waste features a form of urban-centered waste activism organized around the community-based social enterprise. Such enterprises can grow to be "Zero Waste millionaires," organizations "that make a profit in the name of supporting their social mission" (Lombardi and Rogers 2007). They follow the model of the community recycling center of the 1970s but now aspire to provide a "diversified 'eco-system' of local services," organized around the profitable recovery of all types of waste—not just cans, bottles, and newspapers (Lombardi and Rogers 2007). Zero Waste enterprises may handle different materials, they have two common features. First, they seek to adhere as closely as possible to the model of the locally closed loop. The locally closed loop is a preferable alternative to the present unsustainable state of affairs organized around large-scale materials recovery facility processing and long-distance trash disposal. In this model, commodities enter the urban scale from larger scales of production and distribution, flow back out again as garbage transported to disposal *or* as bales of recyclables sent to regional, national, and, most of all, global markets. Under the locally closed loop model, commodities flow into the urban arena from outside markets, but the hope is to have them stay there. The ideal goal is local processing of discards, local remanufacture using recycled inputs production, for local consumption using local labor. In theory, the increased local circulation of commodities to discards to commodities and so on will lessen demand for materials from the outside. The locality will become, again in theory, more "self-reliant" (as indicated in the organizational name of one of the leading proponents of this idea, the Institute for Local Self Reliance).

The second common feature of many Zero Waste enterprises is, as discussed earlier, emphasis on reuse. Although these enterprises may include remanufacture, recycling, or composting operations, they maximize their social and (on a per ton basis) ecological impacts when readying discards for reuse (sorting them, setting them out in the shop). This type of work—repair, refurbishment, disassembly for parts—is labor and sometimes skill intensive, promising not just jobs, but good jobs. Because it is well established through life-cycle analysis that reuse is less energy intensive and polluting than recycling, reuse maximizes the environmental benefits of diversion. Reuse enterprises, moreover, seem a good place to "start small" because the technological requirements for rescuing treasures from the trash are low—all that is needed is a building and some hard workers. But if such efforts are to go on to constitute the basis of a much more materially significant change in the way waste is managed, we have to ask about tonnage. How much of what is now going to disposal is available to be "mined" for reuse?

The EPA's biennially updated *Characterization of Municipal Solid Waste* makes a primary distinction between discards that are products and those that are not—including food scraps, yard trimmings, and other residuals (U.S. EPA 2009b). Products are classified by function, breaking down among three categories: *durables* (including appliances, furniture, carpets and rugs, auto batteries, tires, electronics, and a large "other category"); *packaging* (including boxes, wraps, and containers); and a third category of products the EPA calls "*nondurables*" (including printed matter, disposable tableware, garbage bags, diapers and hygiene products, and textiles).

With bottle refill now almost unheard of, discards in contemporary American municipal solid waste that reuse enterprises do or can target include wood packaging, books, textiles, carpets and rugs, e-waste, furniture and furnishings, appliances, and other durable products (see appendix IV). Durable products with the highest current recovery rates are major appliances, some 67 percent of which are currently recovered—sometimes for reuse, but much more commonly for recycling, which entails melting down and recasting products. As detailed in chapter 1, the scrap-metal industry has a long history, with well-established infrastructure for recycling things such as refrigerators, washing machines, and other "white goods." The material properties of metals make them easy to sort and recycle across functional categories of discard—this is why curbside recycling programs take cans as well as things such as toasters and broken frying pans (Bouman, Heijungs, van de Voet, et al. 2000). Tires and automotive batteries make up another sizeable fraction of durables discards and are also reclaimed at relatively high rates, but not through reuse enterprises. In most states, disposal of these materials in the trash is illegal; in many states deposit laws require their return to point of sale.

The same cannot be said for durables made of other substances, including wood, plate glass, rubber other than tires, and a wide range of plastics. These materials—often in combination making up a wide range of goods, including electronics, small appliances, furniture, housewares, and toys—vary widely in their suitability for repair or for reuse even when they are in perfect working order. Building materials—doors, window sashes, fixtures carefully deconstructed before the wrecking ball arrives—are among the easiest to route into reuse and are the basis of a growing, socially organized reuse industry in the United States, albeit one that targets construction and demolition debris and not municipal solid waste (Jain, George, and Webster 2008). Used clothing and shoes can be effectively marketed to a wide range of consumers, although most collections rely on export to Africa, India, and eastern Europe for the bulk of what is collected (Hansen 1999). But many durables—including increasingly cheap furniture, plastic housewares, and short-lived appliances—are difficult to give away if soiled or broken. Such items are not fodder for reuse enterprises, not only because the repair skills needed (woodworking, electrical work, etc.) are underdeveloped after decades of disuse, but also because the nature of most consumer products is that they can't be repaired or even effectively cleaned without massive investments of labor and materials or often even at all.

The estimates of durables and textiles in municipal solid waste discards are therefore only the vaguest of indicators of the potential quantity of material being discarded that might be subject to repair and reuse
as a method of diversion from disposal. There simply are no data on
these metrics, but my estimates suggest that 24 percent is an upper bound
and that the real percentage is probably significantly lower. (See appendix
IV.) This point is important in understanding the reach of the reuse
enterprise as a model upon which to plan for socially just municipal solid
waste management. If under the most unrealistic and optimistic scenarios
24 percent of municipal solid waste is kept from moving through transfer
stations to disposal, 76 percent and likely a much greater fraction than
that in practice still remain and must be handled otherwise. This point
seems obvious and seemingly easily addressed by adding Zero Waste
recycling and composting enterprises to the agenda as complements. Yet
in the current discourse about waste and social issues that characterizes
the meeting point of the environmental justice and Zero Waste movements, this obvious point is frequently underexamined. As a result, the
momentum of business as usual—materialized in big tonnages of industrial-scale mixed recycling and even bigger tonnages of disposal—chugs
on, crowding out space for alternatives.

Take, for example, the shining exemplar of the Zero Waste reuse
enterprise: Urban Ore, a nonprofit located in Berkeley, California (the
site of one of the nation's first ecology center–based recycling operations). Here is one of many descriptions of the organization, taken from
a 2001 report commissioned for Mercer County, New Jersey, and
researched by Rutgers University's Ecopolicy Center for Agricultural
Environmental and Resource Issues:

An alternative to the transfer station might look like Urban Ore in California,
which generates $1.5 million in revenue through its retail store. Urban Ore
salvages materials that would ordinarily be sent to the landfill. Its 2.2-acre site
contains several divisions, including Salvage and Recycling, the General Store,
and the Building Materials Exchange. Approximately 15% of the materials
Urban Ore receives are gleaned from the Berkeley transfer station; local businesses and residents supply the rest. Since Urban Ore buys many types of materials, it has no problem attracting an adequate supply for resale and reuse. Urban
Ore acts as a retail clearinghouse for recyclable and reusable materials and benefits the community by decreasing waste generation while creating high-paying
jobs. (ECAER 2001, 21, emphasis added)

In this account, the Zero Waste reuse enterprise is described as an alternative to the transfer station, the point of refuse consolidation before

transport to disposal. It is important to highlight this claim as it goes to the expectation of the role of such a model—to replace some or all of the infrastructure and practice that structures how solid waste is currently handled in cities. A similar elision can be found in Kenneth Gould, Allan Schnaiberg, and Adam Weinberg's critique of curbside recycling, which urges consideration of reuse as a socially and ecologically more promising alternative. Set within a much larger vision that includes the strengthening of local and extralocal forms of civil society, Gould, Schnaiberg, and Weinberg's alternative highlights organizations geared toward "social reuse," including garage sales, rummage sales, and "thrift stores (run for profit or by nonprofit organizations)," as not only "more socially progressive than remanufacturing" (which is undoubtedly true), but also with potential to "reduce material use [and] maximize the reutilization of material previously involved in production and/or consumption" (1996, 140). After a critical engagement with the question of how environmental justice and sustainability can work in concert at the urban scale, including an incisive discussion of the current solid-waste-management industry and a call for "caution when proposing recycling industry facilities as community economic development opportunities for low-income areas," Julian Agyeman and Tom Evans go on to cite the ReUse Center in Minneapolis as a "regionally based practical model" that addresses both "environmental justice principles while working toward greater sustainability in urbanized areas" (2003, 35).

The ReUse Center, developed by a group of community activists in the Phillips neighborhood of Minneapolis after a protracted and successful fight against the construction of a new transfer station, has since 1995 "kept 300–500 tons of reusable construction materials out of landfills per year" (ReUse Center 2010). Minneapolis's combined municipal solid waste and construction and demolition waste stream is almost 153,000 tons annually, an impressive 35 percent of which is diverted from disposal. The vast majority of this diversion is in the form of traditional commingled paper, metal, plastic, and glass as well as yard trimmings for composting (*Recycling Today* 2004). At the time Agyeman and Evans were writing, in fact, Minneapolis was routing recyclables to two of the largest materials recovery facilities in the country, each operated by a multinational waste giant (Waste Management, Inc., and BFI as of 2004) (*Recycling Today* 2004). Arrangements like the one in Minneapolis, with high-profile but extremely small Zero Waste reuse enterprises flourishing alongside much larger, parallel systems of industrially organized recycling, are typical of cities across the nation.[3]

To the extent that the Zero Waste movement—with all good intentions—promotes Zero Waste reuse enterprises as a solution to the problem of injust waste-facility siting, it behooves all of us concerned with justice and sustainability to take a long, hard, and considered look at the sufficiency of this solution. The historical case of New York City provides insight into what may go wrong if sufficiency is not critically considered.

The History of Local Loop Closure in New York City

Many of the concepts bound up in the ideal-typical Zero Waste enterprise were identified and tested in New York City during the late 1990s and early 2000s. By and large, the sum total of the activism, municipal planning, and combined energy that went into the struggle for just and sustainable waste outcomes during that period has resulted in a situation very much like the one I described at the beginning of this chapter. In communities of color extensively burdened with waste management and other toxic industrial uses, such as the South Bronx, successful reuse enterprises are being cultivated. Together, these enterprises manage tiny quantities of discards, while traditional materials recovery facilities and a local paper mill take on large tonnages of recyclables following an industrial model quite different from that premised in Zero Waste. In the meantime, the majority of discards still go to disposal, although the impacts of the waste transfer stations, most acutely felt in the South Bronx and low-income communities of color in Greenpoint and Williamsburg, are now being somewhat mitigated by the introduction of rail export instead of trucking, with plans under way to alleviate emissions burdens further by moving to barge-based, long-term export (NYC DS 2006). This outcome—the detoxifying of trash transport and the declustering of transfer stations in certain neighborhoods—has been an explicit victory for the New York City environmental justice movement (Sze 2007).

In 2000, the Consumer Policy Institute (CPI) and the Organization of Waterfront Neighborhoods (OWN)—a New York City community-based coalition "formed to address the common threat to New York City neighborhoods presented by solid waste transfer stations" (Warren 2000, i)—jointly published *Taking Out the Trash: A New Direction for New York City's Waste* (Warren 2000). The report responded to the city's imminent closure of the Fresh Kills landfill and the subsequent switch to out-of-city export for all residential waste disposal. Export would entail the use of existing private transfer stations, at which trash would be consolidated for long-haul trucking to distant disposal sites. Such transfer stations were predominantly sited in a few neighborhoods in the Bronx and Brooklyn (Sze 2007). The problems of vehicle exhaust and odor/stigma from the transfer stations constituted a classic case of environmental racism (Sze 2005). Among the pressing goals of the environmental justice community was to limit or close such stations and to ensure that each borough's refuse went only to stations within that borough. The community's struggle represented what Julie Sze describes as "community action by people of color" that links local and community-based demands for a clean, safe, and healthy environment to "political discontent with intensifying trends of the expansion of capital [and] with a simultaneous decrease in government intervention and regulation" (2005, 101).

The CPI/OWN plan was presented as an alternative to the existing arrangement of land-based transfer stations. It was premised on methodically addressing each fraction of waste—preventable, recyclable, compostable, and reusable—to maximize the "sustainability—environmental, economic, and social—of the waste system." It was explicit in stating that environmental justice problems could be resolved by capturing "valuable resources, creating economic development and jobs." It specifically called for public investment in local enterprises: "Much more could be done to attract manufacturers that use recycled materials and to assist small businesses in this field. . . . [M]any remanufacturing businesses are small, some with great ideas that need to be tried on a small scale first. In order to effect change we must change economic development assistance so that it assists small businesses." Such development would "offer economic opportunities in recycling to communities currently bearing the brunt of NYC's solid waste problems" (Warren 2000, i, 53, 54). It is important to stress this aspect of the proposal: *simultaneous* solution of waste, justice, and underemployment problems via the Zero Waste enterprise model.

A similar argument was made around this time by the New York City Waste Prevention Coalition (NYC WPC), self-described as "a network of organizations and individuals dedicated to promoting waste prevention as the most responsible, environmentally sound and cost-effective means to solve New York City's mounting solid waste problems" (NYC WPC 2002, 1). In 2002, when glass and plastics were suspended from the residential recycling program (see chapters 1 and 2), the Coalition issued the response *Why Waste the Future? Alternatives to the Mayor's*

Proposed Waste Prevention, Composting, and Recycling Cuts. The recommendations it made were similar to those made by CPI/OWN: "If recycling and waste prevention are to serve as serious and cost-effective alternatives to disposal, the city must aggressively court entrepreneurs who want to mine the local waste stream" (NYC WPC 2002, 1).

The courting of miners of urban ore had in fact been under way for some time. Shortly after the institutionalization of curbside recycling in early 1992, then Department of Sanitation commissioner Emily Lloyd led a coalition of stakeholders interested in developing recycling infrastructure. Their goal was to use "more of New York's solid waste materials to make products locally, instead of sending the separated trash to recycling plants around the country" (Breznick 1993, 7). Together they hoped to "lure recycling plants . . . find large, cheap plots of land; counter high operating costs; change public-sector purchasing policies; improve the quality of recyclable materials; find the right markets; and speed up the city's time-consuming approval process" (Breznick 1993, 7). During this same period, the New York State Department of Economic Development's Office of Recycling Market Development funded the first of what would be many research-and-development projects geared to developing local processing and remanufacturing industries that would use city curbside recyclables as inputs. In 1993, the Urban Research Center at New York University predicted "a new blue-collar [recycling] industry . . . that could generate up to 4,000 new jobs" in New York, reinfusing the city with an economic vitality that decades of deindustrialization had eroded (Temes 1993, 21). In theory, the city's massive size meant a concentration of supply of recyclables and (potentially) a concentration of demand for recycled products, especially recycled newsprint and office paper. The city's concentration of marketing and distribution networks could provide, under the right conditions, opportunities for either vertical or horizontal integration of processors and manufacturers (O'Neill and Sheehan 1993).

At the same time, there were disadvantages to New York City as an industrial location, especially for remanufacturers—firms that take sorted materials from materials recovery facilities or secondary processing facilities such as glass-beneficiation plants or plastic pelletizers and undertake the business of turning recycled material into something new. Costs for land, construction, electricity, labor, and living expenses were substantially higher in the city than in other zones. New York City's density meant strict restrictions on air and water emissions. Permitting and city contracting requirements were complicated and discouraging, which made risking venture capital in the already volatile recycling market a precarious undertaking.[4] In fact, New York University scholars noted that although "the collection of secondary materials is inherently a local activity, there is no guarantee that the expansion of sorting and consolidation facilities will occur within the city's boundaries." Instead, they predicted that "industry is much more likely to grow through incremental capacity expansion at existing plants [elsewhere], and there is no existing [recycling] production base within the city from which the industry could grow" (O'Neill and Sheehan 1993, 94). These authors did identify some potential exceptions to this tendency. One, they believed, was the manufacture of plastic products and "intermediate goods" (such as pellets) from recycled plastic bottles. In part because of the lack of prior development in this industry, plastics processors and manufacturers could—in theory—operate on the small scale needed to survive in New York's dense environment.

The exploration of ideas that went on in 1992 and 1993 and the flurry of planning that followed in 1994 were expected to lead to the development of a diverse, high-technology recycling industry in New York City founded on the millions of tons of discarded materials generated by city residents annually. This outcome did not happen. An examination of specific cases reveals that a lack of consideration of material qualities of inputs and of scalar requirements for markets limited the success of most ventures. It also highlights the early iterations of a parallel goal for remanufacturing that today is extended to the reuse enterprise—the redress of inequality and social problems through green jobs working on waste.

Plastics

In 1990, Utility Plastics Corporation of Brooklyn received a $400,000 start-up loan from the state Urban Development Corporation and another $500,000 from the state Economic Development Corporation to develop a facility that would transform residential recycled plastics into traffic cones and police barricades. At the time, the idea of using recycled plastic from New York City residents to make products for city procurement was hailed as a promising avenue for recycling economic development. The media and the community enthusiastically greeted the facility as a

new manufacturing venture that could put more than 100 people back to work in the drug-ridden East New York section of Brooklyn. The company is perhaps one whose time has come. . . . Sales could eventually reach $2.5 million. More important than the size of this venture, however, is its significance to Brooklyn and the rest of the city. New York has lost 161,000 manufacturing jobs in the last decade. This is a small step toward reversing that trend. (Temes 1990, 3)

Utility Plastics planned to sell its product to local utility companies as well as to city agencies. It would accept recycled plastics from city collection and local commercial sources and expected to manufacture its products at "costs way below those of other traffic cone manufacturers, many of whom would use more expensive virgin plastic" (Temes 1990, 3). Maintaining low material costs was essential because, the article pointed out, "labor costs will be significantly higher than those of competitors, who don't need the manpower to sort what comes in" (Temes 1990, 3). These advantages and the boost to East New York, a community "badly beaten by poverty, crime and drugs" and abandoned by industrial employers, combined to make the venture out as a "win-win project for everybody involved" (Temes 1990, 3).

Only two years later, though, Utility Plastics was struggling to stay afloat. *Crains New York Business*, which had reported extensively on the company's promise in 1990, now observed that "despite the great fanfare surrounding its launch, the Brooklyn company has had little success selling its plastic traffic cones and police barricades to its prime targets—state and city agencies." This failure was attributed to both market forces and marketing strategies: "The plight of Utility Plastics shows just how hard it is to sell products in the depressed market for recycled materials. The company has run into trouble rounding up enough customers even though its cones and barricades have earned favorable reviews. . . . The company's woes show how risky it can be for businesses to depend on state and city procurement guidelines, no matter how well-intentioned" (Breznick 1993, 7). Despite its market focus, Utility Plastics was depending on government power (albeit procurement power). As with the great plans for glass aggregate in Fayetteville, Arkansas, described in chapter 1, the venture anticipated agency demand that could not be brought to bear in the complex terrain of public procurement. Wrote a spokesman, "[We] couldn't generate much business from city and state purchasing agents seeking the lowest bidder" (qtd. in Breznick 1993, 7). Lack of government demand was compounded by market forces: a slump in plastics markets made products from elsewhere (both virgin and recycled) cost competitive with the home-grown cones. The company's vision of supplying city agencies with products made using municipally collected recyclables ultimately failed to materialize, and the firm went under.

Glass

The problems of glass recycling were discussed in chapter 1, and New York City was not spared the pain of inefficiencies inherent in this form of diversion. Glass breakage and contamination with organic residues in recycling collections were seen early on in the residential recycling program, leading recycling industry executives to complain that "the city is now mixing glass, plastics and aluminum cans . . . a process that breaks and contaminates the glass, making it less valuable than it could be" (Temes 1993, 21). Soon after the city's curbside recycling program went into effect, the New York City Department of Transportation fortunately began accepting mixed crushed glass from processors contracting with the Department of Sanitation, using it in glassphalt production.

This arrangement came to an end in 1997, however, when the Department of Transportation abruptly discontinued accepting glass due to the redesign of its asphalt facility to enable asphalt recycling using microwave heating. With a large surplus of stockpiled asphalt at sites throughout the city and a steady stream of new millings from ongoing road work, the need for glass aggregate in new asphalt manufacture diminished. Moreover, the department was eager to switch back to gravel and stone, as opposed to glass, for its remaining aggregate input needs because of the high rate of organics contamination of the latter and the lack of reliability of deliveries from the city's private recycling processors (NYC DS 2004). Thereafter, mixed cullet became a drain on processors' profits, with most of it going to low-end beneficial use as alternative daily cover[5] in landfills throughout the Northeast.

When Great Harbor Design Center announced plans to locate a facility in Brooklyn, there were new hopes for a local end market for residential glass. Great Harbor was created in 1998 to commercialize a new technology for making an innovative building material called Ice Stone, which is composed of more than 80 percent recycled container glass. Despite delays in building renovation and equipment installation, the firm was up and running by the end of 2001, with a staff of around 60 employees "generating about five marketable panels per day using 12 tons of glass per month" (NYS EDP 2000, 1). But Great Harbor ultimately could not close the loop with New York City's glass. As the New York State Environmental Investment Program, which supplied nearly $300,000 worth of funding to the project, reported, "[Great Harbor] intended to buy recovered glass from generators in New York City, but were unsuccessful in finding suppliers there who could meet their specification for cleanliness, size and color. Instead, they are buying recycled glass from processors in Ohio and Massachusetts that get a portion of their material from New York City" (NYS EDP 2000, 1). As described in chapter 1, glass collected at curbside needed to travel long distances through costly beneficiation processes in order to be able to come home to market.

Paper

In contrast to the cases of plastics and glass, the development of a private paper-recycling plant and board mill on Staten Island was a rapid success. Work on the project started in 1995, when the city began the process of convincing Pratt Industries, an Australian company, to locate a factory in New York City. The company was initially considering locating in sites in Pennsylvania and New Jersey but was persuaded to build in Staten Island by a package of inducements, including more than $50 million in abatements from city and state sources for real estate and other taxes, a construction labor agreement with the Building and Construction Trades Council that included a no-strike pledge and reduced overtime agreement, and a reduced electricity rate from Con Edison. The project received loans from several sources, among them the New York City Industrial Development Agency, which floated solid-waste bonds to finance the project. New York State directed a total $1.4 million into the endeavor, with $1 million from the New York State Department of Transportation for roadway improvements and $400,000 in grants and loans from the Empire State Development Corporation (New York City Office of the Mayor 1995). The bureaucratic aspects of project development were streamlined by awarding the contract without competitive bidding and by enabling fast-track environmental permit approvals (Siegel 1997). In an agreement that entailed revenue sharing and no net processing fee to the city, the New York City Department of Sanitation committed to delivering between 30 and 50 percent of the city's residential wastepaper to Pratt's facility, called the Visy Paper Mill, each year, using the existing, city-owned marine transfer station system (NYC DS 2004).

The facility cost roughly $250 million to build and had the joint support of Staten Island Borough president Guy Molinari, Governor George Pataki, and Mayor Rudolph Giuliani. Its happy constellation of supporters meant that it was made a reality very quickly, in less than one year, and today it is the city's largest contractor for recycled residential paper, with which it produces linerboard for cardboard box manufacture throughout the United States. Located in an unpopulated and heavily industrialized zone next to the closed Fresh Kills landfill and a power plant, the facility's contribution to local employment is modest (less than 100 employees), its community benefits resistant to quantification, and its product exported for consumption all over the United States. Work at the plant is quite different than work in a materials recovery facility, entailing a range of trades involved in pulping recycled inputs, milling new paper, and fabricating boxes. The model of private, corporate employment it offers is similar to that of any large factory—with all the pluses and minuses therein. Although it is not a Zero Waste social enterprise in the sense advocated in visions of urban sustainability and justice, it nonetheless does guarantee the stability of paper recycling in New York City, whose contracts specify the sharing of risks and rewards from fluctuating secondary paper markets over a 20-year period.

The process of developing local processing capacity went on in parallel with the implementation of the curbside recycling program that the EAC had fought for early on (see chapter 2). Collected tonnages of recyclables increased from about 700 tons per day in 1990 to more than 2,500 by 2000 (NYC DS 2004). These tonnages came in two separations, with residents required to segregate paper and cardboard for one recycling collection and metal, glass bottles and jars, and plastic bottles and jugs—commingled together—for a second. Visy Paper Mill was able to take deliveries of mixed paper and cardboard (including high-grade white paper, newsprint, colored and glossy papers, smooth cardboard, and corrugated cardboard) and pulp them together on site, transforming them into the rough brown paper used in box production. Other paper brokers, building on the scrap industry's long history (see chapter 1), were also able to receive and sort recycled paper and board collected off the curb, following a conveyor-belt/trommel model that relies heavily on manual pick labor. Not so with the other start-up ventures that are so much the subject of economic development. Utility Plastics, Great Harbor Design, and the germs of other companies like them were geared to take *processed* metal, glass, and plastic recyclables—that is, recycled materials that had been sorted, graded, and baled in a materials recovery facility. Finding markets for sorted metals, which also had extensive processing precedent in the scrap industry (again see chapter 1), was no problem. Not only did infrastructure and markets exist, but the properties of metal made it easy and cost effective to reintroduce into production. Glass and plastics were sticking points, however. For the reasons outlined earlier, input specifications and weak markets made conditions in which these recycled materials could be profitably turned into new products highly contingent. Effective remanufacturing depended on market factors that could not be replicated in the locality of New York City.

Over the period in which Utility Plastics and similar projects were fostered, primary materials recovery facility processing was subject to quite different forms of economic development than were called for in regard to "great ideas that need to be tried on a small scale first" (Warren 2000, 53). Development of materials recovery facilities entailed the negotiation of planning at the level of direct service provision by local and state government contracting, to the enrichment not of innovative industries with great ideas and antipoverty potential, but of large, horizontally and in some cases vertically integrated firms in the disposal, scrap, and global manufacturing industries.

Lost Opportunity: Lack of Support for Public Materials-Recovery Facilities

In the late 1980s, as EAC and other recycling movement activism pressed for the institutionalization of curbside recycling, there was no public or private infrastructure to process collections (NYC DS 1988, 33). The passage of the recycling law in 1989 made sure the activism of the early recycling movement and the interests of commodity producers would be institutionalized at public expense. Anticipating increasing tonnages of recyclables that would have to be collected and managed, the city viewed publicly owned facilities as an integral part of New York City's recycling future (NYC DS 1988). The first public materials recovery facility project was an intermediate processing center in East Harlem, constructed and operated under contract with Resource Recovery Systems, Inc. The Department of Sanitation paid the facility's operating costs and was entitled to receive a portion of revenue the company made from the marketing of sorted and baled materials. The mix of private and public arrangements were for the time being enough to handle the city's metal/ glass/plastics recyclables stream. But more capacity and more favorable economics would soon be needed.

In a 1990, Department of Sanitation commissioner Steven Polan called the lack of materials recovery facility–processing capacity "the single most significant hurdle" for the recycling program, saying that "the success of the department's short- and long-term plans depends upon the availability of sufficient public and private processing capacity as well as markets for the materials" (qtd. in Gold 1990, B4). In response, Polan outlined plans to construct several additional public materials recovery facilities. They would be owned, financed, and overseen by the Department of Sanitation but constructed and operated under contract to private-sector firms. The first two would be sited in Staten Island and Brooklyn. In the long run, it was anticipated that the city would need "as many as ten large-scale processing facilities to accommodate the tonnage" of expanding recycling programs— at least five of which would be city owned (Gold 1990, B4).

The Department of Sanitation began considering the construction of a materials recovery facility at Fresh Kills in 1990. Plans for construction continued through 1993, and the department applied to the New York State Department of Environmental Conservation to fund half of the $17.5 million price tag for capital costs. The project's financing depended on economies of scale. It was estimated that if a 300-ton-per-day capacity were achieved, processing would run the city almost $40 per ton with an additional $11 per ton in capital costs over twenty years. Revenues, in turn, would generate about $22 per ton, for an overall net cost per ton of around $29. And if capacity were increased to 600 tons per day (which would raise capital costs to $20 million), this net cost would fall to only $16 per ton (NYC DS 2004).

Despite the required efficiencies, political constraints in 1994 caused the project to be downsized. Staten Island Borough president Guy Molinari—at that point deeply engaged in the local fight to close the Fresh Kills landfill—voiced objections to the transport of any additional out-of-borough waste to Staten Island. The scope was reduced to a smaller, Staten Island–only project. Yet just at that time plans for Visy's paper-only materials recovery facility, also to be located in Staten Island, began to take shape. In order to secure the Visy plant, the city agreed to supply it with Staten Island paper, meaning that the envisioned materials recovery facility's scope would be further curtailed to handling only commingled metal, glass, and plastic. At that point, the economies of the system could not be worked out. By the end of 1994, the plan for a public materials recovery facility was officially canceled.

The vision of a system of public materials recovery facilities also started to come under fire from the business community. In 1993, the private recycling industry, organized under the aegis of the New York/New Jersey Coalition of Recycling Enterprises, started publicly challenging the "$125 million city program to build five publicly owned centers in five boroughs" (Breznick 1993, 7). Asserting that their own materials recovery facilities were running below capacity, these enterprises sought to block the Department of Sanitation's requests for capital funds in the city council. The department responded that "city-owned plants would handle more sophisticated sorting and separating, cost less to operate, process more materials more efficiently, . . . stimulate the sagging market for recyclables," and cut down on transportation costs for city sanitation trucks (qtd. in Breznick 1993, 7). The coalition, joined by the New York Chamber of Commerce and Industry, countered that "instead of spending tax dollars, the city should merely set the regulatory standards and let the free market reign" (qtd. in Breznick 1993, 7). Environmental groups were neutral. As the NYPIRG (a leading bottle-bill and curbside recycling proponent organization) put it, "We have no preference . . . we just want to get (recycling) done" (qtd. in Breznick 1993, 7).

In May 1994, the East Harlem recycling processing center was permanently closed. At that point six years old, the facility was considered costly and obsolete. The *New York Times* noted that "the decision came as a blow to community leaders in East Harlem who had lobbied for city, state and Federal money to build the plant in 1985 as a public-private partnership" (Kennedy 1994, 8). It didn't help that 1994 was experiencing a very poor recyclables market, with "recycling centers across the country . . . backed up with empty plastic soda bottles, glass containers, cans, and newspapers" (Shantzis 1994, A14). Manufacturers were, in fact, finding it cheaper to buy raw materials than recycled ones.

Development of public materials recovery facilities was not pursued after that. The development of the Visy Paper Mill met the city's needs for a reliable, cost-effective, and environmentally sound[6] method of handling much of its paper, but that left the more troublesome commingled metals, glass, and plastic still in need of primary processing. The city needed firms of a size and capacity capable of taking large tonnages of commingled materials, day in and day out, no matter how tough the market became. This imperative limited the range of options available. The only firms able to take on the daily tonnages reliably were enterprises owned and operated by established waste-hauling and disposal firms in the New York area, some of which had been active in commercial refuse carting for decades. None of these firms engaged in remanufacturing. Instead, their profits depended solely on selling sorted and baled recyclables from both residential *and* commercial sectors on an open secondary-materials market. This market included brokers, buyers, and remanufacturers located throughout the United States and abroad.

In 2001, shortly before the onset of the post–September 11 fiscal crisis, the constellation of firms holding processing contracts for commingled metal, glass, and plastic rebid en masse, asking double the processing fees they had charged previously. This rebid would lead in early 2002 to the temporary suspension of glass and plastics recycling that so angered the New York City public. In the early 2000s, the firm Hugo Neu Schnitzer East, a leader in the scrap-metal industry, held a small city contract for bulk metal processing.[7] In the aftermath of September 11, "Ground Zero" turned out to be a major source of scrap metal that, after forensic analysis by the FBI, was processed just like any other bulk metal for which the city had responsibility. The collapse of existing contractual arrangements with waste-management firms processing metal, glass, and plastic and Hugo Neu Schnitzer East's enhanced role in the wake of the events of September 11 opened the contracting field to new directions for primary processing. The scrap-metal firm was among those most qualified to respond to the Department of Sanitation's 2003 request for proposals for the long-term processing of commingled metal, glass, and plastic (at such time as the latter two could be reintroduced to the curbside recycling program). Hugo Neu Schnitzer East was tentatively selected as having the winning proposal in 2004. The relationship ultimately grew into an economic development project for a publicly financed, barge-accessible materials recovery facility in Brooklyn when the multinational firm SimsMetal acquired Hugo Neu Schnitzer East in 2006. This time the package included a parcel of waterfront land transferred to Sims from the New York Police Department and a pledge by the city to split all capital costs of building and operating the multimillion-dollar materials recovery facility. Like Visy, this arrangement was initiated by actors within local and regional governments and negotiated with a large firm that would market sorted New York City recyclables globally.

As with the Visy deal, local environmental groups hailed the Sims-Metal project and interpreted it as being the result of their continued advocacy to show the economic benefits of the curbside program. On its Web site, the NRDC excitedly welcomed the resumption of the collection of glass and plastic, echoing a position within the Zero Waste community and the recycling movement overall that the city had "woken up" to the error of its ways in cutting plastic and glass recycling two years earlier: "NRDC and other environmental groups joined forces to prove that recycling is cost-effective—and, just one year later, New York City was on course to fully restore its recycling program" (NRDC 2004). A year later the New York City Independent Budget Office issued a report that angered this same community, which fully expected the this report to support the defense of recycling on economic grounds. The report concluded that "recycling metal, plastic, paper and glass in New York is more expensive than simply sending all the refuse to landfills and incinerators, even if city residents resume the habit of separating a sizable share of those kinds of waste" (Lipton 2004, B5). Since that time, members of the recycling movement in and around New York City, including those advocating Zero Waste, have celebrated the Sims project as they have endeavored to re-research the economics of recycling to show its cost effectiveness (Dimino and Warren 2004). They have also continued to champion local remanufacturing projects organized around local self-reliance and other very recent legislative initiatives to force extended producer responsibility or public provision of recycling service for electronic waste, plastic bags, rechargeable batteries, and household hazardous waste (thus echoing the tensions of the early 1970s between bottle bills and curbside recycling.)

I address these most recent developments in producer responsibility in the next chapter. For now, I return to the subject of the Zero Waste enterprise—its social meaning and its material significance. The successes and failures of recycling economic development in New York City in the 1990s suggest that there are structural barriers to realizing many of the assumed benefits of this model. As I argue, these same barriers apply even with other examples of flourishing Zero Waste enterprises elsewhere.

Locally Closed-Loop Assumptions

Stripped of particular political, geographic, or historical context, the concept of the closed loop can be thought of in the following way. The linear order of business is the progression of materials through stages of extraction, manufacture, distribution, consumption, and disposal. The closed loop, in contrast, bends the end of the arrow back to its beginning, with discards entering at the stage of manufacture (with recycling) or retail (with reuse). In either case, the materials targeted are frequently metaphorically likened to mineable deposits (ores) or to stands of renewable resources (forests).

Applying the idea of the closed loop to the question of urban waste requires application of jurisdictional scale to the abstract cyclical model. If the benefits of a closed-loop scenario are to accrue directly or even indirectly to urban residents (as taxpayers, potential employees, and community members), then at least some—but preferably all—of the post collection steps of processing, remanufacturing, and marketing must take place within city limits as well. Who are the consumers of remanu-factured goods made from local, residential recycled content? They may be individual residents or local businesses or, as is often the case when closed-loop scenarios are envisioned, the local state. Whether voluntarily or in response to procurement guidelines, public-agency procurement of locally made recycled-content products is frequently called for as an integral step to local loop closing (Dimino and Warren 2004). Public purchasing, it is often stated, will "create local markets," which will have salubrious effects backward in the loop for marketing and distribution, remanufacturing, and primary processing ventures that work within city limits (O'Neill and Sheehan 1993).

The success of large-scale, private primary processors and the failure of specialized secondary processors (remanufacturers) in New York City is not, I argue, unique to this location. It indicates, albeit in a form spe-cific to the Big Apple, some of the inherent barriers to realizing the envisioned benefits of local-loop closure. These barriers stem from scalar incompatibilities between the goals of loop closing and the spaces of materials exchange. One such incompatibility is that most remanufactur-ers need a clean supply of materials but do not necessarily require large volumes—especially if they are the type of small enterprise that thrives in a dense urban environment such as New York City. Thus, their input requirements are frequently at odds with what the recycling citizens "supply." At the same time, thanks in part to a recycling movement that historically and currently focuses on the quantity of curbside collections, the local state must continuously collect and move along large quantities of recyclables, whatever their composition. But municipal recycling col-lections are not, despite the allure of the comparison, akin to urban forestry or mining. They are not the gathering of inputs to production; they are the management of by-products of consumption. Unlike suppli-ers of raw materials, consumers do not respond in quantity or quality to producers' needs.

Any remanufacturer seeking to use residential recyclables has to adjust to the reality of the feedstock. The feedstock is stuff that has been used at home and put out in mixed form in a bin or toter for recycling col-lection in a compacting truck, taken to a materials recovery facility, and sorted out in a variety of steps using methods designed *not* to set aside and clean every particle of use carefully and lovingly, but to chug great quantities of material through and extract exchange value based on old-fashioned business calculus. For this reason, in most cases residential recyclables will underperform alternative secondary sources. Presorted

streams of recyclables from businesses, scrap from other industrial processes that by its nature is cleaner and more homogenous (think of cuttings on the factory floor), and even reclaimed deposit containers will be
vastly more efficient to use in manufacturing due to their cleanliness and
quality. Although this difference does not absolutely preclude the development of small-scale manufacturers that make goods out of residential
recyclables, it makes other kinds of development far more likely. Primary
materials recovery facility operators, who do not engage in the challenge
of manufacturing and can devote space and labor to the task of processing, are far more adept at handling recyclables from residents. Not only
are the jobs created by these firms low wage, unskilled, dirty, and sometimes dangerous (Weinberg, Pellow, and Schnaiberg 2000), but the
outputs are not fashioned into goods for local consumption. The outputs—bales of plastics, scrap metal, crushed glass, and loads of waste-
paper—are sold to a wide array of brokers and manufacturers, seeking
prices on regional, national, and global markets.

Locally based recycled-content manufacturers who actually take in
more than tiny quantities of secondary input tend to be for-profit enterprises that can handle large quantities of mixed, low-quality recyclables.
These firms extract a profit by marketing their product on markets wherever those markets may be. Visy Paper is an example of such a firm. In
its case, a multimillion-dollar package of loans, tax incentives, and con-
cessions from the city, the state, and other local interests were instrumental in wooing a cost-effective processing capacity to locate within
New York City. Unlike other ventures that failed (such as the recycled
paper mill subject of the book *Bronx Ecology* [Hershkowitz and Lin
2002]), Visy did not have to secure investment from a coalition of private
developers—it was an established concern with an existing Northeast
presence. What enabled it to come to New York City and make new
stuff out of city discards was its ability to accept a less-than-clean, mixed
stream of recyclable paper without fail. This stream was remanufactured
into a useable product within city limits but didn't stay there.

The migration of recycled commodities out of localities is the rule,
not the exception, and government procurement can do little to keep
materials close to home. Maureen Smith has noted this phenomenon at
the federal scale as well. In her detailed analysis of the forest and paper
industry, she observes that Clinton's 1993 Executive Order mandating
recycled-content procurement by the federal government was "quite out
of proportion to both the complexity of the task, and, ultimately, the
limitations of the tool." She writes, "Although consuming a good deal

of paper and symbolically important, the federal government neverthe-less accounts for less than 3 percent of domestic paper consumption. Assuming (generously) that half the government's paper purchases were affected by [the new recycling standards] . . . this still left about 99 percent or so of domestic paper unaddressed in direct terms" (1997, 185–186). The federal scale at least has the virtue of influencing move-ments of recyclables to remanufacturers across state lines. The stimula-tive effect of municipal procurement must by definition be even more circumscribed—although a priori reasoning to this effect has failed to dampen constant enthusiasm among recycling advocates for the untapped potential of city purchasing to create local markets. The "limitations of the tool" has been borne out empirically, though. As far as localities go, New York City would seem in a better position than most to spend enough to influence markets. Its agencies spend $7 billion annually on goods and services. A portion of these goods might, in theory, be fabri-cated using recycled content. Hence, there are frequent calls for the city to mobilize its massive purchasing power and "buy recycled." Yet it stands to reason that if local economic development gains are expected to flow from public procurement of such items, they must be made in New York City or out of city content or both. Each condition significantly narrows the potential field of impact that city purchasing can make.

This situation can be seen most clearly in the case of paper. The City of New York purchases a significant quantity of recycled-content office paper each year. This paper is produced by a variety of large paper manufacturers with plants nationwide. Visy Paper produces linerboard for corrugated boxes that it markets nationally and internationally. Given the difficulties that firms manufacturing finished products from residential recyclables face in New York City, the selection of recycled-content products made in the city or out of city residential recycling is quite limited. The city is then left with some very weak options. It can buy products made outside the city that contain materials processed by materials recovery facilities that accept New York City recyclables, or it can commit to paying artificially high prices for a few locally made supplies—some of which may not meet specifications in the best manner (such as the cones from Utility Plastics). This dilemma becomes particu-larly pressing when city agency purchasing and contracting are subject to competing demands for thrift and accountability by the public and oversight agencies (Lueck 1994). The potential impact of the city's pur-chasing power on local recycling markets becomes even more constrained under such pressures. The probability that a local remanufacturing industry will emerge in response to city agency demand thus becomes very tenuous.

Most important for this argument, the recycling/Zero Waste advocacy community ends up overstating and underexamining the link between recycling, city purchasing, and local economic development. In her study, Smith noted a similar degree of confusion among citizen groups, such as in the case of a city, West Sacramento, California, bent on attracting a vastly overscaled paper mill to it. The proposed mill, which would absorb all of Sacramento's paper recycling as well as much of the state's supply, offered local jobs and potential tax revenues but was geared toward profit maximization at scales of exchange well beyond the city, which meant, among other ills, a burden on local environmental quality that was disproportionate to expected benefits. Smith writes: "The city seemed immune to an appreciation of the difference between local impacts and regional or state benefits and to the idea that it actually mattered *where* the various environmental and economic costs and benefits would be distributed" (1997, 218, emphasis in original). In the case of New York, it was the local Zero Waste community that failed to consider scale with regard to impacts and benefits. What this community overlooked most obviously was the need for reliable primary processing capacity at a scale large enough to take in the very mixed curbside collections that earlier generations of this same community had fought tooth and nail to have picked up at public expense (see chapter 2). Absent support for the construction of public infrastructure to provide this capacity, New York City had little choice but to turn to the only other providers available—the waste-management industry—until such time as it could secure processors that operated outside the disposal-maximizing paradigm of big waste management.

California as Comparison

How unique is New York City's case? Can closed-loop approaches work locally or even regionally under different legislative and institutional circumstances? The case of California offers an additional perspective.

Both California and New York are economic powerhouses, situated on coasts with proximity to port-based export of scrap and sorted recyclables. Both states have container-deposit laws and statewide recycling, economic-development programs. In these senses, they are comparable. At the same time, California's regulatory structure for waste management is much more highly developed than New York's. California has the nation's most comprehensive recycled-content laws for glass, plastic trash bags, and rigid plastic container manufacturers. Its State Agency Buy Recycled Campaign requires and coordinates state agencies' purchasing of recycled-content goods and the putting of state-certified recycled-content manufacturers in touch with procurement personnel through an extensive database. And its Recycling Market Development Zone program oversees a statewide initiative in which loans, technical assistance, and product marketing are provided to businesses that use materials from the waste stream to manufacture their products within any of 40 separate areas of the state, each with its own "zone administrator." These and other aspects of waste management are overseen by one well-funded agency—CalRecycle (formerly the California Integrated Waste Management Board [CIWMB]).

Alameda County, located to the east of San Francisco and home to Berkeley, has its own well-developed and progressive regional waste-management agency that operates under the Web address "stopwaste. org." The quality and comprehensiveness of both California's statewide and Alameda's countywide efforts to create markets for processed recyclables and stimulate recycling-based business make the Zero Waste enterprise, closed-loop approach a prime candidate for success. If it can make it anywhere, it would be in Alameda County, California.

The statewide recycling economy in California has been studied in depth using the NRC's *Recycling Economic Information Study* framework, which has also been applied to the U.S. economy as a whole as well as to the Northeast region in which New York is situated (NRC 2001). As with nationwide studies and studies of the Northeast, NRC evaluations of California and its municipalities show that reuse and recycling activities create substantial sales, income, and jobs. The *Recycling Economic Information* framework examines the "interdependencies that industries, institutions, and households have with each other in a region of study" in terms of economic impacts such as employment rates, industry receipts, revenues, and value added (NRC 2001, i). It is beyond their scope, however, to assess the degree to which materials flows are kept local. Focus is instead on economic impacts of collection, processing, remanufacture, and reuse as part of the "big economic picture" for California, which includes import and export of materials across city, county, state, and even national borders (NRC 2001).

In fact, reports published by the NRC and CIWMB confirm that the export of secondary materials remains a major feature of the state's recycling economy. In the mid-1990s, the CIWMB wrote that "the current reality of secondary material markets in California is that large quantities of material from California or other States are exported through California because transportation costs to domestic markets are prohibitive, domestic markets are not available, or foreign markets provide better prices than domestic markets." In reference to the idea of the closed loop at a national scale, the CIWMB acknowledges the "drawbacks of shipping industrial feedstocks overseas when they could be used to produce higher value goods in the United states." Yet it also draws attention to what I discussed earlier as the "reality of the residential feedstock," noting that "export markets for secondary materials have played an important role in markets for California's postconsumer materials by absorbing large quantities of the secondary materials generated . . . that local recycling facilities do not provide demand for . . . with most secondary material characterized by high volumes and low values" (1996, 1). At the same time, California's recycled-content manufacturing laws, in combination with its proactive recycling-market development and state procurement efforts, have succeeded in stoking the state's economic engine with regard to recycling. Although California does export processed recyclables and recycled-content goods out of state and correspondingly imports recycled feedstocks in order to meet content mandates, its robust regulatory structure has succeeded to a degree in closing the loop at the state scale (CIWMB 1996).

But what about closing the loop locally? The NRC's *Los Angeles Recycling Economic Information Study* (City of Los Angeles 2001) and my informal discussions with Recycling Market Development Zone administrators there and in San Francisco suggest that very little of the residential recycling collected in either city is remanufactured into new goods, much less subsequently consumed, within city limits. Despite successful residential programs and highly developed market-development efforts, these materials tend to flow where they can obtain the best price—and more often than not this price is beyond the urban scale.

The case of a project specifically designed to stimulate *regional* market development in Alameda County sheds further light on challenges to closing the loop at smaller scales, especially for large-volume residential materials. In 1998, the U.S. EPA and the CIWMB launched the Jobs through Recycling program in collaboration with the Alameda County Waste Management Authority and several other entities to "establish regional recycling markets for locally generated waste" (CIWMB 2003). This project was notable in that it was *not* conceived primarily to address a problem with waste diversion (the county had a 50 percent diversion rate already), but specifically to "reduce reliance on out-of-region export markets" and to "demonstrate the economic and environmental benefits derived from regional recycling markets" (CIWMB 2003, 2). Economic benefits would be measured in terms of jobs created, investments kept regional, and cost savings; and environmental impacts would be assessed in terms of diversion beyond 50 percent as well as reduced traffic congestion, air emissions, and fuel consumption.

As a result of the project, nine businesses were started or expanded, providing roughly 100 new jobs and infusing more than $10 million in capital outlay in infrastructure in Alameda County. These businesses included two firms specializing in remanufacturing wood reclaimed through deconstruction (one a mill, one a cabinetry manufacturer), a nonprofit salvage operation for felled trees, a nonprofit reuse center for building materials and bicycles, another nonprofit reclaiming and reusing old computers, a tire recycling and crumb rubber–manufacturing facility, a mattress-recycling operation, a construction and demolition waste–reclamation facility, and a glass-recycling plant. In total, these businesses diverted more than 140,000 tons of material in a year, over and above the 1.9 million tons of diversion already taking place in the county in the absence of the program. The lion's share of the additional diversion was by the glass recycler (60,000 tons of material) and the construction and demolition debris firm (65,000 tons) (CIWMB 2003).

Although the project was clearly successful in adding to diversion and attracting business to the county, there was mixed evidence that it contributed to closing the loop at a countywide or even larger regional scale. Specialty Crushing, the construction and demolition waste–reclamation company, reported that the majority of its feedstock *did* come from Alameda County, but Alameda County supplied the Container Recycling Alliance glass facility with only a "small fraction of the total . . . feedstock required," with the balance coming from "throughout the Western United States and from as far away as Hawaii and Washington" (CIWMB 2003, 26). Both firms, furthermore, marketed materials outside the county but within the state—Specialty Crushing to "customers throughout California," and Container Recycling Alliance (a subsidiary of Waste Management, Inc.) to the Gallo Winery in Modesto, south of Alameda County (CIWMB 2003, 27). Firms processing relatively small tonnages of specialized items from the waste stream (wood and other deconstruction materials, tires, mattresses, and electronics) did subsist by and large on feedstock primarily from Alameda County, with end products going to regional and national markets throughout the United States and in certain cases to Mexico. However, only two of the businesses, Community Woodworks lumber mill and Ersch Recycled Millworks, were not reliant at all on extracounty export markets. Overall, one major finding of this project was that "large processors, as well as small businesses, need specialized types and larger quantities of feedstock," than are currently available through Alameda County's two materials recovery facilities (CIWMB 2003, 10). As the CIWMB noted, "Although most of the businesses [assisted by Jobs through Recycling] primarily receive feedstock from Alameda County, just about all depended on [feedstock] from" four neighboring counties (CIWMB 2003, 10). This configuration, in the CIWMB's opinion, demonstrated that regional recycling markets cross jurisdictional lines to serve a "wasteshed," which is defined for each business by the volume and specialization of feedstock it requires (CIWMB 2003, 2). Another major finding of the project was the difficulty in assessing the success in meeting the environmental goals of reduced traffic congestion, air emissions, fuel consumption, and toxics as a result of regionalizing markets that had previously operated at larger geographic scales. The CIWMB noted that "the [Jobs through Recycling] team was challenged to quantify the environmental benefits of regional markets" due to the continued need for businesses to transport materials in and out of the county, to and from destinations throughout California and beyond (2003, 10). Although some of these challenges were methodological (relating to inadequate transportation models or insufficient data), others stemmed from the fact that "as the definition of the 'regional market' changed [from Alameda County to a larger multicounty area], greater distances had to be traveled" (CIWMB 2003, 11).

Models of Planning: Great Ideas at Small Scales

The CIWMB's *Benefits of Regional Recycling Markets: An Alameda County Study* (2003) profiles a number of reuse operations, although Berkeley's Urban Ore is not among them. CalRecycle features on its Web site the now famous operation of a resource-recovery park, noting its plans (still tentative as of today) to add

subtenants whose businesses focus on reuse or manufacturing from recycled feedstocks. The park will operate like a mall, based on recovering materials and keeping resources in the economic stream. Although no subleases have been signed yet, potential subtenants include: A nonprofit organization that rebuilds and upgrades computers and then sells them at low cost to low-income people; A company that makes high-quality countertops out of recycled glass embedded in Portland cement (similar to granite); an overflow warehousing for another reuse company; and a blacksmith who makes products from scrap steel. (CIWMB 2007)

Although this expansion is still in the planning stages, the success of Urban Ore's current operations is already widely acclaimed. The Mercer County, New Jersey, planning study (ECAER 2001) that cites Urban Ore as a waste transfer station alternative also references a profile of the organization in a widely circulated report published in 1997 by the Institute for Local Self Reliance (Platt 1997). Today, visioning documents worldwide continue to point to Urban Ore as an alternative model to existing structures of waste management. As one Canadian Zero Waste consultant stated, "The firm (Urban Ore) advocates the end of the age of waste and designs disposal facilities for zero waste. Every community in North America should have a retail store for used goods like Urban Ore" (Jesson 2000).

Urban Ore featured prominently as a planning blueprint in the first formal articulation of Zero Waste activism in New York City as well. In 2004, the coalition of New York City waste activists that had authored *Taking Out the Trash* (Warren 2000) and *Why Waste the Future?* (NYC WPC 2002) reorganized as the New York City Zero Waste Campaign and released a document meant to inform the expected 2006 update of the city's Solid Waste Management Plan. The document, *Reaching for Zero: The Citizens' Plan for Zero Waste in New York City*, presented recommendations formatted with milestones and timelines so as to be easily incorporated into the bureaucratic structures of city waste planning. As with prior documents, the *Citizen's Plan* explicitly acknowledged the ties between the Zero Waste campaign and the environmental justice movement, both in the nation and within New York City. Its stated objective was to reduce

New York City's waste exports to very close to zero in 20 years, through a combination of waste prevention, reuse, recycling and composting. This plan will not only reduce and ultimately eliminate the crushing expense of waste exports from the City, but it will also keep dollars spent on waste management circulating within the City's economy, creating industry and jobs here rather than shipping our dollars along with our waste to out of state locations. (Dimino and Warren 2004, 7)

As such, the plan represented, in its own words, "considerable public input" into the policymaking process (17). One of the features of this input entailed the notion that reuse enterprises are a viable method to divert much of the "hundreds of thousands of tons of perfectly useful items [that] are thrown away in New York City at an enormous cost to taxpayers and businesses" (59).

The *Citizen's Plan* specifically proposed a series of "municipal sorting facilities and community managed reuse complexes supported by both municipal and supplementary truck fleets" (Dimino and Warren 2004, 61). It called on the city to fund periodic collections of reusables using designated "reuse fleets." Deliveries would be routed to municipally funded, yet-to-be-built "reuse materials recovery facilities" that would act as points of triage, identifying which items might be sold as is, which need repair, and which would be suitable only for spare parts. State-funded job-training and apprenticeship programs would teach restoration skills and "prepare jobs seekers for jobs in reuse" (61). Reuse coordinators, funded by the city and located in each community district, would coordinate the collection of reusables and moreover facilitate periodic neighborhood swap meets, at the end of which remaining items would be collected by the municipal reuse fleet. Each recommodified discard would feature a New York City "Seal of Approval" indicating that it met quality-control standards (66).

The vision was of a careful, considerable, municipally funded yet community-based effort to go through discards fastidiously and conserve use value at every conceivable point, providing jobs, low-cost needed goods, and community cohesion in the process. I find something deeply satisfying in such a vision; I believe many share this satisfaction when they realize that a discard can be used in some way by someone (Botha 2004; W. King 2008). But it is important to step back from the allure of such thrift and examine what was being proposed in terms of tonnage. The *Citizen's Plan for Zero Waste* considered this vision achievable at the level of hundreds of thousands of tons per year. This point is important: hundreds of thousands of tons, in relation to the New York City residential waste stream of some 3.7 million tons annually, *are* materially significant. The advocacy of a plan to address these tonnages through reuse makes a claim that the model of the reuse enterprise, the Zero Waste enterprise, can, with enough state support, substantially diminish quantities of waste going to export. This end is to be achieved by "developing the reuse infrastructure and raising public awareness" (Dimino and Warren 2004, 60). And according to those who advocate this plan, the makings of momentum are already here: "New York City has a network of small but successful reuse programs already in place. Reuse enterprises range from non-profit programs to for-profit businesses and include thrift stores, used equipment stores, reuse centers, salvage yards, refurbishers, food recovery and distribution, and on-line material exchanges and web posting sites. While they are limited in resources, these programs have had a significant impact" (Dimino and Warren 2004, 60).

Is it reasonable to think that discards treated through reuse will be able to overcome the scalar and economic barriers that those destined for recycling have not been able to? Or if scalar barriers to the marketing of reusables are ignored (i.e., if reusable discards of New York City origin that are restored to use value are marketed outside the city), to think that such enterprises will address far more substantial tonnages than the network of "small but successful reuse programs already in place"? According to the *Citizen's Plan*, yes, it is reasonable: "The most noted example of a successful reuse operation is Berkeley's Urban Ore, which receives a wide variety of reusables . . . [and] resells them to the public. Supported initially by the city of Berkeley, CA, it is now a thriving business, receiving no subsidies. *About half of the four hundred tons of reusables per day it receives is delivered directly by the city of Berkeley*" (Dimino and Warren 2004, 60, emphasis added). Half of 400 tons per day, or 200 tons per day, is 73,000 tons per year. Were this the actual tonnage being delivered by the city of Berkeley to Urban Ore, diversion through the operation would constitute half of Berkeley's overall annual diversion. This amount indeed would be materially significant. But this figure is not the tonnage—the tonnage is at most 8,000 per year. And the city of Berkeley delivers nothing directly to Urban Ore. Urban Ore's arrangement with the city allows it to cull materials from the transfer station, using its own labor. Urban Ore presently handles 7,000 to 8,000 tons of materials per year, 10 percent of which come from the City of Berkeley's transfer station (Hess 2005). The City of Berkeley contracts with Urban Ore, paying it $40 per ton to take materials salvaged by Urban Ore employees from the tipping floor, saving the city $60 per ton in avoided disposal costs (Kamlarz 2008). The remainder of its input comes mainly from deliveries from individuals and businesses within and outside Berkeley. Berkeley generates more than 250,000 tons of municipal solid waste per year, recycling about 57 percent of it through curbside collections, yard-waste composting, and deliveries to Urban Ore. Out of the more than 140,000 tons diverted, at most 8,000 tons go through Urban Ore (assuming all Urban Ore deliveries come from Berkeley, which is most likely not the case).

In the imagination of the New York City Zero Waste community, Urban Ore as enterprise model has become abstracted from its measureable material achievements and has been mobilized in contexts far afield to hold out the promise of something that has very little chance of being realized. However, it should be noted that reuse is but one "piece of zero" advocated by the *Citizen's Plan*. As with the recycling movement that concurrently advocated for curbside recycling and producer-focused legislation, the New York City Zero Waste movement has proposed multiple, simultaneous strategies for waste reduction. Among them are to build on the successes of the Visy Paper Mill and the soon-to-be established contract with (then) Hugo Neu Schnitzer East as models for local-loop closure. Ignoring the vast differences between community-based remanufacturing (à la Utility Plastics) and the state-initiated, multinational deals of Visy and Sims, the *Citizen's Plan* argued:

We have a homegrown example of what investment in recycling in NYC can achieve[:] Visy Paper. . . . *Reaching for Zero* proposes that the City focus on using its discarded materials and waste management policy as a tool for economic development, thereby accomplishing several objectives: diversifying the entities that process materials in the City's waste stream; *making the City less dependent on a few large multinational corporations* . . . building industries within the City, like Visy Paper that will utilize recycled materials to make new products, creating jobs. (Dimino and Warren 2004, 14, emphasis added)

The scalar exigencies of primary and secondary processing of recyclables were muddled and elided in this proposal, which went on to state that " the zero waste infrastructure will most likely be made up of hundreds of smaller businesses, instead of large companies like Visy Paper, the zero waste office should plan for staff sufficient to attract remanufacturers, to target particular materials and to develop innovative incentives for existing and potential new businesses" (Dimino and Warren 2004, 108). The plan also overlooked the history of private-sector opposition to public materials recovery facilities and the apparent consent by the recycling movement to the private alternative, calling for a reversal of the city's past "failure . . . to invest for the long term in modern technology" with the construction of a new municipal facility (Dimino and Warren 2004, 65).

In sum, the *Citizen's Plan* showed little understanding of the political economy of reusable and recyclable commodities within and outside New York City, nor was it informed by historical experience. Its proposals were premised not just in factual error, but in a fundamental lack of contextual perspective about the solutions advocated. It was therefore not surprising that the "considerable input" of many dedicated Zero Waste activists was hardly felt in the 2006 Comprehensive Solid Waste

Management Plan that it hoped to inform substantially. The *Citizen's Plan* was in fact sufficiently optimistic about the viability of its proposals that it purposely mimicked the format of the city's earlier drafts of the Comprehensive Solid Waste Management Plan so as to ease incorporation of the *Citizen's Plan* ideas. Here is how its contribution was acknowledged in the city's final 2006 Comprehensive Solid Waste Management Plan: "While the advocates of 'Zero Waste' are to be lauded for setting the diversion bar high, the City must be realistic and recognize that many decisions regarding what individuals and businesses do with their waste are beyond the City's direct or indirect control" (NYC DS 2006, 2-8). The point here is not to attack the Zero Waste movement in New York City, but to ask how and why its advocacy, which reflects a great deal of energy, study, organizing, and genuine commitment, has resulted in proposals that show such little material promise in terms of "reaching for zero." Outside of New York City, such efforts are frequently embraced rhetorically or on small scales to generate goodwill, even as the local state recognizes them as marginal (see, e.g., Brand 2007 and Saha 2009). Seattle and San Francisco, both considered leaders in sustainable waste management, are among cities that have formally adopted Zero Waste as a guiding framework for municipal-solid-waste-management planning. Each city contracts with private haulers and processors to collect vast quantities of commingled paper, metal, glass, and plastic for processing and sale to markets on a variety of scales, including on global markets. The high residential diversion rates that each of these cities achieves are attributable to their added collections of food- and yard-waste organics for centralized composting at local and regional scales.

Within New York City, the city council required extremely watered-down portions of the *Citizen's Plan* to secure its political support of passage of the Comprehensive Solid Waste Management Plan, premised on continuation of the same mix of trash disposal and curbside recycling programs that have been implemented since recycling came to New York. Although the Zero Waste movement celebrates the Sims deal as a vindication of its advocacy, the local government proceeds on its own path, working with scrap and remanufacturing firms to process recyclables and disposing of the rest via export contracts with the private waste-management industry.

The Eco-Industrial Park

An alternative to this outcome would be one in which stages of primary and secondary processing were organized not just at smaller scales, but in safer and more fulfilling workplaces than industrial-scaled materials recovery facilities, generating outputs that would be locally remanufactured into items for which there was stable local or regional demand. The resource-recovery park planned by Berkeley's Urban Ore, but not yet operational, is an example of a model for such an alternative. The most famous existing example of this phenomenon is in Kalundborg, Sweden, although there it is premised on industrial and not municipal by-products. In Kalundborg, a coal-fired power plant provides surplus heat to local residences and a nearby fish farm and sells steam to a large pharmaceutical plant. The fish farm converts its waste sludge to fertilizer; sulfur dioxide from the power plant's scrubber yields gypsum, which is then sold to a local manufacturer of drywall. Finally, fly ash and clinker from the power plant are used for local road building and cement production (Ehrenfeld and Gertler 1997).

Kalundborg's interfirm relationships arose without intentional planning and have been extensively studied as models for intentional projects (Desrochers 2002). Several scholars have identified the practical difficulties of replicating Kalundborg's organic model, arguing that enthusiasm surrounding its promise has elevated it to mythic status (see, e.g., Boons and Janssen 2004). Its municipal counterpart, the resource-recovery park, figures heavily in Zero Waste municipal planning, Here is the *Citizen's Plan* articulation of such a park for New York City:

The park would include both recycled material processing operations and manufacturers that can use the recycled materials to create new products. It can include one or more large firms that process several materials, like a traditional material recovery facility (MRF), as well as several smaller operations that add value to materials through repair, remodeling, refurbishing or remanufacturing. For example, in addition to a MRF, a park could have one or more companies that process the MRFs' glass output for markets like aggregate and sandblasting medium; take the MRFs' plastic and manufactures plastic lumber; and/or take in used tires and manufacture crumb rubber for use in playing fields or as an asphalt binder. (Dimino and Warren 2004, 65, 109)

Such parks remain on the drawing board not just in NYC but across the nation. Geographers David Gibbs and Pauline Deutz found in their 2003 survey of 10 actually existing eco-industrial parks throughout the United States that they were at best "in their early stages" of development, observing that "their contribution to both economic development and environmental policy, let alone social policies, is complicated and inchoate" (2005, 452). Gibbs and Deutz indicate that scalar constraints on the economy of by-product exchange, in particular the difficulty of matching outputs to inputs in the space of a park footprint, leads to, among other things, failure of projects to move beyond planning stages; cases in which eco-industrial parks become simply conglomerations of unrelated industries that integrate some sustainable energy, water, and other practices into their operations; or instances in which the ecotheme is dropped entirely, and the project continues as a manufacturing development zone.

Gibbs and Deutz note that their findings do not "argue that adopting [eco-industrial park] elements is not worthwhile. These [parks] can make a measureable, if undoubtedly modest, impact on the environment" (2005, 462). However, they are careful to distinguish modest gains from those that "make a significant environmental impact.The latter require both a larger scale and more critical engagement with often depoliticized visions of industrial ecology so as not to fall prey to the "danger of ambiguity" that casts aspiring projects as "sustainable" regardless of their material outcomes (2005, 456).

These authors' warnings highlight the importance to the Zero Waste movement of taking a stance that goes beyond the equivalent of saying, "We must try harder to integrate reuse enterprises, within the context of resource recovery parks, into comprehensive zero waste planning." Such an approach is political in that it casts the local and regional state, often allied with a solid-waste industry that offers industrial-scale materials recovery facility processing, as acting in opposition to the true outcomes of material sustainability in terms of tonnage and toxicity. At the same time, it misses questions of justice that are deeply bound up in the continued geographies of race and class as they relate to waste infrastructure in the United States. It bears repeating that, as of today, the Zero Waste movement advances the resource-recovery park model as a means to address past environmental injustice through labor and opportunity as well as to reroute materials flows away from noxious disposal and toward clean, creative revitalization. To the extent that its successes in the former sphere obscure its failure in the latter, the Zero Waste community must take note. The fact is that most stuff is still moving in ways that burden the same communities that have always borne such burdens. It is to this contention that I next turn.

Sufficiency and Justice

If reuse enterprises or envisioned resource-recovery parks offer good jobs and community benefits to neighborhoods sorely in need of them, with no pollution or stigmatizing downsides as industrial-scale waste facilities do, where is the harm in fostering and celebrating them? Moreover, is it really supposed to be up to residents of such communities—activists or otherwise—to factor comprehensive, sustainable planning for materially significant Zero Waste into their daily work and life? After all, such communities not only have borne the brunt of older, antiecological methods of disposal and recycling, but have enabled overconsumption among the white, affluent majority to proceed without nuisance. And with the proper support from government, who knows but that these small outfits can coalesce into something greater, something really able to stem the flow of trash to disposal? These responses are some I have received in my informal discussions with community-based activists and reuse practitioners in New York City. They raise valid points and require fully fleshed-out answers. In particular, they get to the question once again of responsibility—not only as it breaks down between producer and citizen, but among citizens unequally. As I argue in this book's conclusion, I differ from many in the environmental movement in that I do not believe that ecological activism and resistance require rolling up one's sleeves to take responsibility as "part of the solution," a precondition to making critique. We don't expect community residents to dig up and remediate Superfund sites with shovels and garden soil, so why should we expect them to divert large tonnages through reuse enterprises? But nor do I suggest that engaging in any material practice that revitalizes discards, at a small scale and even with little material impact, is a waste of time. To the contrary, such acts are fulfilling and sometimes financially rewarding acts of learning and creativity.

At issue here is material sufficiency, which raises some disturbing questions about the Zero Waste movement as a potential iteration of mainstream environmentalism in that its solutions are structurally though not ideologically (as with mainstream movements) inattentive to questions of the distribution of risk and health along lines of race, class, and power. In 1990, more than 100 leaders in the environmental justice movement confronted 10 of the largest environmental organizations with their failure to consider the role of racism in the identification of and solutions to environmental problems, critiquing their emphasis on wilderness protection to the exclusion of people's health and welfare (Shabecoff 1990). The relationship between mainstream environmentalism and the environmental justice movement has improved since then, if measured in the rhetorical support that the former shows for questions of justice. And the Zero Waste movement, in its explicit alliance with environmental justice movements in the struggle against incinerators and other waste facilities, certainly has lent more than rhetorical support. Yet in advancing great ideas that need to be tried at a small scale as first steps to a Zero Waste society, the movement commits many of the same errors that led recycling activism over the twentieth century to be diverted toward material insignificance, while big flows of materials continued not only to grow, but also to flow along lines that reproduced racism and classism geographically. As Sherry Cable, Tamara Mix, and Donald Hastings ask trenchantly, over the past two decades

what major structural changes occurred to facilitate a more equitable distribution of the environmental costs of production? None. No risky facilities are routinely constructed in white, affluent communities. No federal system of compensation pays citizens for the privilege of contaminating their communities. No national policy discussion has emerged to plan the redistribution of environmental costs and benefits of production. Instead, the organization of production remains entrenched in social institutions whose bureaucratic routines frequently produce racist outcomes, whether intentionally or unintentionally. (Cable, Mix, and Hastings 2005, 56)

The Zero Waste movement has quite unintentionally had a small role to play in maintaining the status quo. The tenacious adoration of the "small step" and the "start" that weaves through the recycling and Zero Waste imaginary has its naive and inadvertent companion in positive can-doism. Can-doism can be very counterproductive. There is a serious problem with the celebration of reuse or remanufacturing enterprises as solutions to too many problems at once, but in America we dearly love the notion of what the *Citizen's Plan for Zero Waste* hailed as "accomplishing several objectives" at the same time (Dimino and Warren 2004, 14). Win-win winism is premised on the three E's: equity, environment, and economy. Ecological modernization, discussed in chapter 3, sees the equity advanced through enlightened forms of corporate organization and "fair-trade" material sourcing, with environmental protection and green profit to be cultivated organically within a factory now understood ecologically. In quite a different context, Zero Waste reaches out to environmental justice at the moment when a victory of opposition has been achieved in terms of resisting an incinerator, a transfer station, or a landfill. Calling such moments achievements of "the early focus on the 'NO!'" Omar Freilla, a leading New York City–based environmental justice activist, writes that

while the focus of much of the environmental justice movement has been on directly opposing polluters this doesn't mean that community-based groups haven't been dreaming up visions of a better world. Yet while many of these groups imagine zero waste; pollutionless industry; green neighborhoods; and solar power as possible answers to the question "what other way is there?," most of them haven't had the luxury of time or resources to focus on bringing the alternatives they'd only dreamed of into reality. (2005, 2)

Zero Waste entrepreneurs have had such a luxury, and to their credit they want to share what they have learned and built. Here we find the Zero Waste–environmental justice nexus.

From a political standpoint, the social considerations behind the environmental justice movement's question "What other way is there?" are fully mature. Freilla's organization, Green Worker Cooperatives, takes direct aim at the structural inability of the treadmill of production to solve its own problems, noting that "the social injustices inherent in the capitalist marketplace cannot be ignored merely to reduce environmental impacts" (2005, 2). It is the material solution premised in Zero Waste that is insufficient. Among a variety of projects Freilla's organization undertook was the ReBuilder's Source, a worker-cooperative reuse center that sells salvaged building materials. Freilla notes, "The stuff you see here, if you look at it for what it is, is a toilet or a cabinet, it's not garbage. If you put it in a Dumpster, then it becomes waste. Context is everything. All we're doing is changing the context." Says Freilla, "The waste that exists depends on having a community that is also considered disposable. . . . Having a cheap place to throw everything away means having an easy way to keep stuff out of mind. You end up with a community that is dumped on" (qtd. in Gonzalez 2008, B1). The redefinition of neighborhood reputation away from waste stigma is fair enough, but a serious distortion occurs when we move from symbol and local opportunity to diversion of tonnage and reduction of toxicity. Sustainable South Bronx, a group allied to Freilla's and one of New York City's most active and influential environmental justice groups, noted in 2009 about its Zero Waste Campaign,

If city-wide garbage equity is important for shorter-term reduction of impacts from waste, the mid-term elimination of the root cause is Zero Waste. If New York City plans and invests appropriately, by 2025 it could have virtually no waste in need of export and it could create jobs and save money in the process. [Sustainable South Bronx] is a part of a city-wide coalition that helped to create the report *Reaching for Zero: A Citizen's Guide* [sic] *for Zero Waste* . . . which lays out an action plan for the City to achieve that goal and which influenced the City's Solid Waste Management Plan. (Sustainable South Bronx 2009)

In a critique of the contemporary environmental justice movement, Robert Benford traces the development of interactive, contested, and constantly renegotiated sets of meaning that characterize the discourse and practice of groups resisting environmental racism and classism. At the movement's outset in 1982, its explicit definition and denunciation of environmental racism and the linking of everyday as well as medically measured health outcomes to the practices of institutions of power, including the state and industry, made it innovative and potent. Regarding one of the movement's founders, Reverend Benjamin F. Chavis, then director of the United Church of Christ's Commission for Racial Justice, Benford writes that "Chavis identified racial discrimination in all matters pertaining to the environment as a problem, pointing a finger at government, industry, and mainstream environmental groups as the culprits. But whereas he explicitly and cogently articulated a diagnosis, the prognosis remained unstated and thus has to be inferred" (2005, 41). The prognosis—the vision of a better world—in Benford's view had to be articulated for the movement to continue. The early focus on the NO! would take it only so far. What was conceived of in terms of "YES!" was defined very broadly as "justice."

It was here that the environmental justice movement, says Benford, began to lose its potency. "Justice" was defined extremely vaguely and shallowly to encompass noncontroversial human rights for all. As such, the movement began to pose less of a threat to "white cultural narrations than its predecessor, 'environmental racism'" (2005, 43) and at the same time began to lose what Benford considers essential for any environmental or social movement—its critical edge, the criticality or radicality aimed at fundamental restructuring of global systems of production and consumption that undergird racism and other forms of power domination. Benford's conclusion is consistent with much critical environmental thought that sees the fundamental transformation of capitalism as the only fair and effective means of addressing the complex of environmental crises, of which solid waste is only a tiny vestige (O'Connor 1998; Burkett 1999; Foster 2000). Such transformation, through insurgency or radical restructuring of production and consumption, is tremendously difficult to get going, for reasons that can only be summarized here as having to do with the domination of all aspects of human life by priorities of market transaction.

With regard to solid waste, the construction of even faintly radical solutions has met with periodic and effective diversion in ways I discuss in previous chapters. When it comes to poor industrial neighborhoods of color burdened by waste facilities, resistance is extremely resource intensive and the object of only periodic and site-specific battles. The task is exhausting, and at moments of exhaustion, after a draining, protracted fight against a facility, when those who have been fighting look up and find a modicum of "time or resources to focus on bringing the alternatives they'd only dreamed of into reality," vexing and somewhat abstract questions of the scales of material exchange and the insufficiency of small starts don't find purchase. Mary Nelson, an environmental justice leader in Chicago, talks about this moment:

> I think there is a role for the protest, and a whole lot of things wouldn't happen if those protests didn't occur. But we've got to have people to find the way to go beyond the protest into the larger program, into long-term beneficial outcomes. I think this environmental stuff is so easily overwhelming because you are up against Goliath. You are little David, and it is very easy to feel isolated, to feel unappreciated, to get worn down. So, I can understand where people who are in the midst of the struggle, at the end of the struggle, have a hard time moving to the next place. They may feel that energy is taken away from them, leaving them more isolated and abandoned. So I can understand that, and all I can say is that, at some point, you need new energy in your group. And envisioning something beyond what you don't want does give us new energy and does give sense of new life and purpose and possibility. It is just really exciting stuff! (qtd. in Lee 2005, 225)

Gould, Schnaiberg, and Weinberg's study of curbside recycling of the 1980s and 1990s identifies (white) citizens' movements as inadvertently instrumental in enabling a "subtle redirection of political and social discourse" effected by institutions with a stake in continued growth (1996, 162). It was easy for producers to enlist the grassroots recycling movement, they argue, because of citizens' "lack of extralocal knowledge about both the economics and ecological impact of postconsumer wastes" (127). We should not expect activists in the environmental justice movement to be any more or less savvy about the scalar exigencies of waste valorization, but it is incumbent upon the Zero Waste movement, if it really does intend to work with the environmental justice movement, to pay attention to the scales of reuse and recycling so as not to reproduce busy-ness in a new form.

This attention should start with being frank about what the actually existing Zero Waste enterprise and the dream of a locally self-reliant recycling and remanufacturing economy can deliver. The history of actual successes and failures needs not to be taken as a limit, but rather as a practical guide. In 1970s New York City, groups that established community recycling centers went on to push for the institutionalization of curbside collections at scales too large for such centers to handle. Once curbside collection was mandated by law, the recycling movement immediately called for economic development around remanufacture that would provide multiple benefits to communities; however, that same community did not support the development of a series of medium-size materials recovery facilities on a public-works model. As the recycling movement continued to celebrate the promise of small, innovative firms with great ideas, not just in remanufacture but also in reuse, it also welcomed (and sometimes took credit for) city contracts with large, multinational firms outside the waste-management industry. Pratt Industries and SimsMetal are inheritors of the legacy of a scrap industry that fought so often and early for support from the recycling movement and against the waste-management empire (chapter 1). Even as arrangements with these firms were finalized, the (now) Zero Waste environmental community continued to champion the promise of the small Zero Waste enterprise, not just as a vehicle for creating jobs and building community ties, but in the face of all evidence as a method for increasing diversion to the point that by 2025 communities in the Bronx and Brooklyn would be spared the burdens of sited waste infrastructure.

This set of contradictory positions will not serve the interests of environmental justice in the near-term future. As the community-based reuse enterprise is championed as the structure for "justice," new inroads for producers' cultivation of busy-ness open up. It is important to point out that Zero Waste enterprises are today totally irrelevant to activities of producers who sell new goods. When demand is highly elastic, as it is with many goods that are sold for reuse, secondhand markets supplement rather than substitute for firsthand ones (Thomas 2003). A lack of one-to-one substitution is also seen on an economy-wide level for remanufactured goods—the aluminum and paper industries, for example, easily integrate secondary inputs into overall industrial-growth patterns, using primary and secondary sources selectively to increase profits (Barham, Bunker, and O'Hearn 1994; Smith 1997). Most important, Zero Waste enterprises, which work either on a social entrepreneurial model using grants from foundations and the state or on a private entrepreneurial model that follows the classic form of the "small business," do not tax producers directly or indirectly to fund the social and (minor) ecological benefits they provide. They either take it upon themselves or draw funds from the common pool. In fact, there is likely a monetary plus for producers (akin to "goodwill" on an asset balance sheet) in the fact that the Zero Waste enterprise, so optimistically celebrated as not just a success story, but also as a "can-do" model for solving several problems at once (poverty, pollution, waste) through good old American entrepreneurialism, provides the sense that progress is being made even though tonnage measures show that it isn't. This scenario is busy-ness in all its glory.

At the same time, projects such as Mary Nelson's—which featured extensive residential and commercial "green" development of her neighborhood to emphasize safe, livable distances from mass transit, energy efficiency, pollution mitigation, and good jobs—*are* truly exciting. So are projects such as Urban Ore, the ReBuilder's Source, and myriad others across the nation, including centuries-old institutions such as Goodwill Enterprises that have flourished in the reuse business alongside mass-scale disposal. But such projects need to be considered separately from solutions to the global-to-local flow of ever-increasing, heterogeneous products and packaging that can be efficiently moved into remanufacture today only through the model of the industrial-scale materials recovery facility. To humanize the materials recovery facility would require making it smaller, returning ownership to the community or to worker cooperatives, but the model of the small, public materials recovery facility clashes fundamentally with parallel exigencies imposed on municipal programs by the recycling movement—the collection of large quantities of mixed, curbside materials of a wide variety, with expense to taxpayers kept to a minimum. At the heart of the problem is the material composition of discards, the reality of the feedstock, which has to be addressed through larger scales of intervention into production that shift the costs of managing some materials away from citizens and back to manufacturers and that lead, under guidance from a data-gathering and data-disseminating state, to real and thorough redesign of products for repair and reuse as well as to homogenization of the range of synthetics making up discards today. It is to this challenge that I now turn.

5

Extended Plastics Responsibility: Producers as Reluctant Stewards

In 2009, Jill Fehrenbacher, a Brown-educated architect who writes a blog on environmental design called "Green Rant," fumed to her readership about her recent discovery that New York City's curbside recycling program limited the plastics it accepted for recycling to bottles and jugs only. Why, she asked, couldn't concerned citizens put other types of plastic packaging such as margarine tubs, deli containers, and salad trays out for curbside collection—especially when they bear the same number 1 or number 2 recycling codes that most plastic bottles and jugs do? Fehrenbacher's comments were an articulation of the confusion, frustration, and anger that many committed members of the U.S. recycling public feel about inconsistent and sometimes mystifying rules for municipal plastics recycling (Burton 2009). Noting correctly that most plastic bottles and jugs bear a number 1 or number 2 code stamp but that similarly coded number 1 and number 2 tubs and trays and other nonbottle plastics were excluded from the city's list of what to recycle, Fehrenbacher asked, "What does it matter what shape the container is in terms of its ability to be recycled?" (2009). In fact, the shape of the container does indeed have a great deal to do with all aspects of plastics recycling, and this little understood point is only the beginning of a set of complex and contradictory qualities of plastics production, consumption, recycling, and disposal.

In the context of the long history of urban trash, plastic wastes are *modern*. They occupy a status along with electronics and other potentially harmful household products—including auto batteries, household chemicals, thermostats, and products ironically marketed as environmental preferable alternatives to older, less-toxic equivalents (rechargeable batteries, compact fluorescent lightbulbs)—as wastes of the twentieth century. Modern wastes contrast with longer-historied discards such as metal, paper, wood, glass, and natural-fiber wastes that have remained steady or declined in municipal solid waste since the 1960's. (See appendixes I–III.) Yet neither their newness nor even their rate of growth is central to what makes modern wastes particularly problematic. In contrast to older materials more directly harvested from nature, modern wastes are synthetic, unpredictable, and above all heterogeneous.

Complex and differentiated products surge at constantly increasing rates through the economy, responding innovatively to expanding needs and desires, with efficiencies of light weight, strength, and low-input costs inscribed in their design (Krausmann, Gingrich, Eisenmenger, et al. 2009) At the same time, modern materials have unique downsides at end of life. Recycling, as has been discussed in previous chapters, requires the separation and sorting of discards into clean, homogeneous streams of inputs to remanufacture. Among other hurdles, heterogeneity within a single product or bound up in a mixed load drives up the cost and difficulty of the recycling process. Disposal, instead of recycling, is one favored option in the face of such costs; another is to seek out disadvantaged labor (prison workers in the United States, manual sorters in developing countries) to sort cost effectively (Puckett and Smith 2002, SVTC 2006). In both cases, the handling of modern discards frequently entails the slow or rapid release of uncertain risks to health and ecosystems at multiple points on local and global scales. These risks by and large stem from the ingestion of large or small pieces of modern materials by people and other forms of life as well as the release of heavy metals and toxic compounds into surrounding media when these materials are dismantled, burned, or buried (Grossman 2006; Lundberg 2010).

The problematic aspects of modern wastes in the United States have been countered by policy in an ad hoc, product-specific fashion that in past decades has increasingly called into question the curbside recycling collection model. Municipalities struggling to manage modern wastes in municipal solid waste and producers worried about future freedom to produce scramble to collect and sell modern materials on insufficient markets that are highly dependent on export to the developing world (Pellow 2007). As these methods fail to grapple with most plastics and many other hazardous products (including electronic waste, or e-waste, such as computers), competing policy models advanced by government–nonprofit coalitions have emerged. Producer-focused policies of the late twentieth and early twenty-first centuries include product bans, fees designed to reduce product consumption, and policies that transfer some or all of the responsibility of planning, financial, and operational aspects of product recovery to brand owners. As of 2010, hundreds of producer-focused legislative proposals are being contested in states and localities across the nation, entailing both conflict and coalition building among trade associations, regional and local governments, and waste-related policy and advocacy groups.

This chapter looks at plastic wastes as a case study of twenty-first-century U.S. modern-waste policy, as cities and states across the nation struggle with an overall waste-management system that still routes most materials to disposal. The problem of plastic wastes, I argue, cries out for a large-scale, comprehensive approach that roots out toxic plastics and routes nontoxic forms back to the production of things people actually need. In this regard, there is much to be learned from studies of the political economy of e-waste (Puckett and Smith 2002; Puckett, Westervelt, Gutierrez, et al. 2005; Grossman 2006; Pellow 2007). The dangers of export of e-waste for "recycling" to the developed world and the toxicity of heavy metals, brominated plastics, and other components of electronics have been thoroughly investigated. In the past decade, e-waste has been the subject of some of the strongest U.S. extended producer responsibility laws. Many have been developed with the participation of grassroots environmental groups that continue to document ongoing problems of hazardous e-waste dumping on developing countries (Sheehan and Spiegelman 2005; Pellow 2007).

Yet there are important differences between the two streams of modern wastes. Plastics, present in municipal solid waste at far greater tonnages than e-waste, have a different and quite varied status in solid-waste policy. Some varieties (bottles and other rigid containers—roughly 17 percent of all plastic wastes; see appendix V) constitute one of the four pillars of curbside recycling programs. Others (plastic shopping bags and Styrofoam,[1] accounting for roughly 12 percent of all plastic wastes) have a special status in litter and ocean debris due to their light weight and ingestibility and are today subject to various policies aimed at reducing their consumption or recycling them. Still other forms (plastics made of the polyvinyl chloride [PVC] or polystyrene [PS] polymers, including Styrofoam, which constitute another 12 percent of all plastics; and plastics containing certain additives, for which there are no separate percentage estimates) are strongly linked to human health problems, although as of yet there are no systematic policies in place to address these concerns. This varied status reflects the extreme heterogeneity in the group of materials we refer to with the common term *plastic* and importantly leaves almost 60 percent of all plastic wastes unaddressed by prevention or recycling programs or by policy initiatives of any kind.[2]

I argue in this chapter that producer-focused policies, which I define as those that ban products outright or discourage consumption using fees and those that require producers to take responsibility for managing spent products, are particularly appropriate for modern materials in general and for plastics in particular. These policies are potent, but they are also highly contested, state specific, and often product specific. As such, they leave big questions about materials flows unanswered. If producer-focused approaches are to be ecologically and socially meaningful in the long term, we need to know much more about the quantity, in total, of all materials—including plastics and their alternatives—that are being produced, consumed, wasted, recycled, or exported as scrap as well as where and how risks from these big flows are distributed unevenly. Although grassroots organizations concerned with health and justice have documented some of the most egregious cases of harm export, data on materials flows remain underdeveloped, incomplete, and often distorted. In many cases, governments and nonprofit organizations working on the tough job of tracking materials flows depend on voluntarily reported data from the very industries they seek to monitor. There is insufficient information about the displacement of one material problem to another or on metrics that would enable us to assess whether a policy is truly "making a difference" in measurable ways. Plastic wastes are the poster child of this lacuna.

To address this lack, I discuss two analytic approaches that can be used to gather and disseminate needed information on plastics as well as all other materials in wastes within a policymaking context. Materials management and sectoral analysis are two approaches to asking big questions that will be indispensable if we want to make serious rather than token inroads into the environmental problems that attend solid waste. As I argue, there is great potential for collective action to achieve meaningful reductions in disposal and to promote real material sustainability when people press for mandatory, audited information on what industries are doing. As one U.S. EPA official I interviewed put it, "We've got a huge problem in terms of the data. . . . People haven't ranted and raved that we cannot get what we want to do. We can't move [forward] until we have better data to know what's happening. You know the industry knows what's happening."[3] I advocate such ranting and raving, communicated through democratic channels, as far more potent and relevant than the much of green ranting that has taken place to date around plastic recycling and contemporary recycling in all its forms.

Plastics Recycling in the Twenty-first Century

If you live in North America, you have probably seen code numbers stamped on the bottom of plastic bottles, tubs, trays, and even some plastic bags, surrounded by the three chasing arrows that since 1970 have symbolized recycling. Although consumers widely construe these code numbers, which run from one to seven, as instructions to recycle the item in question (Rademacher 1999), the numbers are, in the words of the plastics industry itself, "not intended to be—nor ever promoted as—a guarantee to consumers that a given item bearing the code will be accepted for recycling in their community" (SPI 2010). The use of seven codes, which correspond to six different polymers and a seventh catch-all category, suggest a limited range of types of plastic, when in fact hundreds of different varieties of plastic resin formulations make up plastics today. Plastics that are hard-sided (called "rigid") containers are distinct in terms of material and recyclability from bags, wraps, and other pliable plastics called "film plastic," which are in turn distinct from foamed plastics such as the ubiquitous and hated expanded polystyrene (EPS, commonly known as Styrofoam), which are fundamentally simpler in composition than plastic durable goods made up of multiple varieties of plastic and possibly other substances. The number 3 stands for PVC, a form of plastic that has been singled out for concern among environmental groups concerned with health because of its potential to form dioxins when incinerated (Markowitz and Rosner 2002; Gilpin and Solch 2003). Yet the number 3 is stamped only on rigid containers and not on other PVC or vinyl products such as pipes or shower curtains. The number 6 stands for PS, a polymer whose production and consumption entails risks as well (CAW 2010). A number 6 surrounded by chasing arrows may or may not appear on the bottom of clear clamshells commonly used in salad bars or on modular Styrofoam packaging for shipped products— both items are made of the same polymer but are formed differently and as a consequence not able to be recycled as a mass. The same holds for CD cases, foam coffee cups, and many types of white puffy or crinkly/ crystalline clear packaging—all of which look quite different but are made of PS. Polycarbonate, which is frequently used to make baby bottles in conjunction with the additive Bisphenol-A, as well acrylonitrile butadiene styrene, polyphenylene ether, and polyphenylene oxide— which are frequently used in electronic products—are among many other polymers that have no numerical code at all (Howe and Borodinsky 1998; Kang and Schoenung 2006).

Out of this diverse range, only two types of plastic are recovered consistently and viably in the municipal curbside collection systems of every U.S. city: number 1 and number 2 bottles and jugs (*Waste News* 2010a). Plastic bottles and jugs—in contrast to plastic products of other shapes—are nearly always made of one of two polymers: polyethylene terephalate ethylene (PET or PETE), which bears a number 1 code; and high-density polyethylene (HDPE), which bears a number 2 code. Their substantial presence in discards, their ability to be hand or optically sorted from other types of plastic, and their rigidity (which makes cleaning them of contaminants possible) come together in a critical mass of sorted material emerging from a material recovery facility that is worthwhile for domestic plastics processors to buy and use in remanufacture. The same cannot be said of any other plastic waste in the United States.

Why not? As many in the recycling public who call for more plastics to be collected have observed, most varieties of plastic are theoretically recyclable if kept clean and separated from other materials. But the variety of any plastic item reflects more than the polymer it is made of. Molding method—the process by which a plastic item gets is shape by being blown, extruded into a form, or stamped—determines variety over and above the resin indicated by numerical code (Andrady 2003). Bottles are blow molded—formed with air like a glass bottle is—whereas tubs and trays are fabricated by injection into a preformed mold or stamped out of sheet plastic. Inputs to these molding processes have different melting points. The result is that at end of life, after being tossed in the recycling bin, a PET bottle and a PET tub or tray have to be sorted and separated from each other at the material recovery facility and put through different processes to be remanufacture into end products. Here is where the costs of labor and technology to separate, clean, and grind up different varieties for use in remanufacture come into play. In order for labor costs to be recouped, there have to be strong, reliable markets upon which to sell sorted plastics. Markets develop in response to, among other things, quantity and quality of discards. PET and HDPE bottles are far more prevalent than PET and HDPE tubs and trays (U.S. EPA 2009b; see also appendix V). The average New Yorker, for example, consumes and discards 16 pounds of PET and HDPE bottles per year in comparison to 0.8 pounds of HDPE and PET tubs or trays (NYC DS 2010).

This dynamic plays out again and again with other common types of plastic wastes. Yogurt tubs, which are typically made of polypropylene

(PP, number 5), are economical to recycle only when collected clean and presorted—which is why mailback services such as Gimme 5 or in-store drop-off programs such as those run by Aveda or Whole Foods are able to recover them and why material recovery facilities find them so troublesome. If kept clean, dry, and separate from rigid plastics, plastic bags, most of which are made of low-density polyethylene (LDPE), do have a domestic market in the United States, primarily for the production of plastic lumber (ACC 2010a). Mixed with curbside collections of bottles and cans, however, they are not just unmarketable, but also tend to jam material recovery facilities' sorting machinery (Fickes 1998). Plastic durables composed of a multiple varieties of plastic pose even more of a challenge to recycle because they have to be disassembled or broken apart to extract the varieties of plastic they contain. With hundreds of different resin-molding method combinations and many complex and multiple product parts, the outcome of plastics production is hundreds of relatively small-quantity types of plastic that add up, when the term *plastic* is applied en masse, to an extremely heterogeneous agglomeration of long-lived and in certain cases potentially toxic material in landfills and incinerators as well as of litter in huge quantities in oceans (Duchin and Lange 1998; Davis 2007).

Costs to sort recycling are highest under conditions of commingled collection (described in previous chapters) and are in such cases borne by municipalities and taxpayers. Some of the expense may be minimized under bottle bills because deposit redemption ensures presorted, clean streams of incoming materials. But bottle bills target bottles, not non-bottles. And only 10 states have them. Despite the inclusion of plastic bottles and jugs in curbside recycling programs since the mid-1980s and high rates of (primarily PET) plastic-bottle reclamation in bottle-bill states, the overall supply of PET and HDPE bottles struggles to sustain a domestic market (Toto 2004; NAPCOR and APR 2009; U.S. EPA 2010c). There is little domestic infrastructure for recycling nonbottle rigid plastics, in particular those collected under curbside scenarios that require sorting at a material recovery facility (APR 2009).[4] Most important, although ranting designers such as Fehrenbacher believe that "New York City recycling workers are simply too lazy to sort out recyclable plastics from non-recyclable plastics" (2009), the reality is that when cities are forced by public pressure to collect a wide variety of rigid plastics along with bottles and jugs, the recycling workers who sort the recyclable from nonrecyclable plastics are likely to be in Asia and working in conditions that may vary from good to execrable, but for whom laziness is an unknown concept (Ali 2002; Pellow 2007; Schuh 2009; Gill 2010).

As Feherenbacher notes, "Most other cities (such as San Francisco) DO recycle all plastics!" (2009). Export to Asia is what enables them to do so. The majority of U.S. cities have in recent years bowed to pressure, organized through mainstream environmental groups and articulated via elected politicians responding to voter outrage, to expand their curbside programs to allow residents to toss anything from flowerpots to CD cases into their curbside recycling bin (*Waste News* 2010a). Although most cities still exclude Styrofoam from curbside recycling because it is impossible to recycle when commingled with other materials, some (such as Los Angeles) take even this material (Los Angeles Bureau of Sanitation 2010). Agreeing to do so simplifies public education and calms nerves among the recycling public, leaving contracted recyclers to struggle with the mix of tubs, trays, and housewares that are collected (Gurnon 2003). At issue are once again the practical realities of moving large quantities of materials. There are a plethora of success stories featuring small, local, pilot-scale facilities that take nonbottle rigid plastics and make them into niche products. Details on the feedstock requirements, input capacities, and life spans of these enterprises are less featured (Best 2000). Many, like the boutique remanufacturers profiled in chapter 4, need specific, clean, small streams of input, and many go quietly out of business after a few years. All the while, most rigid nonbottle plastic collections are exported in mixed loads to Asia, meeting a shadowy and undocumented end that includes some recycling, some burning for energy, and some residual disposal (Zhang, Zhu, and Okuwaki 2007).

The problems inherent in the export of recycled plastics to developing countries for recycling are in many cases akin to those that the Basel Action Network and other groups have graphically portrayed for U.S. and European recycled electronics, with low-wage laborers, sometimes children, engaged in sorting of mixed, contaminated loads of recycled materials by hand in unsafe conditions (Ali 2002; Pellow 2007; Gill 2010). Such problems have led China, for example, to ban the import of whole plastic bottles; only preshredded plastic that has gone through initial sorting procedures in the countries of origin may be received in Chinese ports (or so the law is on the books) (Toloken 2009). It is difficult to get straight answers about exactly how much plastic from curbside recycling programs (as opposed to industrial scrap) is being exported from the United States and to where. Port-level statistics compiled by the Foreign Trade Division of the U.S. Census Bureau track information on the weight of waste and scrap exported from the United States. Between 2003 and 2009, U.S. exports of commodity code "3915 Waste, Parings and Scrap Plastics," climbed from roughly 570,000 tons to 2.1 million tons to all importing countries, with China by 2009 receiving more than half of these exports. This tonnage reflects preconsumer industrial scrap as well as postconsumer recycling collections.[5] In 2007, 62 percent of postconsumer nonbottle rigid recycled plastics were exported from North America, although in 2008 this fraction had dipped to only 38 percent, due in part to the economic crisis's dampening of Asian appetites for scrap of all kinds (ACC 2010a). In contrast to diversion rates, exported quantities and destinations are not reported to the public in even the most progressive recycling cities. Nor are material recovery facility operators eager to discuss publicly the dilemma they face when, after sorting saleable PET and HDPE bottles (along with metal, paper, and glass cullet) out of the mix, they look at a mass of tubs, trays, bags, and assorted plastic doodads at the end of the sort line and weigh landfilling or export as alternatives. It is not in anyone's interest to be frank about what it means to recycle what one material recovery facility operator told me is known behind closed doors as "Chinese plastic."[6]

The upshot of this state of affairs is that whereas more than 30 million tons (conservatively) of plastic wastes are estimated to be generated annually, only 2.1 million tons are recovered for recycling, with the majority (about 1.3 million tons) of that amount consisting of PET and HDPE bottles and jugs. Much of the remaining 400,000 tons in diversion is clean LDPE (consisting of plastic bags that consumers bring back to the store and the clear wrapping on bulk deliveries of goods to retailers) (U.S. EPA 2009b). Combined, these forms of plastics recycling divert 7.7 percent of all plastics marketed, a rate that is low in comparison to the other three pillars of curbside programs (paper, 55.5 percent; metal, 34.6 percent; and glass 23.1 percent) (U.S. EPA 2009b).

In some ways, the problems with recycling plastic are similar to those for recycling glass in that commingled collection makes the process far more costly and inefficient than deposit redemption. The common problems for these two materials explains why they and not paper and metal were infamously suspended between 2002 and 2004 from the New York City curbside recycling program, causing outrage that reverberates to this day (Gotbaum 2007). But there is a crucial difference in the two materials in terms of risk. Whereas inert glass, used once or many times over, imparts nothing molecular to the consumer of the solid or liquid it holds,[7] the range of polymers cum additives that make up not just containers for food and drink but baby toys and shower curtains may do so (CHEJ 2004). And although glass in a landfill or incinerator can be said to be a problem because of its weight or the space it occupies, there is again no toxicity at the point of disposal, whereas certain types of plastics so disposed do have the potential to release toxins in the near or longer term, particularly when incinerated. At the same time, care must be taken not simply to cast all plastics as satanic. The risk of littered broken glass to hands, feet, and paws was real before plastics came along for soft drinks and other away-from-home beverages. The risk of plastics to health and environment exists to various degrees, based on the variety of plastic in question, requiring careful empirical demonstration of harm on a case-by-case basis. The toxicity of polymers containing chlorine and styrene and of plastics containing certain additives in the phthalate category is well documented, while polyethylene and polypropylene do not suggest risk (Andrady 2003; Rossi and Lent 2006).

Regardless of documented toxicity, plastics are uncanny—their material properties are as far away from natural substances as any in our lives. Their uncertain status in relation to risk, and the problems of nondegradability for litter and ingestion by animal life, with clusters the size of U.S. states congealing in certain ocean vortices (Dautel 2009), have spelled a public-relations problem for the plastics industry for a long period. Styrofoam, in particular, has been cast as inherently wasteful over and above other plastics of far greater weight and volume in trash— with anti-Styrofoam activists in the environmental community eliding empirically grounded concerns about food-grade consumption safety with unfounded alarm over quantities of this material going to waste (Rathje and Murphy 1992; de Blasio 2009). In general, public uneasiness with plastics is pervasive enough that no amount of response from the plastics industry casting such concerns as exaggerated can quell it. From an engineering-naive standpoint, public calls for "more recycling!" are, given the history of such calls in the past to address other systemic problems (health of the planet, forests, ravaged wastescapes in urban neighborhoods), quite understandable. Fehrenbach's blog was after all posted on Inhabitat.com, a Web site devoted to the principle that "design will save the world," reprising, under its masthead, the refrain that "a small step can make a big difference." Adding number 1 or number 2 tubs and trays to the curbside recycling program would indeed be a small step, given that such material composes a relatively small quantity of additional plastics in waste.[8]

If, as the leading voices in industrial ecology aver, design will indeed save the world, there is much still to be done in the area of plastics and their waste. Redesign has led to light-weighting of plastic packaging—the rate of growth in plastics discards by weight dramatically slowed between 2000 and 2010 as compared to previous decades (Subramanian 2000). But design for recycling remains a concept that runs counter to the actual makeup of plastic products on the market (Walls 2003). If anything, there has been increasing complexity in the range and composition of durable plastic products, with materials such as metal and wood giving way to plastic alternatives, many of which are made of a variety of plastics in conjunction with metal fittings (Duchin and Lange 1998). The plasticization of durables makes them resistant to reclamation through recycling or under a model of repair and reuse discussed in chapter 4. Recent efforts to promote "bioplastics" as a design-based approach to sustainability have in fact further interfered with plastic recycling. Developed in the context of the discovery of the use of corn and other monocultural cash crops as substitutes for petroleum, bioplastics are touted by producers as biodegradable and compostable, but in reality they are not so at all in many cases. Indistinguishable from petroleum-based plastic but requiring sorting out as contamination at the material recovery facility, bioplastics have succeeded only in muddying and messing up the problems today with the recycling of traditional plastics wastes (Vidal 2008; CalRecycle 2009).

The heterogeneity of plastic wastes, their risks to health and ecosystems, and their export to the developing world for processing under uncertain conditions raise questions of global environmental justice as well as the proper role of cities in collecting and diverting mixed materials set out at curbside. These problems are not at all addressed by the ad hoc addition of different-numbered rigid containers to curbside collection programs, with much hope but no evidence yet that, given enough material collected, domestic markets will spring up that can absorb plastic discards and remanufacture them safely into something useful (APR 2009). From a redesign standpoint, a clear solution to the problems of plastic would be to reduce the range of different types used in most products, design out the hazardous variants (in particular polymers containing chorine or styrenes), and promote truly compostable alternatives in tandem with systems for collecting and carrying out composting (discussed further in the conclusion) (Ackerman 1997b; Duchin and Lange 1998). But talking about redesign is not enough; pressure has to be applied to producers to change materials and processes in ways that are meaningful for health and environments, not just for profits (as light-weighting does). I have argued in previous chapters that no amount of consumer choice or voluntary refraining from buying plastics in the first place will be enough to effect such pressure. What is needed is a strategy to bring about change at an industrial scale such that real diminution in tonnage and toxicity can be measured and maintained.

Zero Waste activists and progressive policymakers in government are currently turning to a range of new policy models, including extended producer responsibility product bans, and product fees as solutions to U.S. plastic-waste problems. These solutions are quite different from the curbside recycling approaches that have been advanced since the1970s. Often considered as a group because they assign various degrees of responsibility to producers for plastic waste problems, extended producer responsibility, product bans, and product fees have important differences with regard to materials flows. Bans and to a lesser extent product fees are today being advanced in localities across the United States to target plastic shopping bags and Styrofoam takeout containers. The overall objective of such initiatives is to root out problematic products from the materials economy by direct intervention at points of production and consumption. In contrast, extended producer responsibility policies, also under contestation in many states, seek not to directly influence production or consumption, but to eliminate the subsidy to industry that curbside municipal collection, sorting, and marketing of mixed collections of spent products entails. Extended producer responsibility advocates hold that this reallocation of costs will not only be more fair to municipalities and taxpayers, but ultimately will lead producers to implement changes in product design to reduce management burdens on themselves.

There is promise in these alternative approaches, but also cause for caution as they proliferate across the United States. Although there are many cases in which bans and fees are compatible with extended producer responsibility policies, tensions among these options open up a terrain of negotiation for producers who seek weaker, nonregulatory alternatives of materially dubious relevance to environmental problems. The strength of bans and user fees—their goal of reducing production and consumption—also brings with it the tendency to cause unintended consequences when less environmentally preferable alternatives spring spontaneously from the market to fill the void that bans and fees leave behind. Extended producer responsibility policies, for their part, may be highly successful at routing materials back to producers for end-of-life management, but they do not in and of themselves address the labor that producers will choose to employ to manage returned materials, nor the technologies employed to recycle or otherwise handle them. And although the promise of extended producer responsibility is to act as a firm but flexible push toward good, green design, evidence is mixed as to whether such policies result in design changes that bring substantial, measurable relief to communities and ecosystems suffering from waste-related pollution. In the next section, I sketch some of the many local- and state-level conflicts around extended producer responsibility in general and plastic waste in particular that are taking place today and urge Zero Waste activist and progressive policymakers to keep a watchful eye lest the past repeat itself. Today, as citizens and environmental groups call for more (curbside) recycling, product bans, and conscious consumption simultaneously, fine-grained channels of diversion offer themselves up to producers strategically concerned with freedom.

Extended Producer Responsibility in the United States

The core concept of extended producer responsibility is that some or all of the financial or operational burden, or both, of managing consumer products, including packaging and finished goods, should be borne by the producer of the products in question (Lindqvist 1992). Producers, for entirely rational reasons, seek to avoid this responsibility whenever and wherever they can. In a producer's ideal world, he or she would be free to seek out raw materials at the lowest price, transform them into saleable commodities at wages determined by the supply of labor, and sell them anywhere in the world on a free and open market. In this scenario, the capacity of wind and water to take away manufacturing pollution and of ecosystems to yield up bounteous renewable and non-renewable resources to use as input materials would be among what many scholars have called nature's "free gifts" to capital (Burkett 1999). The only rational instance in which producers would take responsibility for the pollution or resource depletion they caused would be if, on a time horizon relevant to the business cycle, the outcome were so bad that it interfered with the functioning of the producer's business (O'Connor 1998). And the only instance in which the producer would be interested in his or her spent product would be if it could be had as a cost-effective substitute for a more expensive raw input, such as was the case with the refillable bottle of a century ago.

Much to producers' dismay, governments have intruded into this ideal with environmental regulation, at times prohibiting certain particularly egregious practices and more often seeking to make the polluter pay something for nature's free gifts. In the language of neoclassical economics, "negative externalities"—the harm to nature and costs to society that occur when nature's gifts are overused—justify market intervention. In the case of extended producer responsibility, the negative externalities in question are the environmental effects of littered and disposed products as well as the publicly borne costs of the preferred alternative—reintroducing these products to the economy (Walls 2003). Producers have recently argued, in their opposition to extended producer responsibility policies, that the act of product purchase is an implicit contract between producer and consumer that transfers title from the former to the latter. Embedded in the price of a product, they argue, is an assumption that the buyer will pay for its disposition at end of life (NAM, NEMA, ALA, et al. 2009). Extended producer responsibility challenges the transfer of title not so much on legal grounds, but more broadly in construing the dispersal of certain products through sale as akin to the dispersal of pollutants in air and water, which externalize costs of production on society and nature without consent.

Independent of the justification for extended producer responsibility policies is the question of whether they are necessarily a good or efficient way of stemming waste problems. One aspect of the answer has simply to do with costs—extended producer responsibility policies require some form of expenditure by producers and thereby enable the construction of infrastructure, provision of public education, and administration of programs that would not have taken place without such funding. This point is particularly salient when governments are in fiscal crisis and not the strongest argument for extended producer responsibility if such funding merely enables the continuation of an overall system of recycling that does not function well in the first place. A far stronger argument for extended producer responsibility has to do with its relevance to modern wastes, specifically their heterogeneity and potential toxicity. In most forms, extended producer responsibility policies target specific products and route them back to remanufacture through mechanisms other than the local, compacting recycling truck and its mixed, dirty loads. At their best, extended producer responsibility policies ensure clean, presorted streams of material—they bypass the modern material recovery facility described in chapter 4. This fact is core to extended producer responsibility's special applicability to wastes that by their nature cannot and should not be handled with cans and newspapers. Such wastes certainly include e-waste and other products containing hazardous constituents, but also, I argue, extend to plastic wastes because of their extreme heterogeneity.

Extended producer responsibility's history dates to the emergence of modern wastes. The profit-enhancing qualities of disposability and planned obsolescence made their way into marketing and industrial planning after World War I. The effects of the introduction of single-use, highly packaged, cheap, made-to-break items—in which the use of plastics featured prominently—began to be felt in municipal waste streams by the 1960s. The changing economics of disposability and planned obsolescence set the stage for the transfer of responsibility to the municipality as the representative of collective consumers/householders. Not only were packaging and short-lived goods generated in greater and greater quantities, but they were also liberated from backward-bending circuits of reclamation through new forms of industrial organization that no longer relied on producers' recouping of their own spent products. The latter job fell to the public as a function of local governance. Bottle bills were a first, early, and partially successful attempt to institute extended producer responsibility by forcing producers—as an industry—to reinstate container deposits and take back returned products. The taxes on packaging that NYC EPA chief Jerome Kretchmer advocated in New York City were an early instance of a failed form of extended producer responsibility—albeit one that only assessed fiscal and not operational responsibility on the producer. In both cases, industry's entrenched response was a fierce NO! at all costs, and a fostering of curbside recycling, financed by taxpayers, as the preferred alternative.

As Bill Sheehan and Helen Spiegelman's history of extended producer responsibility in the United States chronicles, overt industry opposition to proto-extended producer responsibility policies characterized the politics of the 1980s. Battles against bottle bills took place in states nationwide, and manufacturers mobilized at the federal level against the NRDC-initiated National Recycling Act of 1988. That act outlined recycled-content utilization standards that would oblige producers to develop end markets for their spent products (Sheehan and Spiegelman 2005, 213). Such legislation coincided with the RCRA reauthorization process that, as described in chapter 3, also included weak attempts to regulate on-site disposal of nonhazardous industrial waste. As the 1990s progressed, manufacturers' efforts prevented passage of producer-focused legislation at the federal level, but during that time in some states laws did pass that established take-back programs for used oil, tires, and lead-acid batteries. In the latter cases, trade associations such as the American Petroleum Institute and the Rubber Manufacturers Association participated in the crafting of legislation that they saw as inevitable. Their activism ensured a strong operational and fiscal role for government, consumers, and retailers (but not producers) by requiring states to organize collection and processing of material returned to retailers (Sheehan and Spiegelman 2005).

Sheehan and Spiegelman observe that in the mid-1990s environmental organizations switched tactics, retreating from strong advocacy for national or state-level extended producer responsibility legislation and pursuing a more collaborative approach with a now "softened" industry receptive to some form of responsibility sharing. This approach, consistent with the "third way" centrism of the Clinton administration, emphasized a voluntary and joint form of extended producer responsibility called "product responsibility" (Fishbein, Ehrenfeld, and Young 2000). Producers warmed to this variant of extended producer responsibility, seeking to redefine the concept with an emphasis on shared burdens with taxpayers and governments and on industry self-regulation. Producer responsibility under such proposals was in some cases defined as merely providing consumer education (Fishbein, Ehrenfeld, and Young 2000). In others, the model of retail drop off, with distributors providing bins for motivated consumers to fill on their shopping trip, were advanced as voluntary alternatives to mandatory schemes (Sheehan and Spiegelman 2005).

During this period of what Sheehan and Spiegelman refer to as "co-optation," producer coalitions pursued nation-scale voluntary arrangements as a method to preempt more direct regulation at the state level. In the early 1990s, for example, Minnesota and New Jersey passed laws requiring manufacturers to fund take-back programs for rechargeable batteries, which contain the toxic elements nickel and cadmium. Enactment of these laws at the state level pushed a voluntary effort by the Portable Rechargeable Battery Association to organize nationally and start a program for the collection of recyclable batteries in boxes in stores and through free mail-back options for consumers. Today, the program, Call2Recycle, is administered by the Rechargeable Battery Take Back Coalition, a nonprofit trade group that has signed up 30,000 retailers and other organizations as drop-off locations. Firms within the rechargeable-battery and portable-electronics industry fund the program by paying a licensing fee to use the organization's seal, which urges consumers to return spent items to drop-off bins voluntarily. The program claims to have diverted some 50 million pounds of batteries from disposal since 1994 but does not provide baseline data on the quantity of such materials that are generated annually or the rate at which the program recovers total generation. Most important, the program is dependent on consumers' initiative to take batteries back to retail outlets——a practice that has been shown to yield relatively little of what is out there to be recycled (Folz and Hazlett 1991). Although most states have banned the disposal of rechargeable batteries in municipal solid waste, it is difficult to assess the effectiveness of store drop off as the alternative without hard targets for recovery imposed at the state or federal level or ongoing data to monitor the quantities recovered. The Rechargeable Battery Take Back Coalition's recently commissioned study on performance metrics for battery recovery in the United States concedes that "battery collection performance with respect to the metric of greatest relevance to those who care about battery recycling most—the extent to which batteries are entering the solid waste stream and potentially contaminating the environment—is unknown" (PSI 2009, 23).

The coalition's willingness to discuss its failures in reporting signals what may be a growing acceptance among some producers of hazardous products that they must engage with extended producer responsibility at some level or other, although ongoing skirmishes continue to occur over how strong the policy is to be. Americans, it would seem, do not like the feeling of throwing an electronic item, a battery, or full can of varnish into the trash. As a result, locally organized voluntary household hazardous waste drop-off events across the United States turn out masses of hoarded household hazardous wastes, some of which have been kept in basements or garages for decades (Matthews, Hendrickson, McMichael, et al. 1997). Moreover, the Basel Action Network's report *Exporting Harm* (Puckett and Smith 2002) and mainstream media profiles such as the *60 Minutes* story "The Electronics Wasteland" (Pelley 2008) have shown the ravages of e-waste export for recycling graphically enough that even electronics industry representatives have found it difficult to ignore the problems portrayed (see also Grossman 2006; Puckett, Westervelt, Gutierrez, et al. 2005). Crucial in the progress made in hazardous product–focused extended producer responsibility has been the engagement by the grassroots environmental movement—including the Zero Waste movement—in activism for strong forms of extended producer responsibility over voluntarist alternatives (Sheehan and Spiegelman 2005). After a series of long, consultative negotiations between the electronics industry and environmental organizations (led by the Product Stewardship Institute, which emphasizes negotiation of voluntary product initiatives) failed to yield a national policy to address e-waste, grassroots groups concerned with the health effects of mercury-laden products and extended producer responsibility–focused organizations explicitly concerned about toxic exports, such as the Silicon Valley Toxics Coalition and the Electronics Take-Back Coalition, acted as a "counterbalance to industry efforts to keep end-of-life management cost burdens with municipalities as much as possible" (Sheehan and Spiegelman 2005).

Today, what scholars of sustainability call "strong" extended producer responsibility policies are gaining ground. Strong extended producer responsibility places most or all of the fiscal and operational work to recover materials on producers to the exclusion of other actors (Barber 2007). Usually instituted at the state level, these policies make it nonoptional for producers (defined as brand owners who market products in a particular state) to plan and implement programs that will route their spent products toward reuse, recycling, composting, or—in some cases— safe disposal. Strong extended producer responsibility policies require producers to set up systems for collecting materials in a way that is convenient for consumers; to meet targets for recovery of a certain quantity of sales; to provide auditable data and to conduct research to estimate baseline amounts of sales—by weight—to begin with; and, finally, to pick up the bill for the whole endeavor. Although consumers of the products targeted under extended producer responsibility policies may contribute to covering the costs in the form of increased prices, taxpayers as a whole are spared the expense of managing wastes as urban trash or recycling covered under such legislation. State-level policies for requiring electronics manufacturers to manage computers and other e-waste items are in place in 23 U.S. states and are the leading example of strong extended producer responsibility policy today (ETBC 2010). In 2009, Maine became the first state in the nation to adopt what is called "extended producer responsibility framework legislation," outlining a process for the state to identify multiple products on an ongoing basis as objects of extended producer responsibility, and codifying the allocation of responsibility to producers for "designing, managing, and financing a stewardship program that addresses the lifecycle impacts of their products including end-of-life management" (PPI 2010). Maine was also the first state in the nation to enact statewide extended producer responsibility legislation for e-waste and to follow with laws covering five other household hazardous products—more than any other state in the nation.

Among extended producer responsibility experts, the passage of the framework law in Maine is believed to have been aided by the existence of such precedent.[9] Maine businesses, in this particular skirmish, saw future extended producer responsibility laws as unavoidable and concluded that the framework law would at least streamline and minimize the administrative hassles of future, product-specific initiatives.[10]

Strong extended producer responsibility, it is important to note, offers producers the incentive of freedom within the confines of regulation in a novel way. With the assumption of all responsibility for managing products at end of life comes, in principle, complete flexibility as to how to achieve this goal. Producers may act as individual brand owners or may join forces in consortia or both. Although they are required to report on what they do and to follow existing laws governing the handling of wastes, the extent to which they must make sure materials are recycled rather than disposed of is subject to negotiation and agreement between them and the governing body. This point is important because negotiation after a law's passage can gut an extended producer responsibility policy of its strength without drawing close attention. It is notable that the original Maine framework bill, introduced in 2009, contained provisions that required the state's Department of Environmental Protection to monitor recovery rates of covered products and specified that all products collected, with the exception of certain hazardous products and residuals, be reused or recycled, not disposed (Maine House of Representatives 2009). These provisions were struck from the final bill that passed, which was substantially simplified based on feedback from the Maine Chamber of Commerce and Maine Merchant's Association (Maine State Legislature 2010; *Impact* 2010).

To date, the social movements organized around extended producer responsibility have been quite sensitive to the manipulation of core concepts of responsibility, funding, and verifiability in the "legislative alternatives" offered under the moniker of "product stewardship" and other producer-crafted initiatives. Moreover, although the recycling public has shown a strong willingness to take personal responsibility for hazardous products in their households or for their own spent e-waste, as high turnouts at municipally organized, voluntary drop-off events attest, environmental groups advocating extended producer responsibility have not allowed the morale-boosting, community spirit-building qualities of these events to create conditions that interfere with legislation that would put much of the onus on firms to take back meaningful quantities of materials. There is still much to be done to divert the most toxic materials from U.S. municipal solid waste and even more to be done to stem the export of mixed e-waste to the developing world, but the stakes are clear. In this case, diversion into busy-ness has not ruled the day.

At the same time, there are indications that industry opposition to extended producer responsibility for e-waste may be only temporarily abating as producers come to grips with the threat this form of policy poses and contemplate more effective forms of resistance. In 2008, New York City followed 17 U.S. states in passing strong-extended producer responsibility legislation for e-waste marketed within its borders. The city's law, like the state legislation it was modeled on, would require manufacturers to design, carry out, and fund a program to recover targeted quantities of e-waste and televisions over a course of years. The legislation was quite strong. Unlike some state precedents, it did not give manufacturers the option of simply channeling funds to a municipal collection program for e-waste; they were required to design and implement programs directly or through contractors. The law also set mandatory minimum collection standards—assessed as a fraction of the weight of sales within New York City—and financial penalties for failure to do so.

As with state laws, the system had to be "convenient" for consumers to use. Convenience was not spelled out in the law, but it was in the Administrative Code rules issued by the city subsequent to the law's passage. This requirement meant something quite different in a megacity of unprecedented density than it did for mainstream America. Some 55 percent of households in New York City have no access to a vehicle; in Manhattan, this rate is 76 percent (NYC DCP 2000). Periodic e-waste collection drives, funded by the city or by nonprofit organizations, routinely draw citizens, who lug equipment on the subway or transport it in the foldable shopping carts that many New York City households feature (MacBride 2008). Such events are hardly convenient. Instead, for New York City, "convenient" was defined as follows: "Convenient collection from a resident shall mean direct collection from a resident's home in the City, which may include a postal or parcel service but need not include collection from inside such home ('direct collection program'). A direct collection program may not include collection of electronic equipment left for collection at the curbside" (City of New York 2009, 7).

This requirement of convenience, which the industry considered unprecedented and draconian, became a rallying cry around which a more far-ranging producer revolt against strong extended producer responsibility would begin to be mobilized. In July 2009, the Consumer

Electronics Association and the Information Technology Council filed a lawsuit against the city, challenging the onerous collection requirements spelled out in the Administrative Code and raising objections to the law itself. The NRDC and the Electronics Takeback Coalition were closely involved in responding to the suit, organizing state governments in Washington and Maine, both of which had strong state-level extended producer responsibility policies on the books, to submit affidavits in support of the city. Local governments, including San Francisco and Portland, collaborated with the product-stewardship organizations, including the Product Stewardship Institute, to submit an amicus brief in support of New York City, followed by a letter to the Consumer Electronics Association and the Information Technology Council calling on them to withdraw the lawsuit (Hiembuch 2009; NYSAR, City and County of San Francisco, Calif., METRO, et al. 2009).

Despite the industry's focus on the inconvenience of collection, requirements spelled out in the New York City rules, what was under attack was much more fundamental—having to do with the constitutionality of the law and by extension with strong extended producer responsibility laws covering activities within subnational jurisdictions (Sindling 2010). The arguments made in the industry suit involved core questions of the spatial distribution of material responsibility and the freedom of states and localities to regulate the exchange of materials within their jurisdictions (ETBC and NRDC 2010). The issues were eloquently and fervently argued in, among other documents, an amicus brief filed in support of the suit by a consortium of trade associations with great stake in extended producer responsibility directed at packaging, including the National Association of Manufacturers and the American Forest and Paper Association. The frankness with which such producers expressed their interest was striking: "Amici are greatly concerned that allowing the E-waste Program to take effect will encourage other jurisdictions to adopt laws that shift disposal costs historically borne by voting local taxpayers who discard consumer products onto non-voting, out-of-state or off-shore manufacturers who make them." They argued that "for over a century, it has been settled law that garbage collection and disposal is a core function of local government in the United States." NYC's law "would abandon this regime of local accountability by shifting most of the burden of disposal for electronics to out-of-state, non-voting manufacturers." (NAM, NEMA, ALA, et al. 2009, 5).

Plaintiffs to the suit argued that that law was spatially discriminatory: by requiring manufacturers outside city limits to provide collection and processing of their wares, manufacturers of electronics within the city (although none existed) would be privileged. Unequal protection was claimed because manufacturers of other products containing toxics, such as mercury, were not targeted. Other objections were articulated around the degree of responsibility to be borne by producers as opposed to retailers, consumers, or government. Consumer responsibility was constructed in this argument as an agreement to "take title" to anything that is purchased. The act of purchase was called an implicit contract that transferred responsibility from seller to buyer (NAM, NEMA, ALA, et al. 2009, 5). All of these arguments related to strong extended producer responsibility as a concept, not to the program rules' convenience requirements.

Most interestingly, the plaintiffs and their friends took the ideal of the locally closed loop and turned it on its head, describing in old fashioned terms the transhistoric inevitability of the shedding of material responsibility for products through channels of distribution, wholesaling, retailing, consumption, and even immigration:

Business and trade associations . . . include companies that manufacture and sell a wide range of consumer products. Many of those manufacturers are neither located, nor do business, in New York. Their production facilities are far outside New York City—and indeed often outside the United States—and they sell their products through independent distributors, wholesalers or retailers, many of which likewise are outside of and have no connection with New York. Nonetheless, some of the goods they manufacture undoubtedly wind up in New York City. Vendors that buy goods from manufacturers out-of-state resell them to consumers at retail outlets in the city. And because New York City has always been a magnet for people from throughout the Nation and the world, individuals move into the city bringing their chattels with them. In either case, the products may wind up being disposed of in New York City by the ultimate consumers. (NAM, NEMA, ALA, et. al. 2009, 6)

To manufacturers terrified of a shift in the division of collection labor that had prevailed for much of the twentieth century, it was imperative that the contractual obligation of the consumer living in a jurisdiction to take ultimate title to waste not give way to the extraterritorial, state-imposed redistribution of responsibility. In the manufacturers' view, contemplation of such a shift was being brought on by the state's fiscal crisis as the great recession proceeded:

If New York City's E-Waste law is allowed to go into effect, it will send a strong—perhaps irresistible—message to other financially-pressed state and local governments that here is a new way to reduce one of their major costs: shifting the burden of collecting and disposing of discarded consumer goods away from their own taxpayers, who actually discard the products, and onto manufacturers located far beyond their own borders, who do not vote in their local elections. (NAM, NEMA, ALA, et al. 2009, 6)

The alternative to extended producer responsibility proposed in the brief—consumer responsibility and curbside collection—should ring familiar: "Consumers, who are the waste generators, are best suited to dispose of such items in environmentally conscious ways, such as special recycling bins for particular types of waste or special curbside pick-up arrangements" (NAM et al. 2009, 10).

The industry lawsuit was ultimately made moot by New York State's passage of extended producer responsibility legislation for waste electronics in May 2010. The rule making that will follow is still in the works, and the industry's response remains to be seen. With regard to strong extended producer responsibility in general and its potential extension beyond hazardous products to packaging, the record is usefully and refreshingly clear. When threatened with strong extended producer responsibility, producers of products *and* packaging will recognize a common interest and will mount fierce opposition, seeking opportunities to displace responsibility back to municipal service provision funded by voting residents.

Attacking the Root of Plastic Waste

Manufacturers have grounds to be concerned about extended producer responsibility in the near future. Grassroots environmental movements concerned with health and aquatic ecosystems, Zero Waste activists, and local governments are looking at packaging in general and at plastic packaging in particular as the next big category on which to turn the power of extended producer responsibility policies, bans, and fees. To use the words of the EAC's Karen Dumont in the 1970s, new extended producer responsibility initiatives are today's "brush fires" starting up all over the country. As she told beverage and bottling industry funders alarmed over bottle bills in the early 1970s, "A credible alternative to legislation must be found" (Dumont, n.d.). Some producers today reprise the outright opposition of the 1970s and 1980s. For example, the American Forest and Paper Association, an early ally of the beverage and bottling industry in bottle-bill resistance, today forthrightly:

opposes EPR [extended producer responsibility] proposals, including mandated take-back schemes, container deposits and advance disposal fees, that impose waste management and disposal costs solely on the manufacturer. To be successful, any policy proposal addressing waste or litter issues must involve the end user of a product or package—the consumer. [The association] believes government bodies should embrace the concept of shared producer responsibility, which connects individual responsibility with industry initiatives and emphasizes joint responsibility between companies and consumers toward our environment. (AF&PA 2008)

In a bold-faced attempt to repeal the oldest bottle-waste law in the nation using extended producer responsibility in name only, a consortium of beverage producers and bottle makers introduced the Vermont Extended Producer Responsibility Act in 2009, which would feature, in exchange for killing the state's container deposit regulations, a system in which they, along with paper-packaging manufacturers, would provide partial funding to municipalities to fund curbside collection and processing of recyclables. Proponents of this bill in Vermont argue that maintaining a parallel system of deposits (which recover glass, aluminum, and PET bottles at high rates) and curbside collection (which recovers glass, aluminum, steel, PET and HDPE bottles, and paper recyclables at much lower rates) is duplicative and makes both systems inefficient. This point is in fact correct inasmuch as curbside recycling is extremely dependent on the sale of aluminum and PET bottles (high-value commodities when sorted), along with paper, HDPE bottles, and steel cans, to subsidize collection of glass and other plastics that may be included in a municipal program. The need to repeal bottle bills, however, hardly follows from this observation. The duplication of both systems can just as easily be resolved by a redistribution of responsibility in which glass and plastic containers would be subject to deposit and the locality would take on the lucrative responsibility of collecting paper and metals as scrap, following the tradition of the scrap industry. The Zero Waste advocacy community engaged in progressive extended producer responsibility policymaking sees the Vermont act as a diversionary sham that it is meant to be—although it may be tempting to cash-strapped local waste authorities in the economically distressed state of Vermont.

In the case of the Vermont Extended Producer Responsibility Act, attempts to use the moniker *extended producer responsibility* to kill producer responsibility are crude and obvious. This approach mimics diversionary options advanced in the 1990s bearing the title "product stewardship" or "shared producer responsibility." Today, other responses to producer-focused waste policies are becoming more nuanced and evolving rapidly—with "credible alternatives" considered strategically in different states and localities and in the context of the menu of policy options up for consideration at any time. With regard to plastic wastes, industry positions are rapidly differentiating in subtle ways. The undersupply of domestic feedstock of recycled plastic bottles has become pressing enough that domestic plastics recyclers, organized under the National Association for PET Container Resources, are beginning to join in the call for some forms of extended producer responsibility to increase supply, although they are careful to emphasize shared responsibility with consumers (Verespej 2009). The American Chemistry Council (ACC), which represents the interests of the plastics industry as a whole, continues to strongly support municipally provided curbside recycling programs for rigid plastic containers and to encourage cities to take as wide an array of plastics as possible in their curbside programs. In April 2010, the ACC enthusiastically testified in favor of legislation introduced in the New York City Council to expand curbside recycling to accept all rigid containers, not just bottles (ACC 2010c). Unlike the beverage and bottling industries, however, the ACC is agnostic on bottle bills. Of most concern to the ACC and its membership are policies that would pose even more serious threats to producer autonomy than strong extended producer responsibility policies: product bans.

In recent years, many localities in California, Washington, and Oregon have enacted bans targeting two distinct forms of plastic packaging—plastic shopping bags and Styrofoam food containers. Both materials are exceedingly difficult to recycle when included in mixed curbside collections because the process involved in preparing them for reintroduction into manufacture is far more compromised by moisture and contamination with organic matter than is the process for recycling other forms of rigid plastics. On the West Coast, coalitions of local governments and grassroots environmental groups have argued for bans rather than policies to promote recycling via extended producer responsibility or other methods in part on these grounds, but more saliently because of the dangers to marine life that ingested forms of both plastics pose in contrast to other forms of plastic packaging. Grassroots groups are also concerned about the health risks of consuming meals and drink from Styrofoam foodware (CAW 2010).

Material bans represent the ultimate incursion on producer autonomy. With bans, entire markets are eliminated quickly, opening the field of product substitution to quite different sets of firms ready to supply alternatives. Given the seriousness of the threat to profit that bans entail, it is no surprise that the ACC, the Society of the Plastics Industry, and other plastic-manufacturing groups seek to oppose bans as the worst extreme on a continuum along which even strong extended producer responsibility would be marginally better, weaker extended producer responsibility or product stewardship would be much better, and inclusion of any plastic material in a curbside collection or in-store drop-off recycling program organized municipally, funded by the taxpayer, and dependent on an educated, concerned public to participate voluntarily would be best of all.

In the case of plastic bags, the ACC has pursued extended producer responsibility policies as a "credible alternative" in California, when a coalition of municipal governments and environmental groups sought to enact a statewide ban in 2010. As with the Vermont Extended Producer Responsibility Act, industry-crafted legislation in California, introduced under the name "producer responsibility" in 2009, contained provisions to kill the feared ban alternative as a condition of its passage. The ACC-supported bill, AB1141, in its first draft would have prohibited local governments in the state from banning bags. In return, producers would agree to pay an unspecified "extended producer responsibility fee" to the state for each bag sold in the state, with revenues used to fund litter cleanup and consumer-education programs and to provide collection of dropped-off bags from retailers upon request (Verespej 2009). In New York State, the ACC warmly supported the 2008 New York State Plastic Bag Reduction, Reuse, and Recycling Act requiring retailers to take back plastic bags at the store (*Environmental News Service* 2008). Under this law, retailers, not manufacturers, bear all costs related to state requirements that bags be routed back to recyclers. This law effectively preempted concurrent bills in the legislature that would have enacted a statewide ban on plastic bags that would apply a five-cent fee per bag sold. Its effectiveness at diminishing plastic bags in the trash can only be guessed at. With no tracking or reporting requirements, it is impossible to know how much in-store bag drop off is diverting from disposal.

Throughout the United States, alternative state- and local-level ordinances are being proposed and enacted to reduce plastic-bag consumption. Instruments range from bans to fees assessed on consumers at point of purchase to mandatory credits for bags supplied by customers. Overall, the position of the plastics industry and of bag manufacturers in particular is to oppose the passage of legislation and where unsuccessful in this initial effort to mount legal challenges to implementation. The ACC's Progressive Bag Alliance leads the industry campaign to promote in-store recycling of bags within the context of weak extended producer responsibility policies that displace the costs of recycling dropped-off bags onto retailers and—reprising the tactics used by Keep America Beautiful in the 1970s to preempt bottle bills—emphasizes shared responsibility by consumers to put litter in its place, even if that litter may blow out of a trash can or off a landfill once it has been deposited there (Verespej 2009).

It is harder for producers to argue for increased recycling and civic-minded litter reduction when it comes to the other target of product bans: Styrofoam containers used for food and drink consumption. More than 100 U.S. cities and counties, including San Francisco, Seattle, and Portland, Oregon, have banned the sale of take-out food and drink in Styrofoam containers. In localities in which bans are up for consideration, industry groups ritually invoke increased recycling as the preferred alternative, knowing that Styrofoam recycling is nearly impossible under all but the most pristine conditions. As with other problematic plastics, Styrofoam recyclers depend on clean, dry, usually commercially sourced feedstock to recycle this material effectively. Eager to publicize the odd case in which a school or restaurant scrupulously cleans and stacks its Styrofoam trays for direct collection by a Styrofoam recycler, the plastics industry cannot effectively argue down the reality that Styrofoam is not practically recyclable in most cases of actual use in food service. The EPA's reported recycling rate for polystyrene (extended and nonextended) in plates and cups is nil, with such foodware comprising some 760,000 tons out of 2.6 million tons annually of total polystyrene generation (U.S. EPA 2009b; see also appendix V). But the issue of recyclability is moot anyway. At issue with food-service Styrofoam is not so much waste per se, but the health impacts of consuming foods and drinks, in particular those that are hot or contain lipids or both, from Styrofoam containers. A parallel concern involves the predominance of Styrofoam in beach and marine litter. Like plastic bags, its exceptionally light weight makes it prone to blowing into waterways.

Producers are astute at noting and quantifying real unintended consequences that arise from bans when alternatives that are potentially worse in terms of one environmental metric or other arise to fill the void (PBA 2008). Cognizant of this tendency, many jurisdictions enacting bans and fees feature legislation that guides the emergence of alternatives to the banned products in sustainable directions (the practice is called "ban with a plan"), drawing localities into the complex task of orchestrating materials flows within their borders. Responding to research—provided by the plastics industry as well as by independent sources —quantifying the greenhouse gas impacts of plastic versus paper bag usage that revealed paper to be the more burdensome of the two, Washington, D.C., recently assessed a five-cent fee on single-use retail bags of any material (Craig 2010). The question of unintended consequences in the wake of material-specific bans is quite relevant in the case of Styrofoam used in food service. Cities that have prohibited the use of Styrofoam in food packaging, including Seattle and San Francisco, have measured an increase in other, heavier rigid plastics as a result, requiring successive legislation to require food retailers to ensure convenient recycling of traditional alternatives or to route bioplastic substitutes toward composting.

At the end of the 2000s, almost 60 proposals exist to ban, assess fees on, or require in-store recycling collection of plastic bags active in states and a few localities across the United States (PBA 2008). In some states where in-store recycling, mandatory or otherwise, has been implemented, such as Delaware, Rhode Island, and New York, no program meets the criteria of strong extended producer responsibility to require producers to document baseline quantities generated and quantities diverted and to achieve mandatory targets for recycling. The ACC, at the pinnacle of a coalition of trade groups supporting plastic-bag recycling laws, reports that some 400,000 tons of plastic films, made mainly of LDPE and including some HDPE, were recovered in 2008. Of that tonnage, about two-thirds were sourced from businesses and roughly one-third from sources that would include bags returned to retailers. In total, 57 percent was exported to unspecified nations other than Canada, with concerns in China leading to restrictions on imports of postconsumer films. Most of the film that remained in the United States went to make composite lumber (29 percent), but very little (4 percent) to true loop closure to make film and bags. It is notable that although the ACC features the fact that the rate of film recovery has increased by 28 percent since 2005, it does not report baseline generation. In fact, the diversion rate for plastic film—a large part of which is clean, clear shrink wrap used in bulk retail deliveries—stands at only 13 percent. And although the ACC has committed to a goal of 40 percent recycled content for bags produced by its membership, there are no guarantees that such a goal, much less a hard diversion goal for plastic bags as a whole, will be met on a state or especially federal level (ACC 2010b).

The 400,000 tons of plastic film diverted to recycling and even the roughly 3 million tons of plastic film discarded need to be considered within the context of some 30 million tons of plastics moving through the U.S. economy annually, some 28 million tons of which go to disposal.

This 30 million figure, derived from EPA estimates, which are in turn derived from statistics supplied by industry, among other sources, is likely an underestimate of the total quantity because it excludes certain products, such as textiles and floor coverings, made of synthetic fiber (Kuczenski and Geyer 2010). To the extent that plastic wastes pose health and pollution problems or represent an untapped resource, it behooves us to know just how much is being addressed in highly visible, politically charged policy developments that run the gamut from adding more numbered rigid containers to a recycling program to implementing mandatory retail recycling programs for bags and even banning take-out polystyrene (Styrofoam and other forms) and shopping bags outright. And the answer is—not that much. Taken together, rigid containers, plastic bags, and polystyrenetake-out containers total about 30 percent of all plastic wastes generated in municipal solid waste (U.S. EPA 2009b; see also appendix V). There is no policy formulation at all for the remaining 70 percent of plastics in municipal solid waste, consisting of other types of polystyrene, plastic durables, single-use foodware, and a broad range of materials the EPA classifies as "other nondurables" and "other plastic packaging" (see appendix V). And 97 percent of the total tonnages of plastics continue to make a linear journey from cradle to grave, watery or otherwise.

The shifts in materials usage that occur when specific bans or user fees are enacted point to one area in which there is a clear need to look at all materials, plastic and alternatives, as they interact through cycles of production and consumption that cross state and national borders. The existence of an extremely varied range of types of plastics and the extent to which import and export play a role in facilitating or hindering environmental and health goals are other areas that need examination. Materials-flows analysis is a methodology that, if developed fully under a framework of mandatory, annual reporting of industrial statistics in ecologically and physiologically relevant ways, can begin to answer big, underlying questions so as to guide the development of new forms of waste policy, including extended producer responsibility, in significant ways. The strong extended producer responsibility framework advocated by the Product Policy Institute specifies that programs must include "reporting on the final disposition, (i.e., reuse, recycling, disposal) of products handled by the stewardship program, including any products or materials exported for processing" (PPI 2010).

Such reporting is essential if extended producer responsibility is to be developed meaningfully. Industrial ecologists Reid Lifset and Thomas

Lindquist, writing of the material insufficiency of product-stewardship policies premised in shared responsibility and industrial voluntarism, caution policymakers and environmentalists to "trust but verify" when it comes to extended producer responsibility. They argue that "the matters of disclosure and verification relate not only to the legitimacy of contemporary policy proposals. They also bear on efforts to genuinely ascertain the cost and efficacy of competing strategies for accomplishing environmental goals. Without access to data, researchers and decision makers cannot determine what works and at what cost. Society is left debating the same claims endlessly" (2001, 10). In the next section, I review two frameworks that can be used to evaluate industrial data with regard to solid-waste problems and solutions so as to move through the cycle of endless claims debate to say and do things that really mean something materially.

Materials Management: A New Framework for Solid-Waste Policy?

In June 2009, several months into a new presidential administration, the U.S. EPA released *Sustainable Material Management: The Road Ahead* (2009e). The report proposed a shift in discourse and practice around solid waste, reorganized under the term *materials management*. Authored by the 2020 Vision Workgroup, a coalition of EPA and state waste officials, it defined materials management as "an approach to serving human needs by using/reusing resources most productively and sustainably throughout their life cycles, generally minimizing the amount of materials involved and all the associated environmental impacts" (11). Formally taking up work on solid waste under this term would be a new and different step, a departure from the EPA's "collaborations to encourage waste minimization, greater recycling, use of more recycled content, and identification of beneficial uses for materials that would otherwise be thrown away" (15). Such past approaches—including those termed "pollution prevention," "product stewardship," and "industrial-materials recycling" under the Resource Conservation Challenge—had, in the 2020 Vision report's words, "not focused on reducing the use of materials or the toxicity of products or manufacturing processes" (16).

What would the new approach look like in practice? The 2020 Vision Workgroup wrote:

This kind of thinking requires us to ask very different questions. For example, we often ask, "What should we do with scrap tires, or electronics, or fluorescent lights when they need to be disposed?" But the question for the future may need to be: "Is there a way to eliminate this waste completely, to provide these same services with fewer resources and no adverse environmental impacts? Can we do this by substituting something else that does not wear out so fast, can be reused, that can be fully or almost fully recovered and repurposed so that it never becomes waste?" (U.S. EPA 2009e, 31)

The 2020 Vision report was notable in several ways. It treated the unacknowledged disparity between municipal solid waste and other solid wastes with unprecedented frankness, stating that "far more materials are being moved or transformed to meet society's needs than most people realize" (U.S. EPA 2009e, 2). In the tradition of Harvey Molotch and Marilyn Lester's (1975) work, the EPA report contrasted issue visibility in the media with the invisibility of underlying social structures, noting that "climate change, energy policy, and the economy all create headlines, but the stories that follow often miss the point that all these issues are, in part, symptoms of how we use materials" (U.S. EPA 2009e, 1). Among its most remarkable qualities was its suggestion of a broader social theory than is implied in conventional arguments for recycling and green consumerism. Rather than talking about success stories and personal choices as gradually constitutive of systemic change, it acknowledged the potential incoherence of accumulated atomized choice, advocating a strong coordinating role for the government with regard to both business and residential behavior:

We . . . observe many people and companies moving to use and spend less that they did previously. *It is not clear what choices individuals and companies will make.* Therefore, it is important that both the federal and state governments make more systematic efforts to enable, encourage, and collaborate with all parts of society to see that materials are used more effectively and efficiently with less overall environmental toll. (2, emphasis added)

Moreover, the report allowed that such enabling, encouraging, and collaborating need not be limited to voluntarist accords with industry but could include as possibilities a "full set of public policy tools [such as] economic policies, regulations, information and partnerships" (7).

The 2020 Vision report built directly on research the EPA had conducted between 2002 and 2008 with the World Resources Institute (WRI), a D.C.-based nonprofit research organization focusing on global environmental and social change through "sound science and objective analysis" (WRI 2009). Among the WRI's areas of specialization was materials-flows accounting, a "systematic method for tracing the extraction, processing, production, use, recycling, and disposal of all major commodities in a nation's economy" by weight and ecological relevance, not primarily by dollar value as in most forms of accounting (Rogich, Cassara, Wernick, et al. 2008, 1). Research over several years led to the WRI's materials-flows accounting in the United States in 2008, which estimated the total materials in the U.S. domestic economy, including all imported and domestically sourced raw materials that underwent some form of manufacturing transformation, net of exports, at 6.5 billion tons. The WRI called this mass "direct material consumption." Approximately 2.7 billion tons flowed back as wastes deposited in air, water, or soil after consumption, termed "domestic processed output." Another 18 billion tons constituted what the WRI called "hidden flows," materials "mobilized or produced" that are not "purchased as finished goods or consumed in the economy," arising during processes of extraction, processing, manufacturing, and use of materials (Rogich, Cassara, Wernick, et al. 2008). It should be noted that the WRI did not use the same forms of classification of solid waste that apply under RCRA's Subtitles C and D. Using WRI definitions, what I have called "manufacturing wastes" in chapter 3 (Subtitle D nonhazardous industrial wastes) would fall partially within the category "domestic processed output" and partly within "hidden flows."[11] Thus, although the WRI report's methodology does not confirm the accuracy of the manufacturing-waste estimate of 7.6 billion tons from the late 1980s discussed in chapter 3, it does substantiate the order of magnitude by which production wastes outweigh urban trash.

The EPA's 2020 Vision drew in additional data on air- and water-pollution releases, energy consumption, and greenhouse gas emissions associated with materials usage that had been provided by other academic research efforts. The synthesized result was a complex, ambitious, and novel set of indicators linking flows of materials to ecological relevance in terms of tonnage and toxicity. In total, the effort examined 480 different materials, products, and services and their interrelation in the U.S. economy, measuring impacts, resources used, and waste disposed directly at each stage as well as indirectly in terms of associated inputs and eventual outputs of their utilization, transformation, and disposition. The complexity of the results do not lend themselves to one "bottom-line" summarization, although it is clear that electrical services lead in environmental impacts assessed across all stages of the lifecycle. Among the 480 materials, products, and service examined, "plastic materials and resins" and "plastic products not elsewhere categorized" ranked highly in terms of ozone-depletion potential and contribution to material waste and were in the top 20 with regard to potential for human, terrestrial, and aquatic toxicity potential. Plastics per se did not directly figure in the report's final list of 38 priority areas, which were identified on the basis of combined rankings across 17 criteria as a "pool of potential candidate materials, products and services which are important enough to be considered for projects to demonstrate the value of using life-cycle materials management" (U.S. EPA 2007e, 23). Among these 38 priorities were, however, services related to food provision and wholesale and retail trades—with final consumption impacts reflecting a range of materials and products utilized in service provision. And among materials worthy of first consideration from a materials-management perspective were plastic precursors, including petroleum, natural gas, and industrial chemicals, all of which ranked extremely high in terms of direct pollution impacts across media (U.S. EPA 2009e, 28).

The analysis of 480 materials, products, and services was conducted in parallel with the conceptual framework laid out in the 2020 Vision. It drew from existing data sets on impacts to health and ecosystems developed by the U.S. Geological Survey (USGS) and other federal agencies and on data from the WRI to estimate materials flows and solid-waste generated. In its own report on materials flows in the United States, the WRI identified what it termed serious gaps in materials-flows data on plastics as compared to minerals, timber, and other raw commodities for which federal institutions have long gathered data, such as the USGS and the Food and Agriculture Organization. In contrast, noted the WRI, data were lacking on "the production and use of organic and inorganic chemicals, plastics, and synthetic fibers. The materials in most imported finished goods cannot be measured, including electronic devices that contain heavy metals and other materials that are hazardous to human health and the environment. Data on wastes released to the environment in the United States are still largely nonexistent" (Rogich, Cassara, Wernick, et al. 2008, 3). The few scholars attempting to undertake materials-flows analysis in this area have also noted the lack of information on materials flows for chemicals and synthetics in comparison to minerals and agricultural/timber products. Brandon Kuczenski and Roland Geyer, in one of the most comprehensive studies of the flows of primary and recycled PET in the United States, note that, "unlike metals, production of polymers is not tracked by governments and data from industry sources is [sic] sparse" (2010, 1161). The ACC, to its credit, has retained the EPA's municipal-waste characterization consultant, Franklin Associates, to perform a life-cycle inventory of nine plastic resins and four polyurethane precursors on a per unit basis and to report aggregate U.S. production and recycling statistics for rigid plastic containers and film. But life-cycle inventories tell us nothing about the magnitude or location of the materials over their life (Bouman, Heijungs, van de Voet, et al. 2000). In the area of plastics and chemicals, there is still a great need for data that would enable the tracking of flows "through stages of transformation, and particularly secondary materials as they flow from generation to remanufacture" (OECD 2004, 13), and there are real drawbacks to relying on voluntarily provided industrial statistics. As one WRI researcher put it,

We tried with this material flow work to look at priority chemicals for the EPA. And some of them are industrially manufactured, and there's amazingly detailed pathological studies that happen on these things, and then you get to industrial production and you know nothing because the industry can claim competition. "There's too much competition, so we don't have to release this." And when you have the flow data that I was able to get, for example, data [on minerals materials flows] from the USGS or data from the forest service or data on fisheries or any of this stuff, [it] requires voluntary relationships with industry at a lot of these government agencies where they have to kind kiss up to these industries to get this data. And so, you know, the only reason that the mining industry gives the USGS data is because it perceives the USGS as an agency within the government that really serves the interests of the mining industry. And so from that perspective they're willing to share some of this data, but it's really a very limited amount, and there's no requirement to report.[12]

In spite of the current limitations to data, the materials-management framework set forth in the 2020 Vision document has begun to be mobilized in the context of a burgeoning interest in the connection between solid waste and climate change that is flourishing as we move into the second decade of the twenty-first century. In September 2009, the EPA's Office of Resource Conservation and Recovery released *Opportunities to Reduce Greenhouse Gas Emissions through Materials and Land Management Practices*. Setting the U.S. economy's total contribution to climate change through carbon emissions at 7 billion metric tons of carbon dioxide equivalents, the report argued that municipal functions of recycling collection and processing as well as increased capture of landfill-gas emissions should be evaluated and encouraged not just on the grounds of resource conservation, groundwater- and air-pollution mitigation, and energy savings that have previously been seen as benefits, but also in terms of their modest but steady contribution to a national and global imperative to stabilize atmospheric carbon release in the long term (U.S. EPA 2009c, 10) . According to this report, if the United States were to reach a 100 percent recycling rate for traditional materials (paper, metal, glass, and plastic) and 100 percent composting of organic fractions of municipal solid waste, the reductions would amount to as much as 300 million and 20 million metric tons of carbon dioxide equivalents per year, respectively (U.S. EPA 2009c, 4).

In addition, the report set forth a novel categorization of sources of the total 7 billion U.S. metric tons of carbon dioxide equivalents burden. For quite some time, the EPA had used a "traditional sector based approach" to attribute greenhouse gas emissions to specific sources (U.S. EPA 2008b). Using this perspective, the sources break out as: electric power (34 percent), transportation (28 percent), industry (19 percent), agriculture (8 percent), with remaining commercial (6 percent) and residential (5 percent) activities constituting quite small contributions (U.S. EPA 2009c,10). The report advocated a different "systems based approach" that would recategorize sources by examining embedded impacts in materials and services, attributing fractions of total emissions in the delivery of goods (29 percent) and food (13 percent), with provision of transport, heating/cooling and lighting, appliances, and infrastructure making up the balance (U.S. EPA 2009c, 11). The argument thus transfers responsibility for emissions from industrial sectors to materials and processes, a classification that, among other things, is meant to enlarge the calculation of potential for municipal solid waste reduction, recycling, composting, and prevention to reduce the U.S. carbon footprint (Allaway 2009). The approach suggests that various municipal solid waste-diversion activities have a role to play in this goal beyond their direct impacts of avoided disposal. Consequent discussions of the systems-based approach in Webinars organized by the EPA and by local and state governments stress the recognition of the potential contribution of localities and counties to the national work of carbon reduction (Allaway 2009). In other words, recycling municipal solid waste is credited for its ripple effect back up the production chain that will be felt in reduction of the carbon burden of associated transport, heating/cooling and lighting, appliances, and infrastructure when recycled or secondary inputs are used instead of virgin ones. This new approach quite obliquely reprises the implicit assumptions of one-to-one substitution that underlie contemporary discourse about individual recycling and waste reduction discussed in chapter 3. In that context, the emerging connection between municipal solid waste and manufacturing waste is constructed backward from the consumer's choice to buy or recycle or both. In the systems-based approach, a similar argument is targeted at localities, saying in essence, "Maintain and step up your local municipal solid waste recycling and composting programs, because the materials you are diverting, if measured in terms of embodied impacts through the life cycle, mean reduced carbon impacts far afield of your terrain of direct action."

Insofar as the EPA's *Opportunities to Reduce Greenhouse Gas Emissions through Materials and Land Management Practices* talks concretely as opposed to systemically, its focus is on existing municipal solid waste programs and practices. The potential of materials-management practices to reduce greenhouse gas emissions are calculated for municipal solid waste-related activities, including the reduction in consumption of packaging and paper, the extension of personal computers' lifespans, a shift from landfilling to combustion for municipal solid waste disposal, as well as municipal solid waste recycling, composting, and landfill-gas capture for electricity generation. These actions estimate a total technical potential—defined as the "estimated [greenhouse gas] emission reductions that would occur if the scenarios presented were achieved, setting aside economic, institutional, or technological limitations"—of between 5 and 150 million metric tons of carbon dioxide equivalents per year for each activity (U.S. EPA 2009c, 22). The report goes on to note, "The total technical potential scenarios provided here are not representative of all possible approaches to reduce [greenhouse gas] emissions through materials management. Many of these scenarios focus on the waste stream because the *data are limited* on materials management strategies that focus on other points in the materials flow" (EPA. 2009c, 22, emphasis added).

Here again we hit a wall when it comes to industrial data. Although materials management as a new way of thinking about waste and the linking of solid-waste reduction to climate-change mitigation represent interesting and potentially fruitful frameworks for considering tonnage and toxicity in the future, it is clear that the availability of data on extraction and manufacturing will be a crucial factor in achieving real gains in materials management as it seeks to eclipse waste management of old. As one EPA official in the 2020 Vision Workgroup I interviewed explained,

The focus really for a long time [was on]municipal diversion, which was pretty small [in tonnages] and that was, you know, on recycling and stuff like that. And fortunately back in the early '90s or late '80s they got Franklin [the firm contracted by the EPA to compile municipal solid waste statistics] to get a characterization—[a] very small piece, but at that time it was sort of the only information around that could be used because we weren't allowed to get data gathering based on . . . what the industry allowed. You know, the burden that we would put on them.[13]

The materials-management framework is at an early moment in its discursive and practical development. It has broadness of scope to recommend it, which opens space for real consideration of the role of producers and production in environmental problems and of its stated aim, the reduction of harm in meeting human needs. Writes the EPA:

A comprehensive materials management approach serves to direct environmental, product, and resource policy to those areas where it will provide the greatest environmental benefit. It will enable us to focus on those material flows which potentially cause the greatest harm and where in the life cycle they occur. It also will allow us to determine which material flows are overly wasteful, where they originate, and where they ultimately end up. It will also help identify which activities or products are primarily responsible for these harmful flows, and devise strategies that have the greatest likelihood of being environmentally and economically effective. (2009e, 17)

At the same time, the materials-management approach stands poised to promise justification only to continue municipal solid waste–focused, largely curbside recycling practices, leaving the activities of industry unaffected except in cases where voluntary process change happens to coincide with profit enhancement (as with the use of coal-combustion products in cement production discussed in chapter 3). It is important to note that the 2020 Vision Workgroup calls for "a national conversation about materials management, engaging multiple networks," encouraging the EPA itself to "open a dialogue on economic instruments to encourage better materials management . . . [and] . . . create ways to share knowledge on materials management" (U.S. EPA 2009e, v). This call can be responded to with words, more of the same actions, or different actions. In the next section, I propose a progressive and promising direction in which to guide materials management and with it the impulse in environmentalism that led to its first articulation.

Environmentally Grounded Sectoral Analysis

Maureen Smith's *The U.S. Paper Industry and Sustainable Production: An Argument for Restructuring* (1997) is a study of the sustainability of the timber, pulp, and paper sectors of the U.S. industrial economy. As part of her inquiry into the flows of materials through this set of industries and the environmental impacts at each point of transformation, she evaluates the effectiveness of actually existing forms of postconsumer paper recycling to achieve stated goals, among them the environmental movement's by now ritualized claim of "saving trees." Neither rates of global deforestation nor rising tonnages of pulp and paper being produced, transported, and consumed nor levels of process pollutants released suggest that paper recycling as we know it is diminishing sectoral impacts, nor does the vision of sustainability in which it prominently features offer a realistic basis for doing so in the future. Instead, observes Smith, "the current sum of objectives held by the extended environmental community around paper recycling, paper procurement, forest use, nonwoods, pulp mill production, and so on, offers something of a bundle of contradictions rather than a coherent perspective" (1997, 238). As an antidote, Smith offers a framework for coherent challenge to the current organization of this sector, which she says can be "alternatively viewed as an industry-centered environmental analysis or environmentally grounded sectoral analysis" (2). Such coherence is crucially needed, she argues, because of the dangers of diversionary phenomena that I have discussed elsewhere in this book. She writes: "In the absence of approaches based on integrative and systemic environmental analyses, expectations are often dashed, and important opportunities overlooked or foreclosed. . . . Serious distortions of intention can and do arise in strange and unpredictable forms and may be as likely to create new environmental problems as to solve those originally targeted" (8).

Like the materials-management framework advanced by the EPA, Smith's approach emphasizes careful cyclical tracking of materials and their embedded impacts as they move through today's materials economy. Smith goes beyond this approach, however, in arguing that measurement is not enough. The goal is "equally about understanding environmental problems in terms of how they are embedded in the forces that define and influence the larger industrial system" (224). These forces, I add, include power, exerted through its three dimensions, which is linked closely to the economic fortunes of business.

Smith urges environmental movements to refocus on the complex relationships that constitute the industry as a whole and to treat the wasting of both trees and paper not as subjects of action in isolation, but as reflections of the "causes and sources of the demand placed on" them (1997, 105). Among the deficiencies of paper recycling as we know it to serve as a coherent solution to any environmental problem is that "its complex relationship to forest issues has been relegated to a status of vague abstraction" in which the degree of integration among sources of wood, pulp, paper, and product is not considered and in which problems of excessive demand for wood and paper are cast "only in terms of rising consumption" rather than in terms of production (105). Approaches to sustainability, Smith argues, have to be understood in terms of industrial sectors first and foremost.

What would this approach look like with regard to other problems of solid waste—specifically plastics? First, clear analytic distinctions must be made among the problematic aspects of the heterogeneous range of materials called "plastics." In ecological terms, these aspects include risks to workers and communities during production of plastics; risks to consumers from ingestion and inhalation of plastic products; risks to terrestrial and marine ecosystems and species from accumulation of plastic litter; risks to communities in the developed world from combustion of plastic wastes in modern incineration; and risks to workers and communities in the developing world from the export of mixed plastic wastes for processing. It is important to acknowledge that, with the possible exception of mitigating litter that migrates from landfills and diverting some plastics from incineration, *plastic recycling as we know it addresses none of these problems.*

In social terms, plastics entail a cost to taxpayers for waste management as well as a potential source of revenues and jobs from secondary processing and remanufacture. We must similarly acknowledge that, with the exception of the revenues from sale of PET and HDPE bottles in mixed curbside collections, the social benefits of plastics recycling are not accruing to municipalities in proportion to their expenditures on plastics recycling overall. Jobs from plastics recycling, to the extent that they are created in the United States as opposed to overseas, cluster in a few regions of the country and only modestly contribute to national employment. While acknowledging the contributions of the U.S. secondary plastics processing and remanufacturing industry as a whole, it is important to be clear that jobs and tax revenues from plastics recycling do not spring up in cities where residents recycle a large quantity of plastic. The scalar exigencies of secondary plastic processing drive recycled plastics far afield, just as they do with paper and other materials.

The bundle of social and ecological contradictions that characterize the complex subject of plastic consumption and waste urgently need different sets of policies entailing source reduction mandated through bans or product fees for the most toxic and difficult-to-recycle forms of plastic, along with methods of recycling benign plastics that are able to capture substantial quantities and route them into closed-loop, preferably regionally scaled, recycling and remanufacture. The combined detoxification of the plastics-materials cycle and diminishment of varieties of plastics used in that cycle so as to create a critical mass of recoverable tonnage should be the overarching objective. From this perspective, required refill of plastic bottles may well be considered among other strategies (Ackerman 1997a). What is definitely not the answer is a ranting insistence by the public or environmental organizations simply to "get plastic recycling done" no matter what the method or how symbolic the effort.

In her treatment of the paper industry, Smith discusses the crucial importance of data and corresponding information-oriented policy as part of a broader elaboration of how materials-flows analysis can be mobilized in the complex and politically contested terrain of real-world production and consumption. Only with consistent, audited reporting of business activity can the requisite understanding of system functioning be worked up enough to adequately inform processes of urban and regional planning needed to ensure socially and environmental optimal scale of economy. Her study of the development of an inappropriately scaled recycled paper mill, discussed in chapter 4, shows the pitfalls of proceeding without such understanding, as did the New York City cases I profiled. What was lacking in these cases was what she urges: "some understanding of larger, long-range issues attached to the industry and . . . an awareness of the degree to which local decisionmaking can consciously or unconsciously support or undercut the prospects for both long-term transformation of industry and maximum local opportunity" (1997, 240).

The patchwork of state and local laws addressing plastic rigid containers, plastic bags, and food-service Styrofoam through alternatives of bans, fees, and recycling points to the need for a similar degree of understanding with regard to plastics, among other modern wastes. Extending on the questions rhetorically posed by the EPA, which show the difference between a solid-waste-management perspective ("What should we do with fluorescent lights when they need to be disposed?") and a materials-management approach ("Is there a way to eliminate fluorescent bulb waste completely, to provide lighting services with fewer resources and no adverse environmental impacts?") (U.S. EPA 2009e, 31), a sectoral approach would enable us to consider the question, "What is the optimal range of types of plastics to use in consumer products if we want to maximize social justice and protect the health of people and ecosystems?"

In regard to the gathering of consistent, audited data, Smith notes that "the need for further and better regulatory support—a central mechanism for dealing with failures that arise out of the segregation of environment and economy—is as compelling as ever" (1997, 247). She points to the efficacy of the Toxics Release Inventory , which requires industry-wide reporting on releases of certain toxic chemicals, providing not only notification of risk to the public, but also the "self-enforcing quality of other reporting requirements" on pushing and pulling change in industrial practice beyond that required by direct regulation (1997, 248). A WRI researcher also articulated the usefulness of such a framework to a far larger range of industrial processes and materials:

I think we're very kind of light on our industries in terms of making them report some of this information, with the exception of kind of the required reporting under TRI [Toxics Release Inventory]. So when you're trying to construct a whole material account, you know a little bit about what's coming out of the pipe with TRI, but then you're like, oh, there's all this other stuff. We have no freakin' clue, you know, and so that's part of it. I mean, you just don't know, and there's no way of knowing, so until we know, nobody's going to pay attention to managing it because it's not being measured. And so that, from my perspective, that's why everybody looks at municipal solid waste because at least it's transparent, and you can start to, you know, you can start to dig in and try to figure out what's going on.[14]

The recommendations of the 2020 Vision Workgroup do call for improvement of data availability. They do gesture at a sectoral approach when they argue that "different materials will require different management strategies."[15] but the 2020 Vision leaves others to follow up, suggesting "a panel that includes stakeholders and outside experts to advise on materials-management information priorities, including types of information needed, key indicators to track, how to make U.S. information compatible with information being generated in other countries, and how to get started in developing the necessary data sets" (U.S. EPA 2009e, 3). As this proceeds, the role of industry as a stakeholder and data provider with a particular set of interests at stake has to be kept in mind. As the WRI researcher put it,

One of the things that [George W.] Bush was very good at was squelching science and squelching information and making it very difficult for EPA and other organizations to publish information. So what you have now is a much more kind of scientifically literate leadership that will allow this stuff to be published. Now, once the data gets published the Obama administration is gonna be not that much more inclined to stand up to business or to sort of, you know, have a show down with business, but what they're willing to do is they're willing to let the numbers out, they're willing to let science stand, and then what that will do is then it will be the job of [nongovernmental organizations] or of others.[16]

In the face of such institutionalized aversion to conflict, civil society in her opinion should protest in an informed manner:

You need . . . the grass roots to sort of digest and process and figure out what to do and then if the public opinion starts to swell, but then that has a chance for the leadership to then pick up on that public. So they can kind of set the numbers out there and kind of let it percolate with the public and some of these larger actors, and then what will happen is the government leadership and the private sector will start to kind of sense this shifting public opinion and sense this newfound knowledge, and then they'll react to that.

The collection of data, the "numbers" from industries hesitant to reveal them, can be achieved only through government coordination, preferably at the federal level, so as to enable aggregation and comparison. Carrying out this collection, let alone "digesting and processing" these data as part of the collective action by civil society, is no easy task, a fact Smith recognizes:

One might think it desirable for regulators—who have the power to establish regulations so significant that they function like a de facto industrial policy—to be more far reaching in their vision. Yet, because they are still digging out from under the burdens of existing medium-specific and other mandates, attempting to integrate, rationalize, and modernize them (all the while facing challenges to their existing authority), it would be at least naïve to pin high hopes in this direction in the near future. (1997, 151)

In fact, mustering the power of systemic data gathering to the task of forging sustainable-materials policy has been a struggle since 1968, when Robert Ayres and A. V. Kneese proposed to Congress a method of inventorying the flow of materials through processes of industrial transformation within the boundaries of the United States. Their argument departed from prior justifications for looking at imports, exports, and domestic production and consumption so as to maintain resources needed for U.S. industrial growth and international competitiveness. The latter focus began shortly after the end of World War II, exemplified in the 1952 President's Materials Policy Commission (called the Paley Commission) and reappearing in congressional testimony and reporting through 1991 (CRS 1983; U.S. House of Representatives 1991a). What Ayres and Kneese urged instead was industrial-materials data gathering in the context of critique of economic growth on ecological grounds. Such an undertaking, in addition to its political threat, was and still is, says materials-flow analysis historian Marina Fischer-Kowalski, "method-ologically quite demanding. It requires, as a database, economic statistics for all materials not only in monetary terms but also in terms of mass (analogous to the more common energy statistics in joules). This totality of materials flows of a national economy is particularly important as a parameter that can be presented in time series and related to economic performance in monetary terms" (1998, 112).

In sum, it will be very difficult to gather, synthesize, and audit industrial data as well as to understand the relations of power among industries in order to make "materials management" as proposed by the EPA a coherent framework for environmentally grounded sectoral analysis. This effort will not lend itself to immediate political action; the temptation may be to do something simpler just to do anything at all. This is what Fischer-Kowalski alludes to when she talks of the tendency to pursue "political relevance and social change . . . at the price of clarity and depth of analysis" (1998, 123). But foregoing the heavy sledding of environmentally grounded sectoral analysis can take a variety of forms that lead to busy-ness. Among them are organizing policies that focus on data that are already being gathered and turning to the community project as a first step in what is imagined will become cumulative social transformation. As Elizabeth Royte says at one point in *Garbage Land*, when she found herself dismayed by statistics on manufacturing-waste tonnages that did not agree among different sources, "I continued recycling and watching what I bought. It was something I could manage" (2005, 284). But data gathering and analysis *are* something we can manage—they are difficult, but they are things we know how to do. The challenge is to get information consistently from those who are unwilling to report.

Conclusion

The information I have presented in this book leads me to propose some specific changes in U.S. solid-waste policy and, far more important, to encourage an opening up of discourse and practice within those aspects of the environmental movement that focus on garbage, recycling, and the excesses of consumption. First, I argue for a strong federal role in data gathering and dissemination, legislation of mandatory extended producer responsibility for what I call "modern materials" (e-waste, household hazardous waste, and most if not all plastic wastes), and leadership in what Maureen Smith (1997) defines as environmentally grounded sectoral analysis, coordinated as part of a national materials policy. As opposed to focusing on the moment of waste or the greening of the economy, the goal of this policy approach should be the detoxification and diminishment of materials flowing into, through, and out of the United States.

Second, I controversially suggest that paper and metal be the only materials collected in commingled curbside form for recycling in cities, to be processed through human-scaled, safe, well-compensated circuits of materials recovery facility processing and remanufacture that are kept regional and national in scope when and where possible. I advocate the separate collection of glass using municipal or possibly local nonprofit labor so as to route it to refill or bottle-to-bottle recycling and to use it as aggregate only as a last resort. In this regard, deposit systems, standardization of bottle sizes and colors across content categories (soda, beer, food uses), and fees assessed on the glass, beverage, and bottling industry so as to encourage glass-container use over plastic should be pursued synergistically on a national or at least regional (multistate) scale.

Third, complementing the recycling of paper, metal, glass, and plastic fractions of municipal solid waste as well as existing separate circuits of construction and demolition debris recycling, I urge cities to pursue composting aggressively, concurrently developing small- and large-scale operations for the transformation of organic materials into soil amendment (which I discuss more fully later).

Fourth, in regard to just waste solutions, I encourage the cultivation of community-based enterprises that yield good jobs associated with reuse and remanufacture, developed at scales large enough and relevant enough to, using the words of Kenneth Geiser, "progressively reduce [the] throughput of materials and energy" through the U.S. economy (2001, 367). This means thinking about regional systems to move masses of materials if and when that is the goal, with a clear distinction made about the role of small enterprises that work in concert with such systems. I suggest specifically that we rethink the notion that small enterprises, if numerous and diverse enough, can absorb the flow of urban discards such that the burdens of disposal cease. The goal instead should be organization of medium- to large-size infrastructure that is truly public in that it serves and is informed by citizens. To this end, it will be essential to harness the historical and present potential of the scrap industry so as to counter the current model in which the disposal industry operates most recycling infrastructure privately under contract to local governments.

Finally and most important, I urge those concerned about waste and its relation to social and environmental problems to relegate notions of personal commitment and responsibility, as well as expectations of social change premised in step-by-step incrementalism, to the back burner. These constructs gird the American approach to saving the earth far too much. Although they are not worthless outright, there is nothing to be lost from turning away from them to cultivate different sets of ideas and strategies that maturely confront the fact that the materials economy is a complex, global system in which businesses employ people and transform things in highly destructive ways outside the gaze or reach of the savviest consumer.

Waste and Citizenship

My proposals are meant to invite discourse and debate about ecological citizenship. By "ecological citizenship," I mean the range of options, strategies, actions, and communications that people concerned about problems of resource depletion, pollution, ecosystemic disruption, health risks, and inequity globally and locally should feel free to engage in.

Ecological citizens should have the right to know and understand issues of ecological concern through accessible data and reporting, but they should understand that digesting such data may take some study and reflection. They should have the right to mount critiques of individuals and institutions in power without necessarily always having to simultaneously offer a constructive alternative. They should be free to introduce the notion that temporary incursions on corporate profit, especially those incursions applied evenly across industries, to internalize what were before externalities are not heretical to the health of the economy or jobs. They should have the right to advocate—through electoral politics, organized demonstration, art, journalism, and other collective and communicative actions—changes to institutions without needing to change the materials practices of their own daily lives.

These forms of citizenship are in fact thriving within the environmental justice movement, but they are ailing within the recycling public, including some aspects of the Zero Waste movement. In these spheres of civil society, ecological citizenship as I have described it is overshadowed and crowded out by other progressive expressions, such as changing material-lifestyle practice (especially via recycling, buying or not buying), establishing businesses or social enterprises, experimenting with design, educating the next generation, and encouraging people in at times vague and at times moralistic ways to "think differently." Make no mistake, I am not suggesting that we do away with any of these activities—except the moralism. I do invite those concerned with finding solutions to environmental problems and to solid-waste problems specifically to consider putting the familiar, established responses, most of which are rooted in notions of the market and personal life, into a different perspective. This perspective grants a far greater role to systemic solutions through governance—in terms of information, regulation, and industrial policy—and ascribes a smaller role to the individual than prevails today. Such a perspective, I argue, surprisingly frees rather than constrains citizens to strive for the common good.

Business, Movements, and Power

What leads me to take this position is what I have observed about the exertion of power by business to prevent, delay, or in some cases refashion social and ecological change. The five instances of socially constructed solid-waste problems and solutions I have reviewed in this book show civil society's altruistic desire to bring about change in a particular area—the material environmental problems that are manifest in solid waste. Groups within civil society, notably the recycling movement and then the Zero Waste movement, in the past constructed solutions to address problems that were close to hand, visible in terms of daily experience as opposed to reported in data. In several of the stories reviewed, affected industries met such solutions head on, bent on keeping any resulting action from interfering with their autonomy. At the inception of the contemporary recycling movement, industrial groups under threat discovered that they could distract civil society and send it in harmless directions, using the substitute of busy-ness. In these cases, producers strategically used the social fact of busy-ness to further their interests at the expense of civil society. Glass and plastic recycling in particular and curbside recycling in general were clear instances of this strategic mobilization. In other cases, however, busy-ness also arose to divert attention from meaningful material action without producers' direct or even indirect intent.

The neglect of textile waste and manufacturing waste seems to have been driven by their invisibility in daily experience: textiles, unlike glass, were not litter; manufacturing waste remained stationary and hidden behind factory gates. Busy-ness in these cases was manifest in a preoccupying focus on other, more visible wastes that were socially constructed as very important but were in reality relatively less important than textiles or manufacturing waste in material terms. In the case of textiles, it also is possible that the existence of the thrift-shop sector overdetermined the invisibility of textile waste. Perhaps such waste seemed less important because of a widespread impression that others (thrift enterprises) were already "busy" at work collecting used clothing and linens, although I have not yet found empirical evidence to support this speculation. In any case, there is no evidence to suggest that primary textile producers were at all involved in deflecting civil-society attention away from textile waste; this happened without the overt exertion of power. And producers' first-dimensional exertion of power to defend manufacturing waste from regulation had little to do with busy-ness. Although representatives from extractive and manufacturing industries may have benefitted from civil society's preoccupation with municipal solid waste, they did not actively foster this preoccupation as bottlers and beverage industry groups did with respect to curbside recycling.

Representatives of extractive and manufacturing industries, however, did articulate a construction of individual responsibility and consumer sovereignty with regard to industrial waste, and they did advocate voluntaristic models of self-governance, predicated on federal grants and technical assistance, as they defended themselves from the threat of manufacturing-waste regulation. Some of this successful defense was achieved through control over definition. Smith notes that during the regulatory deliberation over RCRA reauthorization, as goals were redefined away from setting production standards on process and inputs and toward imposing recycled-content procurement standards for the federal government, there occurred a "finessing of solid waste into hazardous and postconsumer (or industrial and municipal) categories" as part of a broader effort to "channel . . . aggressive tendencies away from producers and toward the consumer and postconsumer waste where they could be more safely debated" (1997, 157). As part of this project, producers also favored devolution of responsibility for industrial waste oversight to states and localities in the name of flexibility. "A single efficiency standard [for manufacturing-waste minimization] is unrealistic," said William O'Keefe of the Petroleum Institute in his testimony against the Baucus bill (U.S. Senate 1987, 238). "The problem with S. 2773 [the Baucus bill] . . . is that it rigidly specifies technology for all industrial surface impoundments without regard to the characteristics or potential hazards of those wastes," said James Petros of the Chemical Manufacturer's Association, arguing that states should be free to enact manufacturing-waste legislation as they saw fit (U.S. Senate 1987, 225). In the articulation of this set of ideas—individual responsibility, voluntaristic self-governance, and subnational legislation—extractive and manufacturing industries found allies in civil society, just as bottlers and beverage producers had found an ally in the EAC in the 1970s. "It is essential that every individual become responsible for our waste management problem," said a representative of the Citizen's League of Minneapolis who had traveled to Washington to testify at the Baucus bill hearings. "We cannot pass laws that put the burden on government or the business sector alone, maintaining the ease and convenience individual waste generators are used to and expect in disposal. Permanent changes will only occur when every individual calls for them" (U.S. Senate 1987, 40). These words came just after a representative from Mobil urged the Senate to consider "the importance of public education as a fundamental requirement that must be achieved. . . . Individuals create an important and central ingredient in this effort. . . . [T]he goods and comforts consumers want and enjoy produce waste" (U.S. Senate 1987, 40).

Self-reliance. A reconnection to markets. Small steps, start small. Local, flexible, voluntary. Responsibility—corporate, individual, personal. Win-win; win-win-win; the triple bottom line, the three E's (equity, environment, economy). Education, partnership, consumer choice. The modern history of recycling in the United States has seen a fostering of agreement among producers and civil society that this constellation of ideas will lead us out of unsustainability with regard to waste and other material matters. This is a very dangerous development. We see these ideas knit together as a coherent worldview, exerting power to foster particular policies to the exclusion of alternatives. This is the third-dimensional power at work. Hegemonic ideas, not actors per se, set the stage for civil society to act against its own interests. The ideas are not hegemonic simply because they reflect agreement among former adversaries, groups that have been structurally at odds with regard to exchange and use value, environmental harm, and environmental healing. It is indeed possible that conceptual harmony can be achieved without someone losing. Rather, these ideas are hegemonic because they lead to an outcome that is contrary to what recycling and Zero Waste seek. Solid-waste policy and practice geared around the recycling and reuse of certain fractions of municipal solid waste, based on a particular mix of privatization and localization, *isn't working* to reduce tonnage, toxicity, and continued growth of materials extractions and transformations in the United States or globally (WRI 2001; Rogich, Cassara, Wernick, et al. 2008; Krausman, Gingrich, Eisenmenger, et al. 2009).

Bit by Bit: The Implicit Theory of Social Change

It is understandably insulting to tell those working hard every day in many different ways to reduce municipal solid waste that much of the achievement of recycling and Zero Waste can be measured in units of busy-ness but not in material progress, and that unbeknownst to them they are being oppressed when they feel empowered. Such a perspective is a wet blanket (to say the least) thrown atop the exciting momentum that is taking place now as the U.S. administration starts to acknowledge global warming and to plan for an economy based on clean energy. To critique such momentum in any way robs agency from a burgeoning movement. In Marshall Bell's documentary "Slowly Growing Greener," Dale Jamieson, a professor of environmental studies, speaks in defense: "People look at small projects, and they say, well, you know you're never going to save the earth by changing the way you do dry cleaning or, OK, so a few more people ride bikes, that's not going to make any difference, but a lot of small differences can add up to significant change, that's the

first thing. The second thing is that making these small changes, partici-
pating in them, empower individuals to do other things" (qtd. in Bell
2008).

But do they? There is a theory of social change in this statement and
in many others like it that undergirds twenty-first-century progressive
politics of environmental change. The small step, the start, the little bit
that helps, the individual contribution to a common problem are all
articulations of the notion of cumulative transformation of social systems,
institutions, economic processes, and ecosystemic additions and withdrawals. In a 1 +1 + 1 fashion, individual actions add up. Collective
action is, if anything, a simple amalgam of individual action. This theory
is conflict free, but it is based on altruistic intention as opposed to rational choice. As Jamieson articulates, this theory has two parts.

First, the critical mass or tipping point can be reached through accumulation of personal choices and small projects (Gladwell 2002). Second,
there is a notion of empowerment through the education of experience;
this empowerment goes beyond the accumulation of the individual act
itself. Both aspects of this perspective draw on an idealist conception of
history in which a change of mind can change the world, and there is,
if anything, a call to individuals en masse to awaken from a slumber. In
the case of environmental problems, this awakening is to a threat that
must be acted upon before it's too late. There are notions that early
socialization will set the mind change, enabling action by enough individuals to tip the scales sooner rather than later.

Donna Lee King studies environmental education and in her book
Doing Their Share to Save the Planet investigates the social construction
of environmental problems through pedagogy. She notes that "often,
crisis themes that arise in one generation are appropriated by society for
socializing the next" and identifies the "fate of the environment" as the
most "pervasive crisis theme aimed at children" in the 1990s (1995, 1).
Her study of elementary environmental curricula in the United States in
this decade shows that it was routine for "children [to be] cheerfully
targeted for environmental concern. They are told to pick up the trash,
recycle plastic, conserve trees and water, and buy 'green' products. In
this lifestyle context, saving the planet becomes a comfortable arena for
feeling socially and politically committed" (116).

According to King, generalized social concerns are connected to hopes
for the future through the medium of the "next generation." This concern
is channeled into consumptive expression that leaves production systems
unexamined and unchallenged, especially through collective social action.

Calling this expression the "rhetoric of liberal environmentalism," King observes that

the discourse of environmental disaster encompasses a broad range of social, political, economic, biological and cultural concerns. But the rhetoric of liberal environmentalism . . . promotes the notion that global environmental degradation—the end result of multinational corporate, military/industrial, and nation-state practices of consumption and production—is really "everybody's fault." The reduction of complex, global problems to simplistic, individualist solutions serves corporate interests much more effectively than it does children. (1995, 117)

In perspectives such as the one expressed by Jamieson, the "other things" that individuals may be empowered to do by starting with small, personal acts are not specified. They may include more incrementalism or acts that inadvertently intensify the problems they seek to solve (such as bogus green consumption). This outcome is particularly likely if environmental education focuses on the small step as something a kid, handed responsibility for the future along with his crayons, can do. What we ask kids to do are things they can manage, projects in the classroom. But the empowerment Jamieson mentions may also lead to collective action to enact change at levels of institutions and economic structures. This type of change *could* entail conflict, and would require environmental groups' willingness to move beyond the small, the everyday, the demonstration project. It's a project not for kids, but for adults. Adults presumably can handle the stress of facing a problem on a large scale and can withstand hearing that some small steps may instead "serve corporate interests."

Or so one would hope. Disappointment, denial, disgust, and the "trash tantrum" I described in chapter 3 are infantilzed American responses to the news that small steps may not be the start of something bigger, at least without different structures of political engagement than 1 + 1+ 1. They suggest how underdeveloped ecological citizenship is in the United States. Nina Eliasoph's studies of civic activism, in which individuals with "compassionate, curious and open-minded ideas" in private ratchet down their public political imaginations, shows us the extent to which critical political engagement has been washed out of contemporary American civil society. She notes that volunteers interested in questions beyond their backyards and personal spheres of life "worked hard to limit their thinking, not just their action. They all worked hard to create a feeling that the world makes sense" by depoliticizing the aims and in particular by restricting their scope of interest to what was "close to home," personal, and manageable (1998, 257).

Here the third dimension of power is at work. The potential for true ecological citizenship gets shut down by a reflexive turn back to the self, the local, the doable, the manageable, the small step—a turn encouraged no less by progressive environmental discourse than by industries eager to continue business as usual. The outcome is a sense of resignation and powerlessness self-cloaked in optimism and reassurance, as expressed here by one citizen who had volunteered to promote recycling in her apartment building:

I think the magnitude of issues facing most people on a daily basis (particularly in New York City) is overwhelming, and as a result, many feel powerless to affect the environment around us and/or to contribute to some overall greater "cause" when it is all we can do to keep up with our own daily lives. Recycling is something small each of us can do to contribute something to the greater effort to preserve our planet, and it has the added benefit of making us feel just a little bit better about ourselves and our place in the world. (NYC DS 2008c, 3)

Michael Maniates points to outright dangers in the dominant view of social change predicated on conflict-free incrementalist change: "the prevailing conceptualization of the 'environmental crisis' drive[s] us toward an individualization of responsibility that legitimizes existing dynamics of consumption and production" and "ignore[s] critical elements of power and institutions." Such individualization, he notes, "has deep roots in American political culture. To the extent that commonplace language and handy conceptual frameworks have power . . . they shape our view of the world and tag some policy measures as proper and others far-fetched" (2002, 65).

The incrementalist theory of social change runs deeply through the recycling and Zero Waste movements today, to their detriment. It needs critical reexamination, although making this critique is dangerous within academia and practiced environmentalism. From personal experience, I can attest that cynicism, resignation, and abdication of responsibility are assumed as its only alternative. More generally, a critique of individual incrementalism is interpreted as reason for people to do nothing. As one journalist writing for a Memphis paper put it, "The excuse many people give for not living a 'greener' lifestyle is that their small gesture to help the environment won't do enough to make a difference" (Adams 2008, 1).

From Local to National

Individualism isn't all there is to the set of ideas guiding waste solutions today, however. If we look at the impulse to create the ReBuilder's Source or the motivation to draft the *Citizen's Plan for Zero Waste* (Dimino and Warren 2004), we might conclude that the "other things" that personal acts can lead to are indeed beyond the scale of incrementalism. Beyond the shopping trip and the recycling bin are institutions, laws, and economic practices—preferably enacted locally. They are "small projects," such as organic dry cleaners or community recycling centers, whose successful existence stands to provide synergistic social benefits at the local scale not only in terms of jobs, but, in the words of the EAC's Karen Dumont, in terms of a return "back to the community. There one can find identity. The community in which you live can be an escape from that larger place with which you must cope. It is home. The ties are racial, social, economic. . . . The community also can give a feeling of identity. Individual identity is wrapped up in a need to accomplish within one's community. It is, in part, the big fish in the little pond principle in action" (1971c).

At its best, individual responsibility is not antithetical to ecological citizenship. At its best, it leads to action at community and local scales; it emancipates not just through the shopping choice, but through the ecology center. It is certainly more mature and overtly political than pure "every-little-bit-helps-ism." But localism as de facto sustainability cannot be assumed (Born and Purcell 2006). The ideal of local Zero Waste enterprise, with its aspirations of lifting urban residents out of poverty, turning them away from crime, and countering past siting inequities, has tried to do too much at once, valiantly applying win-win-winism to urban social problems, urban fortunes, and urban tonnage all at once. This ideal didn't work out in the case of New York City; although it did work in the case of some outfits in California, even there the entrepreneurial effort to turn waste to wealth did not register in terms of tonnages kept local.

At the same time, the recycling and Zero Waste movements have not been wed to the local scale in principle. Zero Waste vision documents call for action at regional and national scales with regard to mandatory extended producer responsibility, taxing landfills and shutting down incinerators, ending subsidies for extractive industries, and establishing national as well as statewide and municipal Zero Waste goals (ILSR, Ecocycle, and GAIA 2008). The time is now to act on these larger-scale ideas, to take up recycling and materials management on a national level, and to demand that federal, state, and local governments regulate the excesses of industrial practice where and when good data show a lack of control. A mistrust of government, federal government in particular, is certainly understandable. To the extent that, as some scholars hold, the federal government has been the servant of industry in its waste policy (Landy, Roberts, and Thomas 1994) or, as others hold, has been instrumental in absorbing the environmental movement's oppositional power into its bureaucratic structures (Dowie 1995), a cynicism about the federal role is understandable. But among recycling and Zero Waste activists, we ironically do not see that same degree of cynicism leveled toward aspects of the business sector that have proven historically to be at least as harmful as they are beneficial with regard to the public good. We do not see, for example, cynicism with regard to the goals of urban economic development, the entrepreneurial model as an emancipatory one, or consumer sovereignty as a driver of industrial change. Each one of these phenomena has been extensively critiqued as a manifestation of the destructive side of capitalism, leading to outcomes against the public good, despite claims to the contrary (Logan and Molotch 1987; Luke 1997; T. Smith 1998; Brenner and Theodore 2002; Szasz 2007). If the nation-state as an organizer of environmental policy is to be suspected and disregarded because of its inherent tendency to favor business interests over people lives, then surely the eco-corporation and the green product deserve at least some of this suspicion as well.

This brings me to the role that green capitalism occupies within the Zero Waste imagination. Inasmuch as the movement recognizes that economic and technological change has to take place beyond the local scale and that such change cannot be indirectly driven through consumer sovereignty or through the incremental accumulation of small-project success, it identifies the framework of industrial ecology and green or natural capitalism as an alternative route to systemic change at the national and transnational scale (Murray 2002). Mobilization from below (individual, local) rises up to meet and impel industrywide enlightenment at the level of process and facility design. Here is how it has to work. Green production must translate into a verifiable branding that in turn will engender broad, consistent shifts in consumer demand and will take advantage of citizen's willingness to sort their discards and send them back to (now willing) producers of "designed for recycling" goods. At the level of by-products, industries will address hazardous waste, manufacturing waste, and air and water emissions synergistically and as a matter of course through effective, efficient engineering and architecture that understand the factory as a metabolizing organism. Overall, the products, the by-products, and the processes will have waste designed out of them. Driving this process will be two motives: the competitiveness of the green branding and the morality of the CEO (McDonough and Braungart 2002). This vision, outlined by William McDonough and Michael Braungart, currently much in vogue in architecture and product design circles, is beautiful but apolitical. It leaves me with this question for the United States and for solid waste: How will we know? How will we know at an industry-wide level, not just a "success story" level, that waste in all of its forms is being addressed?

The answer, I argue, must be via national-scale policy. Precedent for this form of policy is fully developed with regard to solid waste in Europe (Buttel 2006; Janicke 2006). To one degree or another, the United Kingdom, Ireland, the Netherlands, Germany, Sweden, and Norway publish statistics on the equivalent of manufacturing waste and set targets for its reduction (EEA 2003; OECD 2004). They also set national targets for municipal solid waste diversion and, in the case of Norway and Sweden, monitor and regulate the utilization of forest plantations for paper production as part of a paper-materials policy that also covers commercial, residential, and industrial paper recycling (Kumar 2005). It is beyond the scope of this book to describe and assess critically the range of waste and materials policies in place in Europe and other countries of the North. They have their faults and their critics (Fagan 2004; Davies 2008). The body of environmental scholarship most open to the role of the nation-state in waste governance is ecological modernization, a perspective whose guiding social theory is that although "the most challenging environmental problems of this century and the next have (or will have) been caused by modernization and industrialization, their solutions must necessarily lie in more—rather than less—modernization and 'superindustrialization'" (Buttel 2000, 61). Rooted in the experience of national-supranational environmental governance emerging with the bureaucratization of the European Union, ecological modernization as a European school of thought takes McDonough and Braungart's beautiful blueprint of eco-effective factories and assumes, without great dispute, the need for national brakes on the creativity of markets to address social problems. As Martin Janicke states,

in the context of environmental governance the role of government in general needs to be reinvented. Even if voluntary agreements were a general solution, someone would have to make sure that the ultimate goal is finally reached. . . . Participation, "voluntarization," and consensus need to be complemented by competent moderation and professional public management. . . . The question of final responsibility for solving the relevant environmental problems has become crucial. If everybody is responsible, nobody will be responsible. In this regard, there is no functional equivalent to national government. Its role has changed, but it has not diminished. (2006, 91–92)

A U.S. Materials Policy

It is well documented that the most significant, measured reductions in pollution in U.S. history were brought about by sweeping federal acts in the 1970s (Clean Air Act, Clean Water Act) (Hays 1987). The federal scale has, traditionally, stayed out of matters of solid waste management, yet many waste-related state functions are best and most effectively managed at the national scale. Pollutants cross borders; states compete for a race to the bottom via deregulation. Commodities cross borders; poorer states lose out to wealthier ones compensated as hosts for LULUs (Lake 1994). The U.S. nation-state, in the embodiment of the EPA or a similar agency, is institutionally best capable of carrying out the following "first steps" in what, with continued pressure from a movement oriented toward the federal scale, might evolve further.

First, following John Dernbach's proposal cited in chapter 3, the federal state can use its authority to collect and publicize national data about manufacturing waste at a comparable level of detail and frequency as reporting for municipal solid waste and hazardous industrial waste, preferably in a geographical information system–accessible format such as is provided via the Toxics Release Inventory. Even absent process and product regulation, this step alone, in conjunction with the well-developed forms of resistance that have been built up over several decades of antitoxics and environmental justice activism, would force manufacturing waste onto the national scale of debate as a policy issue.

Second, at the very least the federal state can apply regulatory criteria for onsite disposal of manufacturing waste that are as stringent as the criteria for municipal solid waste disposal. Revisiting the definitional problems of industrial waste, including what is and is not hazardous, in conjunction with setting standards for disposal and recycling to maximize safety and quantify toxicity would be well within the federal government's capability.

Third, following requests by municipalities and states that have been mounted over the years, the federal government can undertake a comprehensive evaluation of imports, exports, and domestic production in terms of mass and not just in terms of dollar metrics that apply today. Such input/output data would provide realistic bases on which to consider legislation to ban, tax, and otherwise control the free proliferation of existing and new forms of plastic packaging, electronics and appliances, plastic durables, and hazardous household substances (glass and paper need not be addressed, for reasons I discuss later in this conclusion). Using fee and tax incentives, the federal state can intervene in the materials economy, as it did during the world wars, to steer these commodities as a whole toward forms that are reusable and at the same time free of toxics and to route such materials back to the manufacturer for nondisposal handling. The simplest and easiest first step would be to institute a national bottle bill or a national rigid plastics container bill.

Finally, following the European Union's landfill-tax model, the United States can tax each ton of landfilled or incinerated municipal solid waste and redirect tax funds toward support of locally organized reuse, recycling, and composting projects, with funding on a per ton diverted basis, established through audited weighing or heavily scrutinized demonstration of tons prevented.

The opponents of such policies would be obvious, the arguments familiar and expected. What must be different is the Zero Waste movement's stance toward the alternatives these opponents will put forward. Alternatives predicated on the offloading of the burden onto citizens and municipalities, or voluntarist compromises absent verification and comprehensive documentation, cannot be taken up anymore as rewarding projects for frustrated citizens to sink their teeth into. The notion of "shared product responsibility" among citizens, consumers, and municipalities must be shelved for the moment, and in its place enacted forms of legislation that equalize the terrain of competition for all producers. For years, state and local governments have articulated this desire in the few forums that allow it, as in the 1987 Baucus bill hearings:

[Regarding] the whole question of reducing waste and what we can specifically do. Cities can establish policies, we can establish programs, but cities have no control over the growing tide of packaging and much of it is non-recyclable. I would say that stopping the source of pollution is always better than treating it, which is what we're doing right now. Congress needs to charge the EPA with strict controls over how American products are packaged. Now, more and more of them are coming in not only plastics, but combinations . . . it's a deluge of plastic and it's there, and we have to deal with it and it's difficult to deal with.

For example, instead of the good old standard glass milk bottles, we now have a packaging revolution that's given us a wide range of potentially toxic, non-recyclable containers; and we believe [the] EPA needs the power to ban certain types of containers. (Virginia Galle, Seattle City Council, chairperson, Environmental Management Committee, in U.S. Senate 1987, 391)

Crucially for the Zero Waste movement, its change in stance will require placing considerations of local economic development, the momentum of existing programs, and the empowerment potential of small steps in a different and less central context, at least for enough time to organize the millions of Americans who profess to be concerned about waste or even the thousands who are willing to mobilize, using tools of collective action—lobbying, protesting, media, and party building. These forms of political engagement decidedly do not include starting businesses, creating green products, shopping, making art, or living like No Impact Man. Let me stress: there is no harm in doing any of these things, but they cannot stand in or substitute for action that demands regulatory action by the nation-state and that holds industries and trade groups accountable for transparency and fairness. Programs and policies that civil society demands need to ask where the big material impacts are. They also have to have the stomach to think big, to contemplate public works that restore use value to waste on monumental and not community scales, if need be. Although not discouraging the freedom to pursue interesting projects, this political position must relieve concerned citizens of the lure and the burden of staying busy sorting cans and bottles when there are more effective alternatives to fight for. Only when the goals of systemic change are decoupled from these individual and local acts of creativity can a revitalized public sphere be fully cultivated around waste. And make no mistake, there is plenty of room for creativity in politics that does not require tending one's own garden (Voltaire [1759] 1959).

The reentry of the nation-state into solid-waste governance need not make the local scale irrelevant at all. To the contrary, the local scale can return to a position in which it can manage urban waste effectively and in which it can realize the beautiful aspects of McDonough and Braungart's (2002) vision, including the notion that waste equals food. What is important here is a division between the wastes of exchange value and those of use value and in particular between the synthetic and the naturally occurring. Synthetics, resulting as they do from the "unnatural" joining together of molecules, are inherently difficult to recycle and to repair for reuse. They have revolutionized the world of commodities, enriching manufacturers who derive them largely from petroleum stocks. They have substitutes in glass, metal, paper, wood, bamboo, clay, and stone. Their husbandry should be the province of federal regulation, forcing manufacture responsibility for all synthetic products and by-products as well as addressing plastics of all kinds, electronics, and other toxics.

With such wastes either federally banned from municipal disposal or carrying a hefty disposal charge, the municipality would be left to manage only a subset of discards. This reduction in responsibility would enable paper and metal, collected at curbside in comingled form, to maximize returns to the municipality through scrap reclamations, offsetting costs of collections. Such revenues might also be used to facilitate municipal funding of not-for-profit reuse enterprises, in particular to facilitate clean collections of textile discards from businesses and residents and the securing of storage space to sort and stockpile materials. These reuse enterprises would provide social benefits such as jobs, job training, and human services, but, more important, this function would not need to be reinvented; it has a long and established history in such organizations as Goodwill Enterprises. To the extent that repairable or reusable durables such as furniture, household goods, hardware, toys, or other durables are not addressed through national policy targeting plastics, electronics, and toxics, such items might be repaired and set back into use, but this activity would not be expected to be a significant diversion in terms of tonnage.

What would be left over once modern materials have made their way back to points of production via noncurbside channels (as bottle bills do today), and once valuable paper, metal, and textile collections have been collected and routed back to scrap, would be the stuff of cities. This stuff would consist of a great deal of organic matter and a small amount of inert inorganic matter. Food waste, yard trimmings, wood wastes not suitable for reuse, ceramics, stones, brick, and dirt. These leftovers, garbage in the old sense of the term, are suitable for large-scale composting along with biosolids (sewage). Wastes of social reproduction, the intimate wastes of kitchen and bathroom, can safely and naturally become amendment for soil, with an endless outlet of uses that do not necessarily rely in markets or prices, if a collective decision is made to fund their transformation as an act of public works.

The national experience with sited hazards and environmental justice shows us that American civil society is well capable of such mobilization when the problem is rooted in a particular space and is risky and frightening. We *have* RCRA Subtitle C; the process of siting facilities *is* fundamentally different and more difficult than it once was. Sited resistance is the starting point for widespread industrial change. Polluting industries, if opposed consistently and long enough, find they can no longer site their facilities anywhere and are forced to detoxify their processes (Heinman 1990).

One of my major points is that we ignore at our peril both data on tonnage and toxicity, and businesses' driving imperative to remain free.

This is not at all to say that business is inherently a negative thing, but to say that the destructive half of its creative–destructive potential will always arise. Here the words of a researcher from the WRI are useful: "I don't want to paint this picture of, as kind of the folks in these companies as being sort of, like, evil, because they're really not. Most big corporations have an environmental sustainability representative." Such a representative, she notes, today works quite efficiently at monitoring the materials flows within the firm and is driven to interact with nonprofit groups such as the WRI when the firm is subject to critique. "When they get enough pressure from, you know, protestors and that sort of thing they'll come sort of knocking on our garage doors saying, hey, we're getting a lot of heat, can you help us?"[1] And the help here is not to facilitate green business development, but to make material industrial processes transparent through dissemination of data, providing businesses with a chance voluntarily to redefine processes away from toxicity and material burden, but failing that to enable civil society to force such redefinition. This researcher elaborates: "We don't work at the grass roots generally. We work at the grass tops. What I do is collect statistics and put them on a Web site that people look at . . . and there are a lot of folks that use the data that my team pulls together for grassroots activities, I don't learn a lot about what they're doing because for me, when I'm trying to do this sort of global stuff, I'm trying to synthesize what's happening at so many small levels is nearly impossible."

Maximizing the reach of these forms of data is crucial to countering what Kenneth Gould, Allan Schnaiberg, and Adam Weinberg refer to when they write that "environmental movements are often naïve about the political forces that surround local-decision makers. Citizen-workers are even more naïve in failing to recognize that these forces arise from dominant economic interests" (1996, 152). Talking about political forces and dominant economic interests becomes immediately concrete and accessible when the role of producers in controlling the movement of materials is made manifest. And here nothing substitutes for basic statistics on tonnage and toxicity, such as 250 million tons of municipal solid waste versus 7.6 billion tons of manufacturing wastes.

To the Soil

Not everyone wants to, or should, become immersed in the study of how sectors of industry collaborate to move masses of materials globally such that they end up as products that are difficult to get rid of when we are done with them. My argument has been that such a task is incumbent upon those who pour energy and resources into, for example, keeping glass in curbside recycling programs, educating children that recycling saves trees, blogging about the pervasiveness of plastics in everyday life, or becoming a living demonstration project in minimal personal eco-impact. Or at least they should do so if they are to target their power, individually and collectively, in a materially meaningful direction. But most people are not engaged in problems of solid waste beyond partici-pating in their municipal recycling program, nor, I argue, should they be. In contrast to many in the minority who are busy at activities listed here, I do not believe that urging more people to get busy in such ways will do much more than make (some) people feel better.

At the same time, it is altogether reasonable and has historical prec-edent to ask citizens, in their roles as urban inhabitants, to comply with certain requirements as to how they contain and get rid of their house-hold wastes. Today, throwing garbage out the window, befouling the streets with the contents of chamber pots, and shoveling mounds of trash into the nearest pit or waterway are pretty well unthinkable to all but the most antisocial among us. Using standard-size trash cans and sealable garbage bags, putting trash out only on collection days, and so on are further elaborations of what is expected and generally complied with among law-abiding citizens. And inasmuch as the curbside collection of paper and metal can be relied upon to reduce the overall costs of munici-pal solid waste management in general, requiring householders to sort newspapers and cans is no different a civic activity than requiring them to sweep their own sidewalk.

I am arguing that municipal solid waste recycling as we know it today is not an earth-saving activity, nor is it a way to stem industrial waste, nor is it the start of a revolution in eco-consciousness, nor does it more than slightly ameliorate the sited burdens associated with transfer sta-tions, truck routes, landfills, and incinerators. But it *is* a responsible civic activity and can (especially if glass and plastics are not included in the mix) promote the public good by freeing up taxpayer dollars. If we remove the hyperinflated expectations of municipal solid waste recycling, we can see it for what it is and perhaps reevaluate why we are doing it and what we are trying to achieve. Insofar as consumers, citizens, and individuals do bear some responsibility for the wastes they create, we should therefore return to the notion of what a person at home actually does. After all, a person cannot forge steel, refine petroleum, fabricate a container, manufacture an electronic component, or batch process a cleaning compound but does prepare a meal, clean up afterward, rake the yard, and use the bathroom. Since 1970, the home dweller has been called upon to connect herself to the former group of activities—sending metal, glass, plastic, and paper back to industries or refrain from buying one product and seek a substitute—but has had far less asked of her in the realm of the latter.

If we look at the material composition of municipal solid waste, we see that about 23 percent consists of industrially provided products made of materials such as glass, plastic, rubber, synthetic and natural fibers, and composites—all of which are relatively hard to recycle when collected in a curbside arrangement (i.e., mixed and requiring sorting for processing). Another 39 percent consists of materials that, for reasons explained in chapters 1 and 2, are far easier and more lucrative for cities to recover and recycle—metal and paper. Another 32 percent, however, consists of materials that rot—food, yard wastes, and wood. (See appendix VI.)

At present, most food and wood waste in municipal solid waste is going to disposal, whereas the recovery rate for yard trimmings is quite high at 65 percent (see appendix IV). Composting, the controlled decomposition of organic matter to produce soil amendment, is the technology of transformation for nearly all recovered yard waste. Recovery of uneaten food to feed the hungry and then to feed animals stands above composting in the food waste–reduction hierarchy. Moreover, some wood waste can be reused in construction or furniture fabrication, and some wood is treated with compounds that make it toxic to include in compost. Nonetheless, composting is an applicable recovery method for much food and wood waste. Some of the 83 million tons of paper waste generated annually is, furthermore, more suitable for composting than for recycling (tissues, napkins, and other paper products made of soft-short fibers that are meant to be soiled through use). And finally, some 8 million tons of biosolids are produced annually, half of which are applied to agricultural lands after treatment as fertilizer (U.S. EPA 2006).

If we desire to maximize diversion of waste from disposal in cities, creating a product that will find a local market as commodity or an immediate direct use in public works of the city itself, does it not make sense to concentrate on biodegradable wastes more than we have?

Biodegradation in the Cities

In fact, such wastes were the first focus of municipal involvement in solid-waste management, which arose historically in response to problems of putrefaction. As cities industrialized and populations swelled, the problem of rotting garbage and the health impacts imagined (through miasma) and actually felt (through bacteriological transmission) became pressing. It was in this context that municipal sanitation emerged as a public-health policy, accompanied by street-cleaning technologies needed to remove offal, excrement, and rubbish from the streets (Melosi 1981; Miller 2000). From 1970 onward, however, the responsibility for the collection and recycling of bottles, cans, and paper for recycling was grafted atop a mandate organized around health and order. As Bill Sheehan and Helen Spiegelman note, local waste management "has been least effective in reducing manufactured product wastes, and most successful in managing certain community-generated biowastes" (2005, 1). Analyzing longitudinal data on municipal solid waste composition compiled by the EPA, they note rapid growth in the fraction of municipal solid waste that consists of discarded products and a more modest increase in organic and nonproduct inorganic materials (rubble, ash, etc.) in municipal solid waste over time. Since the 1960s, the bulk of municipal investment and activity has consequently centered around recovery of product waste. But for many product wastes, especially modern ones, "source reduction, recovery for recycling, and environmentally safe disposal—are either wholly (source reduction) or partially (design for recycling and safe disposal) beyond the control" of localities (Sheehan and Spiegelman 2005, 11).

Not so with organic wastes. There is no shortage of technology or precedent for large-scale composting of urban wastes, including sewage. Such activities go back as far as the twelfth century, when, writes agricultural historian Lihua Wang, "the large-scale channel flow of waste were formed between cities and villages in southern China. To the city residents, it meant removing feces and cleaning [the] environment; to the countrymen, they were accessed to a large number of organic fertilizers" (2009, 23). Several municipally scaled composting systems are currently working well today in North America, including in San Francisco, where residents are required to separate compostable wastes from traditional recyclables for collection (leaving a small, third category of plastic and inorganic product wastes for disposal as well biological wastes from diapers and hygiene products that are unsafe to compost using San Francisco's technology). Separated organics are transported out of the city for processing and used in regional agriculture (Goldstein and Block 2000). Another model, which requires effective removal of household hazardous wastes before treatment, is "mixed-waste composting" practiced in Edmonton, Alberta. There, residents participate in traditional recycling and are offered ample opportunities to drop off household hazardous wastes, electronics, and other toxic waste materials. The remaining garbage is composted with biosolids (processed sewage sludge) using in-vessel technologies at high temperatures, with residual plastics and inorganic materials sifted out at the conclusion of the compost process and discarded. Edmonton claims a 60 percent diversion rate and a clean, safe product that consistently meets standards for agricultural application (Edmonton 2010).

There are substantial barriers to enacting composting at large scales. Among them is community resistance to facility siting. The compost process does produce greenhouse gases and odors, which must be adequately controlled; and truck transport to facilities does entail emissions. In addition, if composting is to be evaluated based on the revenues of generated product, the potential lack of markets for large quantities of compost is a barrier to the functioning of this system, even if siting problems can be overcome.

The final barrier to many forms of large-scale composting (although not to mixed-waste composting as practiced in Edmonton) is the required separation of putrescible materials in the home, their storage separate from other wastes until collection day, and the contemplation of their decay and eventual reuse, especially if this process includes composting them with treated human excrement. Such barriers are greater in dense cities, where space and lack of personal outdoor property bring residents in close proximity to discarded food. Here is a field, I would argue, in which community action and personal transformation have much real capacity to change real-world conditions around waste. If those concerned with municipal solid waste problems redirect concern from glass recycling, plastic use, and the consumer's agency in reducing manufacturing backward through the commodity chain and instead concentrate more on convincing householders to segregate, store, and accept facilities for biological transformation of compostable wastes, vast quantities of city garbage could be directed to greening in the literal sense of the term. There is a great deal of disgust here to be dealt with, entailing quite a different impulse than the pitching in and rolling up of sleeves to work on treasures in the trash. But there is an existing and long tradition of connecting community gardening—an activity that provides manifold social benefits in terms of education and job creation—to composting as a concept. With revenues generated through curbside paper and metal recycling, and with extended producer responsibility instituted through the same distribution networks that bring modern products to market, the goal of Zero Waste or darn close to it in cities not only would be conceivable, but would deliver real, measurable material benefits directly to the urban scale.

The Promise of Recycling

I close with two points of hope. The first is that the technologies for the division of the responsibility for solid waste among the federal government, localities, and producers I have outlined are already in place. What is needed are different forms of action by civil society, following models that have already been established in the history of populist social movements, to challenge the freedom of manufacturers to transform materials without regard to ecology. The federal government has the capacity to track material and economic inputs and outputs within a context of economic competitiveness (Bouman, Heijungs, van de Voet, et al. 2000). The local state has the capacity to enact laws that send modern products back to their producers. There is strong, if unrealized historical precedent in the notion of composting as a method for absorbing large quantities of waste materials and transforming them into wealth for the life of the city and the nation.

The second point of hope concerns the human creativity and desire to change society for the better that runs through the history of social movements' engagement with waste. At present, this creativity and desire are submerged and hobbled within a construct of mythic incrementalism to the point that it is heretical to depart from the notion that atomized individuals, if numerous enough, have the power to move mountains. But if we step back to look at solid waste as it moves across geographies of production, consumption, and contestation, we can begin to appreciate it as a bearer of rich social significance as much as something to be driven to zero. Notions of guilt, moral opprobrium, stigma, and embarrassment attend solid waste as a problem; other notions of creativity, excitement, community solidarity, and satisfaction attend its solutions. These bad and good qualities coexist, presenting themselves sensually in the visibility and tangibility of trash. Garbage is something that you can hold in your hand, something in which you can see traces of meaning worked up through design and use over the life of the thing (Molotch 2003). Such traces are histories in a discard, but they need not stay in the past. Whether industrial by-product, former commodity, or rotting substance, solid waste offers hope because it once held use value and can again. With the application of similar types of labor that transform minerals, trees, and oil straight out of nature into things of use, solid waste can be brought back to life, redefined as an input to production or a useful thing. Even more, this act of regeneration, which sums up the full meaning of the word *recycling*, promises to yield benefits that ripple out through the web of social and natural complexity to heal and protect places—forests, ecosystems, waterways, communities, cities (Geiser 2001). Materials taken from nature will not be used just once, but again and again. This time rejuvenated with *loving* labor, materials in the social realm will cycle and recycle, while those still in nature will be left untouched. That is the promise of recycling.

Appendix I: Summary of U.S. Environmental Protection Agency Data on Solid-Waste Generation, Disposal, and Recycling in the United States

Annual U.S. Tons

	Generated	Disposed	Recovered	Recovery Rate	Data Source
Wastes Directly Addressed in This Book					
Municipal Solid Wastes (MSW)	249,610,000	166,740,000	82,870,000	33%	U.S. EPA 2009b, tables 1, 2, 3, pp. 2–4
Construction and Demolition (C&D) Debris	330,000,000	115,500,000	214,500,000	65%	U.S. EPA 2007a, II – 101
Nonhazardous Industrial Wastes	N/A	7,600,000,000	N/A		U.S. EPA 1987, 2010a
Household Hazardous Wastes	1,600,000	N/A	N/A		U.S. EPA 2010b
Hazardous Industrial Wastes	39,580,000	37,801,000	1,779,000	4%	U.S. EPA 2007c,
Coal-Combustion Wastes (Special Waste)	128,000,000	67,840,000	60,160,000	47%	U.S. EPA 2007a, II-102
Wastes Not Directly Addressed in This Book					
Agricultural Wastes	N/A	1,000,000,000	N/A		OTA 1992
Medical Waste	N/A	3,200,000	N/A		U.S. EPA 1988
Other Special Wastes					
Mining and Extractive Wastes	N/A	1,700,000,000	N/A		OTA 1992
Oil- and Gas-Exploration and Production Wastes	N/A	1,400,000,000	N/A		OTA1992
Cement Kiln Dust, Mineral-Processing Wastes	N/A	N/A	N/A		

Note: In this book, I directly discuss MSW, C&D debris, hazardous industrial waste, "nonhazardous" industrial waste (which I call "manufacturing waste"), household hazardous waste, and coal ash. I do not take up other "special wastes" or agricultural or extractive wastes but list EPA estimates here for context.

Appendix II: Summary of Textile and Glass Disposal and Recycling in the United States and New York City

United States

	U.S. Tons (for Most Recent Year Available)				
	Generated	Disposed	Recovered	Recovery Rate	Data Source
Glass Containers	10,050,000	7,240,000	2,810,000	28%	U.S. EPA 2009b, table 5, p. 6
Clothing and Shoes	8,820,000	7,570,000	1,250,000	14%	U.S. EPA 2009b, tables 15, 16, and 17, pp. 17–19
Linens	1,160,000	960,000	200,000	17%	U.S. EPA 2009b, tables 15, 16, and 17, pp. 17–19
Subtotal (Clothing, Shoes, Linens)	9,980,000	8,530,000	1,450,000	15%	

New York City[1]

	U.S. Tons (for Most Recent Year Available)				
	Generated	Disposed	Recovered	Recovery Rate	Data Source
Glass Containers	144,283	66,137	78,146	54%	NYC DS 2007, vol. 1, sec. 2, table 1-24, p. 2
Clothing, Shoes, and Linens	N/A	149,818	N/A		NYC DS 2007, vol. 1, sec. 2, table 1-24, p. 2

1. Supplementary information from the 2004–2005 New York City Waste Characterization Study (published as NYC DS 2007), which looked at the composition of both refuse and curbside recycling in New York City. A weighted average of glass containers in both refuse and recycling provides information on the percentage of these materials generated in total in curbside collections. It should be noted, however, that deposit glass containers redeemed via bottle bills or kept at home for reuse are not reflected in the generation statistic. Textiles, in contrast, are not collected in curbside recycling collections. Thus, only their fraction in refuse could be measured in this study. An unknown quantity of waste textiles are donated to thrift shops or accumulated at home waiting for an outlet other than disposal.

Appendix III: Changes in Quantity and Composition of Municipal Solid Waste over Time

	U.S. Tons Generated					
	1960	1970	1980	1990	2000	2008
Paper/Paperboard	29,990,000	44,310,000	55,160,000	72,730,000	87,740,000	77,420,000
Glass	6,720,000	12,740,000	15,130,000	13,100,000	12,760,000	12,150,000
Metals						
Ferrous	10,300,000	12,360,000	12,620,000	12,640,000	14,110,000	15,680,000
Aluminum	340,000	800,000	1,730,000	2,810,000	3,200,000	3,410,000
Other Nonferrous	180,000	670,000	1,160,000	1,100,000	1,600,000	1,760,000
Total Metals	10,820,000	13,830,000	15,510,000	16,550,000	18,910,000	20,850,000
Plastics	390,000	2,900,000	6,830,000	17,130,000	25,540,000	30,050,000
Rubber and Leather	1,840,000	2,970,000	4,200,000	5,790,000	6,710,000	7,410,000
Textiles	1,760,000	2,040,000	2,530,000	5,810,000	9,440,000	12,370,000
Wood	3,030,000	3,720,000	7,010,000	12,210,000	13,110,000	16,390,000
Other	70,000	770,000	2,520,000	3,190,000	4,000,000	4,500,000
Total Materials in Products	54,620,000	83,280,000	108,890,000	146,510,000	178,210,000	181,140,000
Other Wastes						
Food Scraps	12,200,000	12,800,000	13,000,000	20,800,000	26,810,000	31,790,000
Yard Trimmings	20,000,000	23,200,000	27,500,000	35,000,000	30,530,000	32,900,000
Miscellaneous Inorganic Wastes	1,300,000	1,780,000	2,250,000	2,900,000	3,500,000	3,780,000
Total Other Wastes	33,500,000	37,780,000	42,750,000	58,700,000	60,840,000	68,470,000
Total MSW Generated (Weight)	88,120,000	121,060,000	151,640,000	205,210,000	239,050,000	249,610,000
U.S. Population	179,979,000	203,984,000	227,255,000	249,907,000	281,422,000	304,059,724

(continued)

	Per Capita Consumption (Annual Pounds)					
	1960	1970	1980	1990	2000	2008
Paper/Paperboard	333.3	434.4	485.4	582.1	623.5	509.2
Glass	74.7	124.9	133.2	104.8	90.7	79.9
Total Metals	120.2	135.6	136.5	132.4	134.4	137.1
Plastics	4.3	28.4	60.1	137.1	181.5	197.7
Rubber and Leather	20.4	29.1	37.0	46.3	47.7	48.7
Textiles	19.6	20.0	22.3	46.5	67.1	81.4
Wood	33.7	36.5	61.7	97.7	93.2	107.8
Other	0.8	7.5	22.2	25.5	28.4	29.6
Total Materials in Products	607.0	816.5	958.3	1,172.5	1,266.5	1,191.5
Other Wastes						
Food Scraps	135.6	125.5	114.4	166.5	190.5	209.1
Yard Trimmings	222.2	227.5	242.0	280.1	217.0	216.4
Miscellaneous Inorganic Wastes	14.4	17.5	19.8	23.2	24.9	24.9
Total Other Wastes	372.3	370.4	376.2	469.8	432.4	450.4
Total MSW Generated (weight)	979.2	1,187.0	1,334.5	1,642.3	1,698.9	1,641.8

(continued)

	Recovery Rates						
	1960	1970	1980	1990	2000	2008
Paper/Paperboard	16.9%	15.3%	21.3%	27.8%	42.8%	55.5%
Glass	1.5%	1.3%	5.0%	20.1%	22.6%	23.1%
Metals						
Ferrous	0.5%	1.2%	2.9%	17.6%	33.2%	33.7%
Aluminum	Neg.	1.3%	17.9%	35.9%	26.9%	21.1%
Other Nonferrous	Neg.	47.8%	46.6%	66.4%	66.3%	68.8%
Total Metals	0.5%	3.5%	7.9%	24.0%	34.9%	34.6%
Plastics	Neg.	Neg.	0.3%	2.2%	5.8%	7.1%
Rubber and Leather	17.9%	8.4%	3.1%	6.4%	12.2%	14.3%
Textiles	2.8%	2.9%	6.3%	11.4%	14.0%	15.3%
Wood	Neg.	Neg.	Neg.	1.1%	9.5%	9.6%
Other	Neg.	39.0%	19.8%	21.3%	24.5%	25.6%
Total Materials in Products	10.3%	9.6%	13.3%	19.8%	29.7%	33.5%
Other Wastes						
Food Scraps	Neg.	Neg.	Neg.	Neg.	2.5%	2.5%
Yard Trimmings	Neg.	Neg.	Neg.	12.0%	51.7%	64.7%
Miscellaneous Inorganic Wastes	Neg.	Neg.	Neg.	Neg.	Neg.	Neg.
Total Other Wastes	Neg.	Neg.	Neg.	7.2%	27.0%	32.3%
Total Recovery Rate All Categories	6.4%	6.6%	9.6%	16.2%	29.0%	33.2%

Note: The EPA characterizes MSW composition in two mutually exclusive ways: by material (shown here) and by product category (durable, nondurable, packaging, and other wastes). For details on the full product category breakdown of MSW over time, see U.S. EPA 2009b, tables 9–24, pp. 11–25.

Source: U.S. EPA 2009b, tables 1, 2, 3, pp. 2–4.

Appendix IV: Fractions of Municipal Solid Waste Suitable for Reuse Using a Model of Repair, Refurbishment, and Retailing

	Annual U.S. Tons				
	Generation	Count as Reusables?	Disposed	Recovered	Recovery Rate
Nonproducts					
Food Scraps	31,790,000		30,990,000	800,000	3%
Yard Trimmings	32,900,000		11,600,000	21,300,000	65%
Miscellaneous Inorganic Wastes	3,780,000		3,780,000	–	0%
Packaging					
Glass, Metal, Paper, and Plastic Packaging	66,090,000		34,140,000	31,950,000	48%
Wood Packaging	10,670,000	Yes	9,090,000	1,580,000	15%
Nondurables					
Printing and Single-Use Paper	37,720,000		20,250,000	17,470,000	46%
Trash Bags	930,000		930,000		0%
Disposable Diapers	3,790,000		3,790,000		0%
Other Misc Nondurables	4,950,000		4,950,000		0%
Books	1,340,000	Yes	950,000	390,000	29%
Clothing and Footwear	8,820,000	Yes	7,570,000	1,250,000	14%
Towels/Sheets/ Pillowcases	1,160,000	Yes	960,000	200,000	17%
Durables					
Batteries (Lead Acid)	2,530,000		20,000	2,510,000	99%
Rubber Tires	4,690,000	Gray Area	3,030,000	1,660,000	35%
Carpets and Rugs	3,220,000	Yes	2,960,000	260,000	8%
Consumer Electronics	3,160,000	Yes	2,730,000	430,000	14%
Furniture and Furnishings	9,610,000	Yes	9,600,000	10,000	0%

(continued)

	Annual U.S. Tons				
	Generation	Count as Reusables?	Disposed	Recovered	Recovery Rate
Major Appliances	3,690,000	Yes	1,220,000	2,470,000	67%
Small Appliances	1,530,000	Gray Area	16,760,000	480,000	31%
Other	17,240,000	Gray Area	1,420,000	110,000	1%
Total MSW	249,610,000		166,740,000	82,870,000	33%
Potential Reusables, without "Other Durable" Category	43,200,000 U.S. tons				
Percentage of Total MSW	17%				
Potential Reusable, with "Other Durable" Category	60,440,000 U.S. tons				
Percentage of Total MSW	24%				

Note: How much of urban waste can be targeted for reuse enterprises, defined as firms that take in and possibly repair goods for resale? To estimate an upper bound, I started by excluding categories of municipal solid waste that clearly don't fit a reuse model: *nonproducts* (food wastes, yard trimmings, miscellaneous nonproduct waste); *packaging* (glass, metal, paper and plastic packaging); *nondurables* (printing and single-use paper, trash bags, and disposable diapers); and certain *durables* (tires and auto batteries).

Given their material properties, the following categories can be subject to reuse: *packaging* (wood packaging—that is, pallets); *nondurables* (books; clothing and footwear; and towels/sheets/pillowcases); *durables* (appliances, furniture and furnishings, carpets and rugs, and electronics).

Combined, these categories total some 43 million tons of MSW generation annually, which is 17% of all MSW.

Gray areas suggesting that more should be counted: An argument might be made to include tires as subject to reuse, although most states have a system in place to recover used tires through deposit. Also, as Dan Knapp (2008) has pointed out, Franklin's methodology does not account for reusables stored over years in basements, attics, and elsewhere.

Gray areas suggesting that less should be counted: Major appliances tend to be white goods that have a high rate of recovery for scrap metal. Given the long history of the metal-scrap trade, existing methods of recovering major appliances would be only minimally supplemented with reuse. Small appliances, furniture and furnishing, carpets and rugs, electronics, and arguably all of the categories I have included as potentially subject to reuse cannot be effectively reused or repaired if soiled or broken. To err on the side of overestimating the potential field for repair to work on, I add in the large "other durables" category to get 24% of MSW.

Note that these calculations do not address the quantity of C&D debris (330,000 tons annually) that can be addressed through deconstruction and resale, which is one of the most viable forms of reuse enterprise in the United States. There are no data available to estimate this fraction.

Source: U.S. EPA 2009b, tables 9–24, pp. 11–25.

Appendix V: Details on Various Quantities of Different Plastics in Municipal Solid Waste

Annual U.S. Tons

Resin/product category, U.S. EPA 2008	Generated	Disposed	Recovered	Recovery rate
#1 PET rigid containers (see note 1)	2,680,000	1,950,000	730,000	27%
#2 HDPE rigid containers (see note 2)	2,060,000	1,580,000	480,000	23%
#3 PVC rigid containers	40,000	40,000		
#4 LDPE rigid containers	40,000	40,000		
#5 PP rigid containers	430,000	410,000	20,000	5%
#6 PS rigid containers	70,000	70,000		
#1 PET bags, sacks, and wraps	–	–		
#2 HDPE bags, sacks, and wraps	550,000	490,000	60,000	11%
#3 PVC bags, sacks, and wraps	80,000	80,000		
#4 LDPE bags, sacks, wraps	2,350,000	2,020,000	330,000	14%
#5 PP bags, sacks, and wraps	760,000	760,000		
#6 PS bags, sacks, and wraps	–	–		
#1 PET durable and nondurable plastics	1,060,000	1,060,000		
#2 HDPE durable and nondurable plastics	2,740,000	2,710,000	30,000	1%
#3 PVC durable and nondurable plastics	1,540,000	1,540,000		
#4 LDPE durable and nondurable plastics	3,490,000	3,490,000		
#5 PP durable and nondurable plastics	3,000,000	2,950,000	50,000	2%
#6 PS durable and nondurable plastics (except EPS food service)	1,790,000	1,770,000	20,000	1%
EPS food service	760,000	760,000		
Nonspecified resin (#7 and noncoded) rigid containers	10,000	10,000		
Nonspecified resin (#7 and noncoded) bags, wraps, and sacks	220,000	220,000		
Nonspecified resin (#7 and noncoded) durable and nondurable plastics	6,380,000	5,980,000	400,000	6%
TOTAL	**30,050,000**	**27,930,000**	**2,120,000**	**7%**
Percenetage of total plastic wastes generated	100%	93%	7%	

---

1. EPA statistics do not distinguish blow-molded PET (which has strong markets) from injection-molded PET (which has weak markets). The following data sources are used to estimate a breakdown. The conclusion is that almost all PET rigid containers are blow molded.

	Annual tons	Percentage of total	Data source
2008 U.S. PET bottle annual production (this equals EPA tonnages on PET rigid containers)	2,683,000	100%	(NAPCOR 2008)
NYC PET bottle weights in residential discards	40,533	99.6%	(NYC DS 2007)
NYC PET tub/tray weights in residential discards	168	0.4%	(NYC DS 2007)
Subtotal	40,701		

2. EPA statistics do not distinguish blow-molded HDPE (which has strong markets) from injection molded HDPE (which has weak markets). The following data sources are used to estimate a breakdown. The conclusion is that 90 to 95% of HDPE rigid containers are blow molded.

Blow molded (beverage, food, cosmetics, other household), 1996	1,283,500	90%	(NC ENR 1998)
Injection molded (tubs, trays), 1996	137,500	10%	(NC ENR 1998)
Subtotal	1,421,000		
NYC HDPE bottle weights in residential discards	31,377	95%	(NYC DS 2007)
NYC HDPE tub/tray weights in residential discards	1,775	5%	(NYC DS 2007)
Subtotal	33,152		

A conservative estimate of 90% blow-molded PET was applied in this note's table.

U.S. EPA 2008 HDPE rigid containers	2,060,000	100%	(U.S. EPA 2009f)
95% estimate for blow molded (bottles)	1,854,000	90%	
5% estimate for injection molded (tubs/trays)	206,000	10%	

Annual U.S. Tons Generated Attributed to Marketability, Policy Approach, and Toxicity Concern

Strong domestic markets for recycled material	Weak domestic markets, use of export markets for recycled material	No markets for recycled material	Target of curbside recycling programs	Target of in-shop drop-off for recycling programs	Target of products bans and taxes	Not targeted under any program or policy	Subject of concern over toxicity
2,680,000			2,680,000				
1,854,000	206,000		1,854,000 / 206,000				
		40,000	40,000				40,000
		40,000	40,000				
	430,000		430,000				
		70,000	70,000				70,000
550,000				550,000	550,000		
		80,000		80,000	80,000		80,000
2,350,000				2,350,000	2,350,000		
		760,000		760,000	760,000		
		1,060,000				1,060,000	
	(see note 3)	2,740,000	(see note 3)			2,740,000	
		1,540,000				1,540,000	1,540,000
		3,490,000				3,490,000	
	(see note 4)	3,000,000				3,000,000	
	(see note 4)	1,770,000				1,790,000	1,790,000
		760,000			760,000		760,000
		10,000				10,000	
		220,000				220,000	
	(see note 4)	6,380,000				6,380,000	
7,434,000	636,000	21,960,000	5,320,000	3,740,000	4,500,000	20,230,000	4,240,000
25%	2%	73%	18%	12%	15%	67%	14%

Political tension between in-shop drop off for recycling and bans/fees/taxes as policy alternatives

Potential to export harm by commingling PVC and/or PS with other plastics exported for "recycling"

3. Durable and nondurable plastics are items other than plastic containers and packaging. In rare case, certain HDPE durables (toys) have an export market. Certain cities (for example, San Francisco and Los Angeles) include toys in curbside recycling collection. Thus, non-HDPE toys of various resins are exported in mixed loads with other plastics.

4. In rare cases, clean, presorted streams of certain fractions of this category may find markets domestically or internationally, but this is not the norm.

Source: U.S. EPA 2009b, table 7, p. 8–10.

Appendix VI: Fractions of Municipal Solid Waste Referred to in the Conclusion

| | Annual U.S. Tons Generated | Attribution of Total Tonnage to Major Category | | |
		Metal and Paper	Organic	Other
Paper/Paperboard	77,420,000	77,420,000	–	–
Glass	12,150,000	–	–	–
Metals				
Ferrous	15,680,000	15,680,000	–	–
Aluminum	3,410,000	3,410,000	–	–
Other Nonferrous	1,760,000	1,760,000	–	–
Plastics	30,050,000	–	–	30,050,000
Rubber and Leather	7,410,000	–	–	7,410,000
Textiles	12,370,000	–	–	12,370,000
Wood	16,390,000	–	16,390,000	–
Other	4,500,000	–	–	4,500,000
Total Materials in Products	181,140,000	–	–	–
Other Wastes				
Food Scraps	31,790,000	–	31,790,000	–
Yard Trimmings	32,900,000	–	32,900,000	–
Miscellaneous Inorganic Wastes	3,780,000	–	–	3,780,000
Total MSW Generated (Weight in Tons)	249,610,000	98,270,000	81,080,000	58,110,000
Percentage of Total		39%	32%	23%

Source: U.S. EPA 2009b, tables 1, 2, 3, pp. 2–4.

Notes

Introduction

1. The term *recycling*, as we know it, refers to recycling in the colloquial sense: the recycling of metal, paper, glass containers, and certain plastics at home or at work. As detailed in this book, other forms of recycling do occur (recycling of plastic bags and electronics generated by households and local businesses, composting of organic wastes, and recycling within other streams of wastes, including construction and demolition debris, hazardous industrial wastes, and coal-combustion wastes).

2. This dimension is also the most difficult to swallow for those who do not study power and other phenomena from a social science perspective because on its face it smacks of a conspiracy theory. Why Lukes's third dimension may appear so is an interesting sociological question in its own right that ultimately points back to the pervasiveness of this dimension.

3. In the United Kingdom and in some U.S. states in the past, diversion has also included routing discards to be transformed into energy.

Chapter 1

1. The term *glass* in this book refers to glass containers—bottles and jars. Plate and other forms of glass are a much smaller fraction of waste.

2. In the spring of 2010, for example, paper commanded between $85 and $300 per ton, depending on grade; steel sold for around $120 per ton, aluminum for $1,500 to $1,600 per ton, and bottle plastic for $400 to $660 a ton, but clear glass went for $20 to $25 a ton, green and amber glass for $4 to $10 a ton (*Waste News* 2010b, 30; 2010c, 18).

3. Pat Franklin, founder and former executive director of the Container Recycling Institute, telephone interview by the author, New York, January 29, 2007. California is the preeminent example of such an arrangement. By managing a wide-ranging, variably priced deposit system; applying mandatory recycled content requirements on the many bottle and fiberglass producers in the state; requiring bottlers to contribute funding to state recycling budgets; and

transferring funds from bottlers and from unredeemed deposits to municipalities on a per ton of glass processed basis, California is able to subsidize glass recycling so that most recycled glass makes its way back into production. California is an exceptional case.

4. The term *rubbish* referred to dry refuse, as opposed to the term *garbage*, which at the time meant food and animal wastes.

5. This revenue estimate derives from my own calculation of the average market value of ferrous and nonferrous scrap and bottle plastic containers between 2000 and 2008, indexed to the composition in collected metal/plastic curbside collections, factoring in the city's contractual terms with its processors over the past ten years.

6. Brian Pugh, recycling manager, Fayetteville, Arkansas, interviewed by the author by telephone, February 5, 2008.

7. See, for example, the New York Public Interest Research Group's critique of suspending curbside glass recycling in New York City; the group is a leading proponent of the bottle bill in New York State. See also the Container Recycling Institute's position on curbside recycling at http://www.bottlebill.org/about bb/mythfact.htm.

8. As a result of the large quantities of textiles found in New York City waste in its 2004–2005 Waste Characterization Study, the Department of Sanitation's Bureau of Waste Prevention, Reuse, and Recycling has facilitated textile-donation events of its own and through its contractors. It is notable that although the New York City recycling advocacy community welcomed this policy development, it did not call for or drive it in the first place. The policy instead emerged from within municipal government in reaction to the fact of large tonnages of refuse and the government's knowledge that existing infrastructure and markets were not absorbing those tonnages.

Chapter 3

1. John Dernbach, legal scholar and former Pennsylvania waste administrator, interviewed by the author by telephone, May 22, 2009.

2. As the EPA's own earlier reports to Congress suggest, "Manufacturing wastes are not subject to the promulgated treatment standards, although they can sometimes contain levels of constituents that are higher than the standards. As a result . . . untreated [manufacturing] wastes—which may contain higher levels of constituents—can be disposed of in surface impoundment and landfills with few or no environmental controls, depending on applicable State regulations, [and] potential environmental and human health risks associated with different Subtitle D wastes may be significant for several reasons—e.g. relatively few controls at Subtitle D waste management facilities, the broad range of toxic constituents in these wastes, and the large volumes involved" (OTA 1992, 9–12).

3. High rates of construction and demolition waste diversion, in fact, are used to boost local or regional municipal solid waste statistics, such that, for example,

San Francisco can claim a recycling rate of 60 percent, nearly half of which consists of construction and demolition reuse (*Waste News* 2007). New York City has construction and demolition waste–diversion rates of between 80 and 90 percent (NYC DS 2008b).

4. U.S. EPA official 2, interviewed by the author, Washington, D.C., May 4, 2009.

Chapter 4

1. There is, however, a disturbing but as of yet unaddressed question in the field of life-cycle analysis as to whether reuse simply delays rather than diverts from disposal. The same question can be raised with regard to "downcycling"—the remanufacture of products that does not displace the use of virgin inputs.

2. These facilities are called "mixed-waste processing facilities" or "dirty-materials recycling facilities."

3. A small number of nonprofit recycling processors operate following the Zero Waste model. One, Eureka Recycling, handles collections from St. Paul and has a facility in Minneapolis but does not contract with that city to receive and process recyclables.

4. See Allen Hershkowitz's *Bronx Ecology* (2002) for a full treatment of the factors that prevented the development of a recycled paper mill in a zone overburdened with transfer stations in the South Bronx.

5. Alternative daily cover replaces earth as the layer that is, by federal law, placed over deposited trash in a landfill each day. Much recycled glass and other nonmarketable forms of recycled materials (fluff from auto shredders, construction and demolition rubble) goes toward alternative daily cover. The distinction between material being disposed of in the landfill and beneficially used on the landfill is understandably lost on those outside the profession of waste management.

6. Visy was environmentally sound in that it entailed barge transport of recyclables to the processor rather than the more polluting truck transport.

7. As part of its cleaning functions, the New York City Department of Sanitation regularly collects scrap metal from abandoned lots, public construction sites, and other ad hoc generators of scrap metal.

Chapter 5

1. Styrofoam is a brand name for EPS, expanded polystyrene, one kind of polystyrene. Although it is not technically correct to refer to all EPS as Styrofoam, I have done so in this chapter to acknowledge common terminology used in discourse about EPS problems. Polystyrene may be expanded or "foamed" or molded using injection or other methods. To avoid double counting, I have calculated food-service EPS in the first statistic pertaining to lightweight plastics and not in the second concerning health risks. See appendix V for details.

2. As shown in appendix V, some 67 percent of all plastic wastes are not targeted for curbside recycling, in-store drop-off recycling, taxes, bans, deposits, or other policy initiatives at all. This 67 percent is a different statistic than the percentage of all plastic that is not recovered but goes to disposal. This latter statistic is 93 percent.

3. EPA official 1, interviewed by the author, Washington, D.C., May 4, 2009.

4. This explains why certain green retailers are able to take back clean, pre-sorted, nonbottle plastics of certain resins (in particular number 5). The degree to which they subsidize boutique recycling of this kind is unknown but probable, given the difficulty of nonbottle recyclers to stay in business even when sourced with presorted, clean recycled plastics.

5. I compiled these statistics from information reported in USTradeOnline®, the U.S. Census Bureau's official source for port statistics. I converted vessel weights in kilograms to U.S. tons.

6. Telephone conversation with a private material recovery facility operator, January 10, 2010.

7. Assuming it is not leaded—as consumption-grade glass no longer is.

8. The EPA does not calculate tonnages of PET or HDPE bottles and nonbottles separately. See estimates of breakdown in appendix V.

9. Bill Sheehan, executive director of the Product Policy Institute, interviewed by telephone by the author, June 8, 2010.

10. Melissa Walsh-Innes, Maine State Representative, interviewed by telephone by the author, July 13, 2010.

11. Researcher at WRI, a D.C.-based, environmental data-tracking organization, interviewed by the author, Washington, D.C., May 4, 2009.

12. Ibid.

13. EPA official 1, interviewed by the author, Washington, D.C., May 4, 2009.

14. Researcher at WRI, a D.C.-based environmental data-tracking organization, interviewed by the author, Washington, D.C., May 4, 2009.

15. "For example, the most important focus for non-renewable materials such as metals often will be to get the most use and reuse from each finite unit of the resource, while the focus for renewables such as wood and forest products has to include protection for the natural ecosystems that produce the resource" (U.S. EPA 2009e, 13).

16. Researcher at WRI, a D.C.-based environmental data-tracking organization, interviewed by the author, Washington, D.C., May 4, 2009.

Conclusion

1. Researcher at WRI, an environmental data-tracking organization, interviewed by the author, Washington, D.C., May 4, 2009.

References

ACC (American Chemistry Council). 2010a. *2008 National Postconsumer Recycled Plastic Bag and Film Report*. Washington, DC: ACC.

ACC (American Chemistry Council). 2010b. Plastic Bag Makers Kick Off Series of Plastic Bag Recycling Events to Celebrate Earth Month. Accessed May 1, 2010, at <http://www.americanchemistry.com/s_acc/sec_news_article .asp?CID=206&DID=10873>.

ACC (American Chemistry Council). 2010c. Plastics Industry Testifies in Support of New York City Recycling Program Expansion. Accessed April 27, 2010, at <http://www.americanchemistry.com/s_acc/sec_news_article.asp?SID=1&DID =10914&CID=206>.

Ackerman, F. 1997a. Environmental Impacts of Packaging in the U.S. and Mexico. *Society for Philosophy and Technology* 2 (2):1–16.

Ackerman, F. 1997b. *Why Do We Recycle: Markets, Values, and Public Policy*. Washington, DC: Island Press.

Adams, L. 2008. Path to Greener World Can Be Taken in Many Small Steps. *The Commercial Appeal*, April 20. Accessed January 7, 2011, at <http://www.commercialappeal.com/news/2008/apr/20/guest-column-path-to -greener-world-can-be-taken>.

Adams, M. 1942. Our Precious Junk. *New York Times*, May 24, SM13.

AF&PA (American Forest and Paper Association). 2008. Extended Producer Responsibility (EPR) Statement. Accessed June 20, 2010, at <http://www .afandpa.org>.

Agyeman, J., and T. Evans. 2003. Toward Just Sustainability in Urban Communities: Building Equity Rights with Sustainable Solutions. *Annals of the American Academy of Political and Social Science* 590:35–53.

Ali, S. H. 2002. Disaster and the Political Economy of Recycling: Toxic Fire in an Industrial City. *Social Problems* 49 (2):129–149.

Allaway, D. 2009. Treatment of Materials in Community-Scale Greenhouse Gas Inventories. Paper read at the Northeast Forum on Climate-Waste Connections, June 24, Eugene, OR.

Andrady, A. L. 2003. *Plastics and the Environment*. Hoboken, NJ: Wiley-Interscience.

Antweiler, W., and K. Harrison. 2003. Toxic Release Inventories and Green Consumerism: Empirical Evidence from Canada. *Canadian Journal of Economics / Revue Canadienne d'Economique* 36 (2):495–520.

APR (Association of Postconsumer Plastics Recyclers). 2009. Non-Bottle Plastic Collection: What to Make of Tubs, Bags, & Film. Paper read at Into the Bin and Back Again, an online Webinar hosted at <http://www.plasticsrecycling.org>, June 4.

ASTSWMO (Association of State and Territorial Solid Waste Management Officials). 2007. *2006 Beneficial Use Survey Report*. Washington, DC.: ASTSWMO.

Atlas, M. 2002. Few and Far Between? *Social Science Quarterly* 83 (1): 365–379.

Ayres, R. U., and L. Ayres. 1996. *Industrial Ecology: Towards Closing the Materials Cycle*. Cheltenham, UK: Edward Elgar.

Ayres, R. U., and A. V. Kneese. 1968. Environmental Pollution. In *Federal Programs for the Development of Human Resources*, vol. 2, ed. Joint Economic Committee, U.S. Congress. Washington, DC: U.S. Government Printing Office.

Bachrach, P., and M. S. Baratz. 1970. *Power and Poverty; Theory and Practice*. New York: Oxford University Press.

Barbanel, J. 1982a. Bottle-Bill Walk Ends with Rally in Albany. *New York Times*, April 23, B1.

Barbanel, J. 1982b. Bottle Bill: Why the Governor Signed It. *New York Times*, June 27, 28.

Barbanel, J. 1982c. Carey Signs Law on 5 Cent Bottle Deposit. *New York Times*, June 16, A1.

Barbanel, J. 1982d. Report Rejects Industry's Case on Deposit Bill. *New York Times*, March 15, B1.

Barbanel, J. 1985. Group Disputes City Incinerator Plan. *New York Times*, August 4, 39.

Barbanel, J. 1986. Pressed by Union, City Postpones Recycling Plan. *New York Times*, July 24, B3.

Barber, J. 2007. Mapping the Movement to Achieve Sustainable Production and Consumption in North America. *Journal of Cleaner Production* 15 (6): 499–512.

Barham, B., S. G. Bunker, and D. O'Hearn. 1994. *States, Firms, and Raw Materials: The World Economy and Ecology of Aluminum*. Madison: University of Wisconsin Press.

Barlaz, M. A., R. B. Green, J. P. Chanton, C. D. Goldsmith, and G. R. Hater. 2004. Evaluation of Biologically Active Cover for Mitigation of Landfill Gas Emissions. *Environmental Science & Technology* 38 (18):4891–4899.

Barringer, S. G. 2003. The RCRA Bevill Amendment: A Lasting Relief for Mining Waste. *Natural Resources and Environment* 17 (3):155–194.

Bartels, A. H. 1983. The Office of Price Administration and the Legacy of the New Deal, 1938–1946. *Public Historian* 5 (3):5–29.

Bayrakal, S. 2006. The U.S. Pollution Prevention Act: A Policy Implementation Analysis. *Social Science Journal* 43:127–145.

Beamish, T. D. 2002. *Silent Spill: The Organization of an Industrial Crisis.* Urban and Industrial Environments. Cambridge, MA: MIT Press.

Beck, U. 1995. *Ecological Enlightenment: Essays on the Politics of the Risk Society.* Atlantic Highlands, NJ: Humanities Press.

Becker, H. S. 1995. The Power of Inertia. *Qualitative Sociology* 18 (3): 301–309.

Bell, M. 2004. *An Invitation to Environmental Sociology.* 2d ed. Thousand Oaks, CA: Pine Forge Press.

Bell, M. 2008. *Slowly Growing Greener.* Documentary film. Accessed January 18, 2010, at <http://marshallbell.blip.tv/#1686721>.

Benford, R. 2005. The Half-Life of the Environmental Justice Frame: Innovation, Diffusion, and Stagnation. In *Power, Justice, and the Environment: A Critical Appraisal of the Environmental Justice Movement*, ed. D. N. Pellow and R. J. Brulle, 37–54. Cambridge, MA: MIT Press.

Berkeley Ecology Center. 2008. History of the Ecology Center. Accessed April 29, 2010, at <http://www.ecologycenter.org/about/whoweare.html>.

Best, R. 2000. Presentation on plastics at the conference Take It Back! Pacific Rim: Forging New Alliances for Waste Reduction, February 28–March 1, Los Angeles.

Beverage World. 1982. *Beverage World: 100 Year History, 1882–1982, and Future Probe.* Great Neck, NY: Beverage World.

BioCycle. 2008. State of Garbage in America. 49 (12):22.

Bird, D. 1967. Kearing Sees a Crisis in Garbage Disposal. *New York Times*, June 19, 37.

Bird, D. 1969. Disposal Charge for Waste Urged: Manufacturers Would Pay a Cent a Pound under Plan. *New York Times*, July 20, 42.

Bird, D. 1970a. Round-up of Bottles Improves Only the Manufactures' Image. *New York Times*, November 8, 60.

Bird, D. 1970b. Wanted: A New Sanitation Chief. The Mayor Again Faces the Task of Filling a Sensitive Post. *New York Times*, July 16, 23.

Bird, D. 1972. Kretchmer Irks Packaging Parley. *New York Times*, February 27, 62.

Bird, D. 1974a. City Environmental Body Is in Turmoil under Beame. *New York Times*, October 13, 1.

Bird, D. 1974b. Waste-Recycling Is Victim of Recession. *New York Times*, December 22, 1.

Blumberg, L., and R. Gottlieb. 1989. *War on Waste: Can America Win Its Battle with Garbage?* Washington, DC: Island Press.

Boons, F., and M. Janssen. 2004. The Myth of Kalundborg: Social Dilemmas in Stimulating Eco-Industrial Parks. In *Economics of Industrial Ecology*, ed. J. C. van den Bergh and M. A. Janssen, 337–355. Materials, Structural Change, and Spatial Scales. Cambridge, MA: MIT Press.

Born, B., and M. Purcell. 2006. Avoiding the Local Trap: Scale and Food Systems in Planning Research. *Journal of Planning Education and Research* 26: 195–207.

Botha, T. 2004. *Mongo: Adventures in Trash*. New York: Bloomsbury.

Bouman, M., R. Heijungs, E. van de Voet, J. van den Bergh, and G. Huppes. 2000. Material Flows and Economic Models: An Analytical Comparison of SFA, LCA, and Partial Equilibrium Models. *Ecological Economics* 32 (2):195–216.

Brand, P. 2007. Green Subjection: The Politics of Neoliberal Urban Environmental Management. *International Journal of Urban and Regional Research* 31 (3):616–632.

BREATHE (Bay Ridge Ecological Action Towards a Healthier Environment). 1972. Breathe Again. *Ecology Action Newsletter*. Copy in the Archives of BREATHE (Bay Ridge Ecological Action Towards a Healthier Environment), Manuscripts and Rare Book Division, New York Public Library.

Brenner, N., and N. Theodore. 2002. *Spaces of Neoliberalism: Urban Restructuring in North America and Western Europe*. Malden, MA: Blackwell.

Breznick, A. 1993. Private Recyclers Trash City Recovery Plant Plan. *Crain's New York Business*, May 24, 7.

Brown, P., and E. J. Mikkelsen. 1990. *No Safe Place: Toxic Waste, Leukemia, and Community Action*. Berkeley and Los Angeles: University of California Press.

Bullard, R. D. 2000. *Dumping in Dixie: Race, Class, and Environmental Quality*. 3rd ed. Boulder, CO: Westview Press.

Bullard, R. D., and G. S. Johnson. 2000. Environmental Justice: Grassroots Activism and Its Impact on Public Policy Decision Making. *Journal of Social Issues* 56 (3):555–578.

Burkett, P. 1999. *Marx and Nature: A Red and Green Perspective*. 1st ed. New York: St. Martin's Press.

Burks, E. C. 1970. "Bounty" for Junked Cars Urged. *New York Times*, February 24, 45.

Burton, S. 2009. Recycling? Fuggheddaboudit. *Mother Jones* (May–June): 52–54.

Business Week. 1978. Corporate Strategies: Waste Management. March 13, 102.

Buttel, F. H. 2000. Ecological Modernization as a Social Theory. *Geoforum* 31:57–65.

Buttel, F. H. 2006. Globalization, Environmental Reform, and U.S. Hegemony. In *Governing Environmental Flows: Global Challenges to Social Theory*, ed. G. Spaargaren, A. P. J. Mol, and F. H. Buttel, 157–186. Cambridge, MA: MIT Press.

Cable, S., T. Mix and D. Hastings. 2005. Mission Impossible? Environmental Justice Activists' Collaborations with Professional Environmentalists and with Academics. In *Power, Justice, and the Environment: A Critical Appraisal of the Environmental Justice Movement*, ed. D. N. Pellow and R. J. Brulle, 55–76. Cambridge, MA: MIT Press.

CA DEC (California Department of Conservation). 2006. *Market Analysis for Recycled Beverage Container Materials*. Sacramento: CA DEC.

CalRecycle. 2009. Compostable Plastics. Accessed July 26, 2010, at <http://www.calrecycle.ca.gov/publications/Plastics/2009001.pdf>.

Carmody, D. 1986. Environmentalist's Report Faults City Plans to Incinerate Garbage. *New York Times*, February 21, B4.

CAW (Californians against Waste). 2010. The Problem of Polystyrene. Accessed May 1, 2010, at http://www.cawrecycles.org/issues/plastic_campaign/polystyrene/problem.

CHEJ (Center for Health and Environmental Justice). 2004. *PVC Bad News Comes in Threes: The Poison Plastic, Health Hazards, and the Looming Waste Crisis*. Falls Church, VA: CHEJ.

Chertow, M. R. 1998. Waste, Industrial Ecology, and Sustainability. *Social Research* 65 (1) (Spring):31–53.

Christian Science Monitor. 1970. Nationwide Program Planned to Use Nonreturnable Bottles. July 2, 10.

Ciplet, D. 2008. Community-Based for Zero Waste. Global Alliance for Incinerator Alternatives. Accessed June 22, 2010, at <http://www.no-burn.org/article.php?id=377>.

Citizen's Solid Waste Advisory Council. 1976. Statement of Concern. Copy in the Archives of the Environmental Action Coalition, Manuscripts and Rare Book Division, New York Public Library.

City of Edmonton. 2010. Edmonton Composting Facility. Accessed July 29, 2010, at <http://www.edmonton.ca/for_residents/garbage_recycling/edmonton-composting-facility.aspx>.

City of Los Angeles. 2001. *Los Angeles Recycling Economic Information Study*. Los Angeles: City of Los Angeles.

City of New York. 2009. Electronic Equipment Collection, Recycling and Reuse, April 15. In *Rules of the City of New York*, title 16, chap. 17. New York: City of New York.

CIWMB (California Integrated Waste Management Board). 1996. *Market Status Report: Secondary Material Export Markets*. Sacramento: CIWMB.

CIWMB (California Integrated Waste Management Board). 2003. *Benefits of Regional Recycling Markets: An Alameda County Study*. Sacramento: CIWMB.

CIWMB (California Integrated Waste Management Board). 2007. Resource Recovery Parks—Case Studies. Accessed December 30, 2009, at <http://www.ciwmb.ca.gov/LgLibrary/Innovations/RecoveryPark/CaseStudies1.htm>.

CIWMB (California Integrated Waste Management Board) Waste Line. 2008. Re: Inquiry Regarding Tonnages, Diversion Rates, and Regulations Relating to Nonhazardous Industrial Wastes

Clean Washington Center. 2001. *Best Practices in Glass Recycling.* Seattle: Clean Washington Center.

Colten, C., and P. N. Skinner. 1996. *The Road to Love Canal: Managing Industrial Waste before EPA.* Austin: University of Texas Press.

Commoner, B. 1995. The Political History of Dioxin. *Synthesis/Regeneration* (Summer), Accessed September 5, 2010, at <http://www.greens.org/s-r/078/07-03.html>.

Congressional Quarterly Researcher. 2007. The Future of Recycling: Is a Zero-Waste Society Achievable? December 14, 1.

Consumer Reports. 1994. Recycling: Is It Worth the Effort? February:92–100.

Corey, S. 1994. King Garbage: A History of Solid Waste Management in New York City. Ph.D. diss., New York University.

Craig, T. 2010. D.C. Bag Tax Collects $150,000 in January for River Cleanup. *Washington Post*, March 30. Accessed September 3, 2010, at <http://www.washingtonpost.com/wp-dyn/content/article/2010/03/29/AR2010032903336.html>.

Crenson, M. A. 1971. *The Un-Politics of Air Pollution: A Study of Non-Decisionmaking in the Cities.* Baltimore: Johns Hopkins University Press.

CRI (Container Recycling Institute). 2008. Bottle Bills Complement Curbside Recycling Programs. Accessed April 29, 2008, at <http://www.bottlebill.org/about/benefits/curbside.htm>.

Crompton, T. 2008. *Weathercocks and Signposts: The Environment Movement at a Crossroads.* London: World Wildlife Fund UK.

Crooks, H. 1983. *Dirty Business: The Inside Story of the New Garbage Agglomerates.* Toronto: J. Lorimer.

Crooks, H. 1993. *Giants of Garbage: The Rise of the Global Waste Industry and the Politics of Pollution Control.* Toronto: J. Lorimer.

CRS (Congressional Research Service). 1983. *Strategic and Critical Materials Policy.* Research and Development Issue Brief no. Ib74094. Washington, DC: CRS.

Cummings, L. D. 1977. Voluntary Strategies in the Recycling Movement: Recycling as Cooptation. *Journal of Voluntary Action Research* 6:153–160.

Dautel, S. 2009. Transoceanic Trash. *Environmental Law Journal* 3 (1): 181–208.

Davies, A. R. 2008. *The Geographies of Garbage Governance: Interventions, Interactions, and Outcomes.* Burlington, VT: Ashgate.

Davis, K. 2007. It's Cheap, Durable, but Plastic Still Carries a Heavy Price; Environmental Cost Is Well Documented, but Ubiquitous Material Also Contains Dangerous Toxins. *Vancouver Sun*, August 4. Accessed January 11, 2011, at

<http://www.canada.com/vancouversun/news/westcoasthomes/story.html?id
=ce13b03f-be20-49cc-bc74-db98e6cc5b49>.

Davis, P. A. 1991. Administration Backing Away from RCRA Reauthorization. *Congressional Quarterly* 2685:47.

De Bell, G. 1970. *The Environmental Handbook: Prepared for the First National Environmental Teach-in, April 22, 1970.* New York: Ballantine.

De Blasio, B. 2009. Press Release: De Blasio Calls on City to Ban Styrofoam in Schools. August 24. New York City Office of the Public Advocate. Accessed May 5, 2010, at <http://www.billdeblasio.com/node/613>.

Delmas, M., and A. Keller. 2005. Free Riding in Voluntary Environmental Programs: The Case of the U.S. EPA Wastewise Program. *Policy Sciences* 38: 91–106.

Dernbach, J. 1990. Industrial Waste: Saving the Worst for Last? *Environmental Law Reporter* 20:10238–10293.

Desrochers, P. 2002. Industrial Ecology and the Rediscovery of Inter-Firm Recycling Linkages: Historical Evidence and Policy Implications. *Industrial and Corporate Change* 11 (5):1031–1057.

Dimino, R., and B. Warren. 2004. *Reaching for Zero: The Citizen's Plan for Zero Waste in New York City.* New York: New York City Zero Waste Campaign and Consumer Policy Institute/Consumers Union.

Dowie, M. 1995. *Losing Ground: American Environmentalism at the Close of the Twentieth Century.* Cambridge, MA: MIT Press.

Dryzek, J., and J. P. Lester. 1995. Alternative View of the Environmental Problematic. In *Environmental Politics and Policy: Theories and Evidence*, ed. J. P. Lester, 328–346. Durham, NC: Duke University Press.

Duchin, F., and G. M. Lange. 1998. Prospects for the Recycling of Plastics in the United States. *Structural Change and Economic Dynamics* 9 (3):307–331.

Dumont, K. 1971a. Draft presentation given to the Business Environmental Action Coalition Committee, New York, n.d. Copy in the Archives of the Environmental Action Coalition, Manuscripts and Rare Book Division, New York Public Library, Box 3.

Dumont, K. 1971b. Speech given to the U.S. Brewer's Association, New York, n.d. Copy in the Archives of the Environmental Action Coalition, Manuscripts and Rare Book Division, New York Public Library. Box 3.

Dumont, K. 1971c. Testimony to Citizen's Council on Environmental Quality. New York, June 18. Copy in the Archives of the Environmental Action Coalition, Manuscripts and Rare Book Division, New York Public Library. Box 3.

Dumont, K. 1972. Statement before the New York City Council Budget Hearings, May 2, 1972. Copy in the Archives of the Environmental Action Coalition, Manuscripts and Rare Book Division, New York Public Library, Box 3.

Dumont, K. 1973a. Memo to staff on EAC finances. April 14. Copy in the Archives of the Environmental Action Coalition, Manuscripts and Rare Book Division, New York Public Library. Box 3.

Dumont, K. 1973b. Second fund-raising letter to Norman Alexander for the Inner City Project, April 17. Copy in the Archives of the Environmental Action Coalition, Manuscripts and Rare Book Division, New York Public Library. Box 3.

Dumont, K. 1974. Statement at Public Hearing on New York State Policy Regarding Non-Returnable Beverage Containers held by the New York State Council of Environmental Advisors Feb 20, 1974 Copy in the Archives of the Environmental Action Coalition, Manuscripts and Rare Book Division, New York Public Library. Box 3.

Dumont, K. n.d. Draft letter to potential funders of a motivational film celebrating "Trash is Cash." Copy in the Archives of the Environmental Action Coalition, Manuscripts and Rare Book Division, New York Public Library, Box 1.

Dunlap, R. E., and A. G. Mertig. 1992. The Evolution of the U.S. Environmental Movement from 1970 to 1990. In *American Environmentalism*, ed. R. E. Dunlap and A. G. Mertig, 1–9. Philadelphia: Taylor and Francis.

EAC (Environmental Action Coalition). 1970–1988. Undated minutes of meetings, undated drafts of various documents, and correspondence. Copies in the Archives of the Environmental Action Coalition, Manuscripts and Rare Book Division, New York Public Library.

EAC (Environmental Action Coalition). 1973. *Progress Report for 1970–1972*. New York: EAC. Copy in the Archives of the Environmental Action Coalition, Manuscripts and Rare Book Division, New York Public Library, Box 3.

EAC (Environmental Action Coalition). 1992. *The Road to Recycling: A New York City School Recycling Manual*. New York: EAC Copy in the Archives of the Environmental Action Coalition, Manuscripts and Rare Book Division, New York Public Library, Box 1.

EAC (Environmental Action Coalition). 2002. History of Recycling in New York City. Accessed January 15, 2002, at <http://www.eac.org> (since removed).

Earthworks Group. 1990. *The Recycler's Handbook: Simple Things You Can Do*. Ashland, OR: Javnarama/Earthworks Group.

ECAER (Ecopolicy Center for Agricultural Environmental and Resource Issues). 2001. *Beyond Flow Control: Economic Incentives for Better Solid Waste Management in Mercer County, New Jersey*. New Brunswick, NJ: Rutgers University.

Eckelman, M. I., and M. R. Chertow. 2009. Quantifying Life Cycle Environmental Benefits from the Reuse of Industrial Materials in Pennsylvania. *Environmental Science & Technology* 43 (7):2550–2556.

EEA (European Environment Agency). 2003. *Europe's Environment: The Third Assessment*. Copenhagan: EEA.

Ehrenfeld, J., and N. Gertler. 1997. Industrial Ecology in Practice. The Evolution of Interdependence at Kalundborg. *Journal of Industrial Ecology* 2 (4):67–79.

Eliasoph, N. 1998. *Avoiding Politics: How Americans Produce Apathy in Everyday Life.* Cambridge Cultural Social Studies. Cambridge, UK: Cambridge University Press.

Enright, W. J. 1942. Scrap Dealers Face Burdens. *New York Times*, October 25, E6.

Environmental News Service. 2008. New York Requires Statewide Plastic Bag Recycling. December 15, 1.

Eriksson, C. 2004. Can Green Consumerism Replace Environmental Regulation? A Differentiated Products Example. *Resource and Energy Economics* 26:281–293.

Erkman, S. 1997. Industrial Ecology: An Historical View. *Journal of Cleaner Production* 6 (1–2):1–10.

ETBC (Electronics Takeback Coalition). 2010. Brief Comparison of State Laws on Electronics Recycling. Accessed June 22, 2010, at <http://www .electronicstakeback.com/legislation/state_legislation.htm>.

ETBC (Electronics Takeback Coalition) and NRDC (Natural Resources Defense Council). 2010. Legal Issues in the New York City E-Waste Lawsuit. Accessed July 27, 2010, at <http://www.computertakeback.com/legislation/Legal%20 Issues%20in%20the%20New%20York%20City%20Lawsuit.pdf>.

Eureka Recycling. 2008. *Our Story.* St. Paul, MN: Eureka Recycling. Accessed January 3, 2009, at <http://www.eurekarecycling.org/abo_ourstory .cfm>.

Fagan, G. H. 2004. Waste Management and Its Contestation in the Republic of Ireland. *Capitalism, Nature, Socialism* 15 (1):83–102.

Feherenbacher, J. 2009. Why Won't NYC Recycle Plastic? Accessed March 22, 2010, at <http://inhabitat.com/green-rant-why-wont-nyc-recycle-plastic>.

Fenner, T. W., and R. J. Gorin. 1976. *Local Beverage Container Laws: A Legal and Tactical Analysis.* Stanford, CA: Stanford Law School.

Fickes, M. 1998. Getting the Best Bang for the Waste Buck. *Waste Age*, June 1, 22–27.

Fischer-Kowalski, M. 1998. Society's Metabolism: The Intellectual History of Materials Flow Analysis, Part II, 1970–1998. *Journal of Industrial Ecology* 2 (4):107–136.

Fishbein, B. K., J. Ehrenfeld, and J. E. Young. 2000. *Extended Producer Responsibility: A Materials Policy for the 21st Century.* New York: INFORM.

Folz, D. H., and J. M. Hazlett. 1991. Public Participation and Recycling Performance: Explaining Program Success. *Public Administration Review* 51: 526–532.

Foster, J. B. 2000. *Marx's Ecology: Materialism and Nature.* New York: Monthly Review Press.

Frankel, R. 1971. Richard Frankel on Recycling Textiles. *Secondary Raw Materials* (March):104.

Freilla, O. 2005. *Green Development for Environmental Justice and Health Communities*. Bronx, NY: Greenworker Cooperatives.

Frosch, R. A., and N. E. Gallopoulous. 1992. Towards an Industrial Ecology. In *The Treatment and Handling of Wastes*, ed. A. D. Bradshaw, 269–292. London: Chapman and Hall.

Gandy, M. 2002. *Concrete and Clay: Reworking Nature in New York City*. Cambridge, MA: MIT Press.

Gardner, G., and S. Payal. 1999. Forging a Sustainable Materials Economy. In *State of the World*, ed. L. R. Brown, 41–59. Washington, DC: Worldwatch Institute.

Gates, S. 2003. Re: The Big Picture on Glass. GreenYes listserv, April 11, 14: 09. Accessed January 3, 2009, <http://greenyes.grrn.org/2003/04/msg00067 .html>.

Gebel, A. 1954. Prices for Nearly All Waste Items Plummet: Dealers Blame Oversupply. *Wall Street Journal*, January 11, 3.

Geiser, K. 2001. *Materials Matter: Toward a Sustainable Materials Policy*. Urban and Industrial Environments. Cambridge, MA: MIT Press.

Geiser, K. 2004. Pollution Prevention. In *Environmental Governance Reconsidered: Challenges, Choices, and Opportunities*, ed. R. F. Durant, D. J. Fiorino, and R. O'Leary, 427–454. Cambridge, MA: MIT Press.

GFN (Global Footprint Network). 2008. *Ecological Footprint Atlas*. Oakland, CA: GFN.

Gibbs, D., and P. Deutz. 2005. Implementing Industrial Ecology? Planning for Eco-Industrial Parks in the U.S.A. *Geoforum* 36 (4):452–464.

Gill, K. 2010. *Of Poverty and Plastic*. Oxford, UK: Oxford University Press.

Gilpin, R., and J. G. Solch. 2003. Production, Distribution, and Fate of Polychlorinated Dibenzo-P-Dioxins, Dibenzofurans, and Related Organohalogens in the Environment. In *Dioxins and Health*, ed. A. Schecter and T. A. Gasiewicz, 57–87. New York: Wiley-Interscience.

Gladwell, M. 2002. *The Tipping Point: How Little Things Can Make a Big Difference*. Boston: Back Bay Books.

Glenn, J. 1997. Moving from Industrial Waste to Coproducts. *BioCycle* 38 (1):54–56.

Gold, A. R. 1990. As Trash Is Recycled, Where Can It All Go? *New York Times*, October 3, B4.

Goldsmith, S. A. 1971. Letter to members of the National Aluminum Association, September 7. Copy in the Archives of the Environmental Action Coalition, Manuscripts and Rare Book Division, New York Public Library. Box 3.

Goldstein, N., and D. Block. 2000. Solid Waste Composting Trends in the U.S. *BioCycle* 41 (11):31–38.

Gonzalez, D. 2008. Greening the Bronx, One Castoff at a Time. *New York Times*, April 21, B1.

Gordon, D. M. 1978. Capitalist Development and the History of American Cities. In *Marxism and the Metropolis*, ed. W. K. Tabb and L. Sawers, 25–63. New York: Oxford University Press.

Gotbaum, B. 2002. Public Advocate Calls for Mayor to Save Recycling. Press release, Office of the New York City Public Advocate, June 14. Accessed May 2, 2010, at <http://publicadvocategotbaum.com/new_news/pdfs/Save_Recycling_press_release.pdf>

Gotbaum, B. 2007. Catching up on Recycling. *Gotham Gazette*, April 23. Accessed January 12, 2010, at <http://www.gothamgazette.com/article/fea/20070423/202/2154>.

Gould, K. A., D. N. Pellow, and A. Schnaiberg. 2004. Interrogating the Treadmill of Production. *Organization & Environment* 17 (3):296–316.

Gould, K. A., A. Schnaiberg, and A. S. Weinberg. 1996. *Local Environmental Struggles: Citizen Activism in the Treadmill of Production*. Cambridge, UK: Cambridge University Press.

GPI (Glass Packaging Institute). 2006. *Glass Recycling and the Environment*. Washington, DC: GPI. Accessed January 3, 2010, at <http://www.gpi.org/recycle-glass/environment>.

Grossman, E. 2006. *High Tech Trash: Digital Devices, Hidden Toxics, and Human Health*. Washington, DC: Island Press, Shearwater Books.

GRRN (Grassroots Recycling Network). 2008. What Is Zero Waste? Accessed December 6, 2009, at <http://www.grrn.org/zerowaste/zerowaste_faq.html>.

Gunther, M. 2006. The Green Machine. *Fortune*, August 7. Accessed July 31, 2010, at <http://money.cnn.com/magazines/fortune/fortune_archive/2006/08/07/8382593/index.htm>.

Gurnon. E. 2003. The Problem with Plastics. *North Coast Journal Weekly*, June 5.

Guttentag, R. 2001. Re: Glass Recycling / What Makes Sense to Recycle? GreenYes listserv, July 8, 15: 58. Accessed December 27, 2010, at <http://greenyes.grrn.org/2001/07/msg00009.html>.

Guttentag, R. 2002. Re: MSW vs. Total Wastes. GreenYes listserv, January 4, 2002, 20:12. Accessed January 4, 2010, at <http://greenyes.grrn.org/2002/01/msg00020.html>.

Hahnel, R. 2007. Eco-Localism: A Constructive Critique. *Capitalism, Nature, Socialism* 18 (2):62–78.

Hajer, M. A. 1995. *The Politics of Environmental Discourse: Ecological Modernization and the Policy Process*. Oxford, UK: Clarendon Press.

Hall, K. M. 2008. Coal-Ash Spill Worse Than Thought. *New York Times*, December 26, A10.

Hall, M. 2010. Emptying Landfills and Debunking Waste Myths. *Cleantech Forum*, May 17. Accessed January 7, 2010, <http://cleantech.com/news/5784/emptying-landfills-and-debunking-wa>.

Hamilton, J. 2005. *Regulation through Revelation: The Origin, Politics, and Impacts of the Toxics Release Inventory Program.* Cambridge, UK: Cambridge University Press.

Hansen, K. T. 1999. Second-Hand Clothing Encounters in Zambia: Global Discourses, Western Commodities, and Local Histories. *Africa (London.1928)* 69 (3):343–365.

Harbin, F. R. 1926. Low-Grade Fuels Hamper Efficiency of Oil-Heat Plant; Attempts to Use Inferior Distillates in Automatic Machinery in Homes Fail. Responsible Concerns Look toward Future, Expert Says, Cracking Process Will Furnish Economical Product for Heating. *Washington Post*, December 5, F11.

Harrison, P., F. Pearce, and AAAS(American Association for the Advancement of Science). 2000. *AAAS Atlas of Population & Environment.* Berkeley and Los Angeles: University of California Press.

Hartford Courant. 1970. Recycled Bottles Pass 42 Million Count for the Year. November 1, 43.

Hawken, P. 2007. *Blessed Unrest: How the Largest Movement in the World Came into Being and Why No One Saw It Coming.* New York: Viking.

Hawken, P., A. B. Lovins, and L. H. Lovins. 1999. *Natural Capitalism: Creating the Next Industrial Revolution.* 1st ed. Boston: Little Brown.

Hays, S. P. 1987. *Beauty, Health, and Permanence: Environmental Politics in the United States, 1955–1985.* Cambridge, UK: Cambridge University Press.

Heather [no last name]. 2007. Best Way to Reduce Waste? Buy Less Stuff. Accessed December 14, 2009, at <http://www.enviromom.com/2007/05/bes_way_to_red.html>.

Hiembuch, J. 2009. U.S. Government Officials Ask Electronics Industry to Take Back NYC Law Suit, and Take Back Gadgets, *Treehugger*, November 5, Accessed January 10, 2010, at <http://www.treehugger.com/files/2009/11/us-govermnet-officials-ask-electronics-industry-to-take-back-nyc-lawsuit-and-take-back-gadgets.php>.

Heinman, M. 1990. From "Not in My Backyard!" to "Not in Anybody's Backyard!" Grassroots Challenge to Hazardous Waste Facility Siting. *American Planning Association Journal* 56 (3):359–362.

Hershkowitz, A. 1998. In Defense of Recycling. Social Research 65 (1, Spring):141–218.

Hershkowitz, A. 2002. *Bronx Ecology: A Blueprint for a New Environmentalism.* Foreword and original designs by M. Lin. Washington, DC: Island Press.

Hess, D. J. 2005. Case Study of Reuse Organizations: Urban Ore. David J. Hess Research Homepage. Accessed December 30, 2009, at <http://www.davidjhess.org/UrbanOre.pdf>.

Hill, G. 1969. Major U.S. Cities Face Emergency Trash Disposal. *New York Times*, June 16, C38.

Hill, G. 1970. A Nation Set to Observe Earth Day. *New York Times*, April 20, 36.

Holifield, R. 2004. Neoliberalism and Environmental Justice in the United States Environmental Protection Agency: Translating Policy into Managerial Practice in Hazardous Waste Remediation. *Geoforum* 35 (3) 285–297.

Howe, S. R., and L. Borodinsky. 1998. Potential Exposure to Bisphenol A from Food-Contact Use of Polycarbonate Resins. *Food Additives and Contaminants* 15 (3):370–375.

Hubbard, S. 2003. The Environmental Impacts of Recycling Glass. GreenYes listserv, April 14, 10: 01. Accessed January 10, 2009, at <http://greenyes.grrn .org/2003/04/msg00085.html>.

Hudson, R. 2001. *Producing Places: Perspectives on Economic Change*. New York: Guilford Press.

ILSR (Institute for Local Self Reliance). 1997. *Recycling Means Business*. Washington, DC: ILSR.

ILSR (Institute for Local Self Reliance). 2005. *Waste to Wealth*. Washington, DC: ILSR.

ILSR (Institute for Local Self Reliance), Ecocycle, and GAIA (Global Alliance for Incineration Alternatives). 2008. *Stop Trashing the Climate*. Washington, DC: Institute for Local Self Reliance.

Impact: The Newsletter of Legislative and Regulatory Issues Facing Maine Business. 2010. March 4 edition.

Jain, R., R. George, and R. Webster. 2008. Sustainable Deconstruction and the Role of Knowledge-Based Systems. *International Journal of Environmental Technology and Management* 8 (2–3):261–274.

Janicke, M. 2006. The Environmental State and Environmental Flows: The Need to Reinvent the State. In *Governing Environmental Flows: Global Challenges to Social Theory*, ed. G. Spaargaren, A. P. J. Mol, and F. H. Buttel, 83–106. Cambridge, MA: MIT Press.

Jesson, M. 2000. Putting Waste to Work. Zero Waste Services. Accessed December 30, 2009, at <http://www.zerowaste.ca/articles/column164.html>.

Kamlarz, P. 2008. Memorandum to Honorable Mayor and Members of the City Council of the City of Berkeley, California, Re: Contract: Urban Ore for Recycling Services. City of Berkeley. Accessed December 30, 2009, at <http://www.ci.berkeley.ca.us/uploadedFiles/Clerk/Level_3_-_City_Council/ 2008/09Sep/2008-09-16_Item_20_Contract_Urban_Ore_for_Recycling_ Services.pdf>.

Kang, H. Y., and J. M. Schoenung. 2006. Economic Analysis of Electronic Waste Recycling: Modeling the Cost and Revenue of a Materials Recovery Facility in California. *Environmental Science & Technology* 40 (5):1672– 1680.

Keane, A. D. 1992. Recent Developments: Federal Regulation of Solid Waste Reduction and Recycling. *Harvard Journal on Legislation* 29:251–276.

Kender, S. 2003. Re: The Big Picture on Glass. GreenYes listserv, April 13, 11: 30. Accessed December 28, 2009, at <http://greenyes.grrn.org/2003/04/msg00075.html>.

Kennedy, R. 1994. Trash Plant No Salvation. *New York Times*, May 15, CY8.

King, A. A., and M. J. Lenox. 2000. Industry Self-Regulation without Sanctions: The Chemical Industry's Responsible Care Program. *Academy of Management Journal* 43 (4):698–716.

King, D. L. 1995. *Doing Their Share to Save the Planet: Children and Environmental Crisis*. New Brunswick, NJ: Rutgers University Press.

King, W. D. 2008. *Collections of Nothing*. Chicago: University of Chicago Press.

Knapp, D. 2008. Re: [ZWIA] Re: [CRRA] Zero Waste, EPR and Total Recycling. GreenYes listserv, April 17, 2008 15: 01. Accessed December 15, 2009, at <http://greenyes.grrn.org/2008/04/msg00099.html>.

Koch, E. 1971. Trash Is Cash. *Congressional Record* 117 (May 20):16142.

Kocha, L., and N. A. Ashford. 2006. Rethinking the Role of Information in Chemicals Policy: Implications for TSCA and Reach. *Journal of Cleaner Production* 14 (1):31–46.

Koehler, S. 1974. Speech at Women's City Club dinner. Copy in the Archives of the Environmental Action Coalition, Manuscripts and Rare Book Division, New York Public Library, Box 4.

Koehler, S. 1975a. Testimony before the New York State Assembly Committee on Commerce, Industry, and Economic Development. Copy in the Archives of the Environmental Action Coalition, Manuscripts and Rare Book Division, New York Public Library, Box 4.

Koehler, S. 1975b. Testimony before the New York State Assembly Standing Committee on Environmental Conservation, Task Force Subcommittee on Solid Waste Disposal. Copy in the Archives of the Environmental Action Coalition, Manuscripts and Rare Book Division, New York Public Library, Box 4.

Koehler, S. 1975c. Transcript of Minutes from EAC Staff Meeting. February 18. Copy in the Archives of the Environmental Action Coalition, Manuscripts and Rare Book Division, New York Public Library, Box 4.

Kolbert, E. 1988. New Albany Session: Hard Issues and Delicate Politics. *New York Times*, January 4, B1.

Kovach, B. 1973. Garbage-Smothered Cities Face Crisis in Five Years. *New York Times*, June 10, 1.

Krausmann, F., S. Gingrich, N. Eisenmenger, K.-H. Erb, H. Haberl, and M. Fischer-Kowalski. 2009. Growth in Global Materials Use, GDP, and Population during the 20th Century. *Ecological Economics* 68 (10):2696–2705.

Kretchmer, J. 1971. Letter of Commendation for the Environmental Action Coalition from the Environmental Protection Agency of the City of New York.

May 11. Copy in the Archives of the Environmental Action Coalition, Manuscripts and Rare Book Division, New York Public Library. Box 3.

Kuczenski, B., and R. Geyer. 2010. Material Flow Analysis of Polyethylene Terephthalate in the US, 1996–2007. *Resources, Conservation, and Recycling* 54 (12):1161–1169.

Kumar, V. 2005. Towards Sustainable Product Material Flow Cycles: Identifying Barriers to Achieving Product Multi-Use and Zero Waste. Paper read at the International Mechanical Engineering Congress and Exposition, November 5–11, Orlando, FL.

Lake, R. W. 1994. Central Government Limitations on Local Policy Options for Environmental Protection. *Professional Geographer* 46 (2):236–242.

Lake, R. 2002. Bring Back Big Government. *International Journal of Urban and Regional Research* 26 (4):815–822.

Lakoff, G. 2004. *Don't Think of an Elephant! Know Your Values and Frame the Debate: The Essential Guide for Progressives.* White River Junction, VT: Chelsea Green.

Landy, M. K., M. J. Roberts, and S. R. Thomas. 1994. *The Environmental Protection Agency: Asking the Wrong Questions from Nixon to Clinton.* Expanded ed. New York: Oxford University Press.

Lee, C. 2005. The Collaborative Models to Achieve Environmental Justice and Healthy Communities. In *Power, Justice, and the Environment: A Critical Appraisal of the Environmental Justice Movement*, ed. D. N. Pellow and R. J. Brulle, 219–251. Cambridge, MA: MIT Press.

Leonard, A. 2008. *The Story of Stuff.* Documentary. The Story of Stuff Project. Accessed November 22, 2009, at <http://www.storyofstuff.com/pdfs/annie _leonard_footnoted_script.pdf>.

Lewis, J. F. 1977. *Goodwill: For the Love of People.* Washington, DC: Goodwill Industries of America.

Lichtenstein, G. 1971. Running for Mayor on a Garbage Truck. *New York Times Magazine*, April 25, SM31.

Lifset, R., and T. Lindquist. 2001. Trust, but Verify. *The Journal of Industrial Ecology* 5 (2) 9–11.

Lindqvist, T. 1992. Extended Producer Responsibility as a Strategy to Promote Cleaner Products. Ph.D. diss., Lund University.

Lipton, E. 2004. Report Calls Recycling Costlier than Dumping. *New York Times*, February 2, B5

Loetterle, F. 1970a. Pollution Foes Seek Recruits for All Levels. *New York Daily News*, July 22, 5.

Loetterle, F. 1970b. Two Hundred Concerns Join Campaign against Trash. *New York Daily News*, July 26, 4.

Logan, J. R., and H. L. Molotch. 1987. *Urban Fortunes: The Political Economy of Place.* Berkeley and Los Angeles: University of California Press.

Lombardi, E., and K. Rogers. 2007. Discovering the Future . . . 2,500 Zero Waste Millionaires. *In Business* (September–October). Accessed December 27, 2009, at <http://findarticles.com/p/articles/mi_qa5378/is_200709/ai_n21298831>.

Los Angeles Bureau of Sanitation. 2010. What You Can Recycle at the Curb. Accessed July 26, 2010, at <http://san.lacity.org/solid_resources/recycling/curbside/what_is_recyclable.htm>.

Los Angeles Times. 1916. Good Value in Old Rags. June 25, III16.

Los Angeles Times. 1921. Lunch Papers Clutter Roads. July 24, V18.

Los Angeles Times. 1931. Useless Waste. July 26, J2.

Los Angeles Times. 1949. Salvation Army Can't Pick Up Any More Papers. July 19, A2.

Loundsbury, M., M. Ventresca, and P. M. Hirsch. 2003. Social Movements, Field Frames, and Industry Emergency: A Cultural-Political Perspective on U.S. Recycling. *Socio-economic Review* 1:71–104.

Low, R. 1974. Letter to Karen Dumont. September 18. Copy in the Archives of the Environmental Action Coalition, Manuscripts and Rare Book Division, New York Public Library. Box 3.

Lueck, T. J. 1994. Ruling Is Seen as a Threat to Preferences in Bidding; Judgment Casts Doubt on Incentive Plans. *New York Times*, February 5, 25.

Luke, T. W. 1997. *Ecocritique: Contesting the Politics of Nature, Economy, and Culture.* Minneapolis: University of Minnesota Press.

Lukes, S. 2004. *Power: A Radical View.* 2d ed. Houndsmill, UK: Palgrave Macmillan.

Lundberg, J. 2010. Plastics Keep Coming after You: A Comprehensive Report and a Call to Action. *Culture Change*, March 15. Accessed June 20, 2010, at <http://www.culturechange.org/cms/content/view/613/62>.

Maantay, J. A. 2002. Industrial Zoning Changes in New York City and Environmental Justice: A Case Study in "Expulsive" Zoning. *Zoning, Projections: The Planning Journal of Massachusetts Institute of Technology* 3:63–108.

MacBride, S. 2008. Throwing Out Our Clothes: The Relation between Income and Textile Waste Generation in New York City. Paper read at the conference Waste: The Social Context, May 15, Edmonton, Canada.

Maine House of Representatives. 2009. *An Act to Provide Leadership Regarding the Responsible Recycling of Consumer Products.* HP 115901, LD 1631. 124th sess., December 21. Accessed June 18, 2010, <http://www.legislature.maine.gov/legis/bills/display_ps.asp?LD=1631&snum=124>

Maine State Legislature. 2010. *An Act to Provide Leadership Regarding the Responsible Recycling of Consumer Products.* Public Law, chapter 516, item 1. 124th session, March 17. Accessed June 18, 2010, at <http://mainelegislature.org/legis/bills/bills_124th/chappdfs/PUBLIC516.pdf>.

Makower, J. 2009. Industrial Strength Solution. *Mother Jones* (May–June). Accessed December 29, 2009, at <http://www.motherjones.com/environment/2009/05/industrial-strength-solution>.

Urban and Industrial Environments

Series editor: Robert Gottlieb, Henry R. Luce Professor of Urban and Environmental Policy, Occidental College

Maureen Smith, *The U.S. Paper Industry and Sustainable Production: An Argument for Restructuring*

Keith Pezzoli, *Human Settlements and Planning for Ecological Sustainability: The Case of Mexico City*

Sarah Hammond Creighton, *Greening the Ivory Tower: Improving the Environmental Track Record of Universities, Colleges, and Other Institutions*

Jan Mazurek, *Making Microchips: Policy, Globalization, and Economic Restructuring in the Semiconductor Industry*

William A. Shutkin, *The Land That Could Be: Environmentalism and Democracy in the Twenty-First Century*

Richard Hofrichter, ed., *Reclaiming the Environmental Debate: The Politics of Health in a Toxic Culture*

Robert Gottlieb, *Environmentalism Unbound: Exploring New Pathways for Change*

Kenneth Geiser, *Materials Matter: Toward a Sustainable Materials Policy*

Thomas D. Beamish, *Silent Spill: The Organization of an Industrial Crisis*

Matthew Gandy, *Concrete and Clay: Reworking Nature in New York City*

David Naguib Pellow, *Garbage Wars: The Struggle for Environmental Justice in Chicago*

Julian Agyeman, Robert D. Bullard, and Bob Evans, eds., *Just Sustainabilities: Development in an Unequal World*

Barbara L. Allen, *Uneasy Alchemy: Citizens and Experts in Louisiana's Chemical Corridor Disputes*

Dara O'Rourke, *Community-Driven Regulation: Balancing Development and the Environment in Vietnam*

Brian K. Obach, *Labor and the Environmental Movement: The Quest for Common Ground*

Peggy F. Barlett and Geoffrey W. Chase, eds., *Sustainability on Campus: Stories and Strategies for Change*

Paloma Pavel, ed., *Breakthrough Communities: Sustainability and Justice in the Next American Metropolis*

Anastasia Loukaitou-Sideris and Renia Ehrenfeucht, *Sidewalks: Conflict and Negotiation over Public Space*

David J. Hess, *Localist Movements in a Global Economy: Sustainability, Justice, and Urban Development in the United States*

Julian Agyeman and Yelena Ogneva-Himmelberger, eds., *Environmental Justice and Sustainability in the Former Soviet Union*

Jason Corburn, *Toward the Healthy City: People, Places, and the Politics of Urban Planning*

JoAnn Carmin and Julian Agyeman, eds., *Environmental Inequalities beyond Borders: Local Perspectives on Global Injustices*

Louise Mozingo, *Pastoral Capitalism: A History of Suburban Corporate Landscapes*

Gwen Ottinger and Benjamin Cohen, eds., *Technoscience and Environmental Justice: Expert Cultures in a Grassroots Movement*

Samantha MacBride, *Recycling Reconsidered: The Present Failure and Future Promise of Environmental Action in the United States*